Whose Goals
for American
Higher Education?

Whose Goals
for American
Higher Education?

Edited by

CHARLES G. DOBBINS *and* CALVIN B. T. LEE

AMERICAN COUNCIL ON EDUCATION • *Washington, D.C.*

Contributing Authors

JAMES E. ALLEN, JR., Commissioner of Education, State of New York

McGEORGE BUNDY, President, The Ford Foundation

HAROLD W. CHASE, Professor of Political Science, University of Minnesota

JOHN J. CORSON, Consultant to the Carnegie Corporation of New York and to the Secretary of Health, Education, and Welfare

JOSEPH P. COSAND, President, Junior College District of St. Louis

J. BROWARD CULPEPPER, Chancellor, State University System of Florida

PAUL DANISH, Vice-President, Student Government of the University of Colorado, 1966–67

NEIL O. DAVIS, Trustee, Agnes Scott College; Editor and Publisher of the *Lee County Bulletin*, Auburn, Alabama

KENNETH EBLE, Professor and Chairman, Department of English, University of Utah

DAVID FELLMAN, Vilas Professor of Political Science, University of Wisconsin

KERMIT GORDON, President, The Brookings Institution

SAMUEL B. GOULD, Chancellor, State University of New York

ARNOLD M. GRANT, Trustee, Syracuse University; Attorney, New York City

W. EUGENE GROVES, President, United States National Student Association, 1966–67

KENNETH KENISTON, Associate Professor of Psychology, School of Medicine, Yale University

CALVIN B. T. LEE, Assistant Director, Division of College Support, U.S. Office of Education; formerly, Staff Associate, American Council on Education

ROGER LEHECKA, Student Coordinator of Project Double Discovery, Columbia Citizenship Program, Columbia College, 1966–67

v

Foreword

Not long ago there appeared in *The Atlantic* an amusing essay by Morris Bishop, "The Perfect University." This ideal institution is described as a pleasant place for both students and faculty. It will build character in youth, cultivate among its undergraduates the "qualities essential to directors of large enterprise," and guarantee that its graduates possess the essential social skills. The majority of the faculty will teach no classes, but the current student clamor for more contact with professors will be quieted by the exclusion of women and the requirement of faculty celibacy. In a world already "drowning in knowledge," members of the perfect university community will devote themselves "not to knowledge, but to the problem of how to find it, or even how to find how to find it." It is also speculated that "since unfettered research is rapidly making the world uninhabitable, the perfect university will not go out of its way to encourage research." The physical setting of all of this, the author goes on to note, will be both beautiful and comfortable, with an architecture suggesting "ease, spaciousness, permanence."

The reader will recognize, of course, that the institution described is very much like eighteenth-century Oxford and Cambridge. Lest we dismiss the model too quickly as being backward-looking and unproductive, we are reminded that its graduates built the British Empire. We are admonished, moreover, to "look what happened to the British Empire" after Oxford yielded to the "pressures of grubby modernity" and dropped compulsory Greek in its general resolve to be more practical!

I cite Mr. Bishop's humorous observations mainly to contrast them with the seriousness of the issues dealt with in the present volume, *Whose Goals for American Higher Education?* Although there may be those who look back nostalgically to a halcyon era when the higher learning was devoted mainly to the education of gentlemen, with little argument about how this was to be done, contemporary American colleges and universities are in the midst of a period of turbulent change, and the exigencies to be coped with are those of the present and foreseeable future.

vii

Higher education has ceased to be an elitist enterprise, and our campuses are no longer enclaves set almost entirely apart from the surrounding society. With the rise of egalitarianism, science, and technology, what was once a prerogative of the few has come to be regarded as a right of the many, and, indeed, as a necessity for millions of young persons.

In this changed situation there is less consensus than there once was about the means and ends of endeavor. The large and heterogeneous population to be served has diverse notions about goals, and every constituency has its own views about priorities; even a particular constituency—such as students, for example—may be far from unanimity about who should be doing what. Despite the perseverance of time-honored platitudes about teaching, research, and public service, these basic functions are undergoing modifications. They are being subjected to expectations that differ, frequently compete, and sometimes conflict.

Under these circumstances, determining the goals for American higher education is not an easy task. In a democratic social order, moreover, a wide variety of objectives must somehow be brought together in the total endeavor. The purpose of this book is to bring together the views of the main constituencies of American colleges and universities —students, faculty, administrators, trustees, and persons from public life. Some of the commentators manifestly draw upon much more penetrating experience than do others, but to reflect only the observations and opinions of the most experienced would not mirror the reality where educational outcomes are determined. Informed professional judgments, as educators are aware, are just one of the components that influence the structure and function of a college or university as a social institution.

As I note in my own chapter in this volume, it is no wonder that institutions of higher education are moving from autonomy toward heteronomy. This is an understandable response to the new and growing demands for their services, and in a sense these pressures are a collective compliment to higher education's increased importance in a rapidly changing society. The responses of American colleges and universities to changing needs demonstrate their viability, but it should be remembered that durable social institutions must display continuity as well as change. No single institution can succeed in trying to be all things to all possible constituents, and hence each campus should have distinctive purposes while sharing in common goals. Furthermore, the maintenance of institutional integrity implies a sensible division of labor in decision and action, and a coherence of principles in setting priorities of effort.

Because of the well-known diversity of American higher education, however, we can hope to accommodate all legitimate expectations *somewhere* without engaging in futile endeavors of trying to do *everything everywhere*. Now as never before, our people should appreciate that a pluralistic society needs and can make good use of a pluralistic system of educational institutions. Adequate public support and understanding, coupled with the adaptability of such a system, can assure the attainment of every worthy goal.

A careful reading of *Whose Goals for American Higher Education?* should prove very useful to all who want to move ahead with the urgent business before us.

LOGAN WILSON, *President*
American Council on Education

March 15, 1968

Preface

THE PUBLICATION of *Whose Goals for American Higher Education?* recognizes that the aims and roles of each of the five main constituencies of higher education—students, faculty, administrators, trustees, and persons from public life—change as the functions of higher education shift and expand. The problem involves not merely competing visions of true purpose, but also competing preferences regarding priorities, means, and forms of governance by which aspirations are considered, articulated, and adopted. With so many underlying disagreements among the constituencies of higher education, there is need for an attempt to understand the dissonances and consonances among them.

It was no simple task, however, to select the authors represented here. If the views of the five constituencies were to be presented fairly, how were the appropriate spokesmen to be identified and selected?

The professors—what should be their disciplines, professorial loyalties, attitudes toward teaching and research? Should the administrators be representative of public or private institutions? advocates of expansion, or of stand-pat quality? serve-the-public types, or we-are-here-to-learn? What are the representative students—activist or professionalist? Hippie or traditional? Doves or hawks? Should the trustees be from labor, industry, or the professions? And public officials —should they be those who declare "Education is a public responsibility" or those who intone, "The student should pay his way"?

This book's list of contributors was chosen, however, with far less regard for such categories than for the selection of individuals with recognized ability to write or speak from a point of view that is of interest and significance to higher education. The papers, with two exceptions, were prepared for the Fiftieth Anniversary Meeting of the American Council on Education in Washington, D.C., October 11–13, 1967. Walter Lippmann's *The University and the Human Condition* was originally delivered at a convocation sponsored by the Center for the Study of Democratic Institutions and is published here with the permission of the author; and Logan Wilson's *Institutional Autonomy and Heteronomy* is a revision of his 1967 address to the Illinois Conference on Higher Education.

The Council's somewhat "over-thirty" staff finds particular satisfaction in the student representatives, who, it will be noted, present their views with force and conviction. Even if at times their trumpets of conflict jar some nerves, they give life to the dialogue.

Essays basic to the book's theme have been contributed by Calvin B. T. Lee, Philip R. Werdell, Lyle M. Spencer, John J. Corson, David Fellman, Kenneth Keniston, and W. Allen Wallis. In related papers, writing from their special points of view, other representatives of the five constituencies have addressed themselves to many of the controversial issues.

Samuel B. Gould's "A New Objective for American Higher Education" and Sir John Wolfenden's "British University Grants and Government Relations" were keynote addresses of the Fiftieth Anniversary Meeting. "Coordination for the Definition of Goals," by Richard H. Sullivan, and "In Praise of Candor" by McGeorge Bundy were the banquet and final luncheon addresses.

The editors express their thanks to the authors represented, and to the many Council staff members who have helped in producing this volume. Mrs. Janet Alwin was responsible for much of the editing of the papers. Finally, we are grateful to Miss Olive Mills, production editor, for her helpfulness at every stage of the task.

CHARLES G. DOBBINS
CALVIN B. T. LEE

March 15, 1968

Contents

CALVIN B. T. LEE

Whose Goals for American Higher Education?

LIKE THE BLIND MEN of the Hindustani parable, each convinced that he could describe the total elephant by the part he felt, the constituents of higher education—students, faculty, administrators, trustees, and public officials—each believes that it alone truly apprehends the goals of the nation's diverse colleges and universities. And all of them are correct, except that each perceives only a part of the whole. For the separate components of higher education, like the parts of an elephant, are not independent and unattached; they compose a total organism, a system comprising many parts with separate functions.

In this, the fiftieth year of the American Council on Education, the annual meeting will focus on the theme "Whose Goals for American Higher Education?" The question is not rhetorical; it is central to the purposes and functions of higher education.

A college or university has three basic goals: to transmit, to extend, and to apply knowledge. Each of these three missions—teaching, research, and public service—is related to a multitude of programs, intermediate goals, and functions, some of which can be identified with the particular interests of one or the other of the five main constituents of higher education. Although the five may agree on many of the goals, they often differ radically in their rank ordering of priority and emphases. As Clark Kerr has said,

> Newman's "Idea of a University" still has its devotees—chiefly the humanists and the generalists and the undergraduates. Flexner's "Idea of a Modern University" still has its supporters—chiefly the scientists and the specialists and the graduate students. "The Idea of a Multi-

1

versity" has its practitioners—chiefly the administrators, who now
number many of the faculty among them, and the leadership groups
in society at large. . . . These several competing visions of true purpose,
each relating to a different layer of history, a different web of forces,
cause much of the malaise in the university communities of today. The
university is so many things to so many different people that it must, of
necessity, be partially at war with itself.[1]

Implicit in Kerr's analysis is the premise that the segments of
the academic community differ in their views about what the ultimate goals of institutions of higher education should be. But if the
academic community is to remain creative and coherent, it must identify the goals common to all of its constituents, it must select goals
appropriate to each academic institution, and it must even eliminate
some goals. Each of the five groups—students, faculty, administrators,
trustees, and public officials—gives different answers to the questions:
Whose goals? Which goals? And how may they best be achieved?
By examining the various answers to these questions, not only will
we arrive at some understanding of the consonances and dissonances
in the academic world today, but also we may gain some insight into
how to resolve the differences, or, if necessary, to choose among them.
We need to look at the specific issues arising out of the views of the
constituents; these issues cluster around (1) ultimate goals, (2)
priorities among goals, (3) criteria for determining the relevance of
intermediate goals to ultimate goals, (4) the best means of achieving
the goals, and (5) the responsibility for decision making.

Our problem then is not merely one of "competing visions of true
purpose"; it involves competing preferences among priorities, means,
and the form of governance by which aspirations are considered, articulated, and adopted. Because the aims and roles of the different constituents of the academic community have changed as the functions
of higher education have shifted and expanded, we must begin by
setting our problem in a historical context.

THE PROBLEM IN PERSPECTIVE

During its early stages, higher education in America was characterized by orthodoxy, conformity, and religious constraint. Up to the
time of the Civil War, the main function of the American college was
to conserve culture. Neither tone nor method encouraged academic
freedom. Professors were drillmasters teaching prescribed and traditional material; students learned their lessons by rote. The faculty

[1] Kerr, *The Uses of the University* (Cambridge, Mass.: Harvard University
Press, 1963), pp. 8–9.

was given little chance for critical comment, and the college student was considered too immature, innocent, and impressionable even to be exposed to controversy or independent thought, let alone to engage in either. Yet the oppression of a narrow and moralistic ethos did not go unchallenged. The very rivalry between denominations which created the many sectarian colleges also offered to some dissatisfied professors an opportunity for diversity of thought and an avenue of mobility; occasionally, the students themselves agitated against authoritarianism, paternalism, and traditionalism.

The authority of the governing board during the seventeenth and eighteenth centuries was broad. It was not unusual for trustees to shape the curriculum, prescribe the work of the classroom, write the rules of behavior for students, hire and discharge faculty, and conduct final oral examinations, as well as select the president. Between 1800 and 1860, however, the colleges faced two overwhelming problems: internal disorder and financial instability. In many ways, the first issue was resolved when the governing boards acceded to professorial demands for more control over educational programs and student discipline. The second grave difficulty, that of money, was alleviated in large part when the colleges turned from the church to alumni for support. Thus, faculty interests were given greater attention, and a profoundly more secularized base for both fiscal operations and policy was established.

The consequent shifts in educational purpose were becoming apparent by the time the guns boomed at Fort Sumter. Research and scholarship acquired a new vitality, old assumptions became more open to challenge, and secular philanthropy loosened sectarian control over the intellect. When the seeds of Darwinism blew over America, the soil of higher education proved ready to receive the new biology and the new geology; and as the potentials of science became more widely recognized, a home was prepared for the traditions of the German university with its emphasis on scholarship, on graduate work, and on the principles of *Lehrfreiheit* and *Lernfreiheit*.

There was, of course, strenuous opposition to these changes. Nevertheless, the professor in the United States was fundamentally transformed from a conserver of traditional wisdom to a seeker of truths to be discovered progressively and to be held only provisionally. The wars over the teaching of evolution and the research set in motion by Darwin's ideas caused faculties to consolidate, an action that produced widespread educational reforms whereby intellectual performance was stressed, the shaping of character was de-emphasized, and the questioner and empiricist was exalted above the traditional figure of authority, principally the clergyman.

Because of its greater flexibility, the free elective system, adopted in varying extent by liberal arts colleges, gave students a chance to choose a more practical and less traditional curriculum. As science, secularization, and the ideal of intellectual freedom were given new emphasis, laymen replaced clergy both on governing boards and in presidential chairs; and, reinforced by their demonstrated practicalities in a society undergoing rapid industrialization, these trends led to such events as the passage of the Morrill Act in 1862, which explicitly established the land-grant institutions for the purpose of developing and applying intellectually based expertise to an expanding agricultural and industrial economy. The academy's sudden diversion into practical fields represented the grafting of distinctively native limbs on the imported German tree—applied research was coupled with its "pure" counterpart, and the function of public service, of responsiveness to social needs, was added to the functions of teaching and inquiry. As the university grew, it radiated an aura of vigorous diversity and eclecticism. In such an atmosphere, multiple goals were often competitive with one another, if not actually in conflict. With no unified purpose, there could be no unity of needs within the already sprawling academic community, just as there could be no comprehensive and accepted concept of academic freedom to fit all occasions.

Although higher education in the United States entered the twentieth century in a high state of health, it was even then committed to three objectives—instruction, research, and public service—that often seemed incompatible and that frequently varied markedly in their attractiveness to faculties and in the valence they commanded in any given institution. These discords, by no means resolved at the present time, are intimately related to the question of whose goals a college or university should represent.

TEACHING AND LEARNING: THE BASIC FUNCTION

The world's increasing complexity, the growing diversity of student bodies, and the clash between new visions of promoting technological efficiency and old traditions of nurturing human individuality are only three of the contemporary conditions that impose distinctive strains on American colleges and universities. If these conditions have offered rich opportunities and given great advantages to our institutions, they have also led to new student movements, to changing relationships between faculty and administration, to uneasiness about the quality of teaching, and to criticism of the curriculum. Indeed, given the wide range of intellectually productive and economically rewarding roles now available to the professoriate, one can legitimately raise the question of whether our institutions still function primarily as *schools.*

It is necessary that we identify the fundamental problems affecting undergraduate education in the domains of the student body, the faculty, and the curriculum—the three awesomely large spheres of interest that the functions of teaching and learning inevitably touch.

Perhaps if we take as our starting point the many expressions of student discontent that have swept the country, regarding them as serious in intention and as prophetic of new and enduring circumstances on our campuses, we will be able to perceive that the characteristics of contemporary student bodies, the climates of our institutions, the roles, backgrounds, and dominant attitudes of faculty members, and the nature of the curriculum (which is, in essence, whatever it is that happens in college classrooms) are closely interrelated.

Students are demanding more freedom both in and outside the classroom. Refusing to be treated like products on an assembly line, they conceive of learning as a process that entails action and participation. Some of them claim that partnership in the enterprise is a necessary condition of effective learning. To the student, the danger inherent in mass education and in the government's present involvement in education is that these will lead to the creation of a "system," which imposes on its end products—the graduates—certain fixed qualities and constrains them to live up to a narrowly conceived set of specifications.

Given this mistrust of The System and this demand for relevance and personal involvement in the learning experience, to what extent are questions about the processes of teaching and the nature of the learning environment questions about the methods rather than the goals of a college education? Are closer contact with professors, a voice in matters of curriculum and tenure, freedom in dormitories, freedom of speech, and freedom in dress an end in themselves, or are they means to some other end?

When students seek greater freedom within the curriculum and the environment of the campus, what are they asking for? What are their objectives in curriculum reform? What do they mean by "relevance"? If students are to become creative and innovative adults, capable of adjusting to the explosion of knowledge and the complexities of the modern age, then are their traditional roles as note-takers and reiterators of bits of fact and opinion sufficient? What equipment must they acquire in college if they are to lead meaningful lives? And who is to determine what that equipment is or how "meaningful" should be defined?

Student demands today are often at intense odds with the time-honored rules that govern campus life, with the typical interests of professors, and with the objectives and content of their courses. To what extent are these conflicts accounted for by the following hypotheses?

1. That student discontent, regardless of its specific content and its often unfortunate forms of expression, constitutes a symptom of nationwide academic failure to meet human needs relevantly and meaningfully.

2. That it is erroneous to regard college teaching (meaning by that the professor's performance in the classroom) as the only profession which requires no formal preparation.

3. That the increased support for research and the rewards given for a greater variety of faculty roles help to reinforce what is most professorial in professors, thereby enlarging the gulf between them and undergraduate students.

4. That the curriculum represents a compound of tradition and the scholarly concerns of men understandably more committed to the advancement of their disciplines than to the issues associated with undergraduate learning and undergraduate motivation.

The central question seems to be "Whose goals are important around here?" To what extent are the goals of government, trustees, administrators, and faculty different from those of students? Although students and other segments of the academic community undoubtedly have some common goals, there are obviously areas of conflict; unless these can be identified, understood, and appropriately dealt with, the basic function—teaching and learning—cannot be maximally performed in our colleges and universities.

THE RESEARCH FUNCTION AND THE ADVANCEMENT OF KNOWLEDGE

Research has been blamed for many of the ills currently afflicting American higher education. It has been held responsible for usurping facilities and manpower from classroom teaching, for taking senior professors out of the classroom, and for draining off funds that otherwise would have been spent for teaching. In addition, scientific research has been accused of subverting the position of the humanities and the social sciences. As long as the debate is posed in terms of mutually exclusive alternatives—teaching *or* research, publish *or* perish —it has little chance of being resolved. Such a view oversimplifies and obscures the problem. For it is not a matter of the incompatibility of functions, but of emphasis and degree, of priorities and goals. If research is one of the three main functions of a university, what kinds of research should be considered inappropriate? How much is too much?

Although the teacher-scholar has long been an ideal in American higher education, no definition of "research" has been agreed upon, and herein lies part of the problem. Before one can decide whether research is good or bad for an institution, one must know what it is. Does "research" include unrelenting inquiry in one's field, the constant synthesis of materials for the sake of advancing both the professor's and his students' understanding? Does it make any real difference if the professor "publishes" the result of this scholarship in classroom lectures rather than in a learned journal or a book? Is the printed word the only criterion of effective research?

The dichotomy between basic and applied research has also made for confusing and unfortunate value judgments. Basic research, it is argued, is proper for an institution, and applied research is not. Fritz Machlup, a proponent of this view, speaks of the "opportunity cost" of basic research:

> The "opportunity cost" of basic research is applied research. Of the three possible uses of the scientist—to produce new scientific knowledge, to produce new technological knowledge, and to produce new scientists—two are complementary with each other, and one is competitive with these two. But if society foregoes some new technological developments at the moment, for the sake of more scientific training and scientific research, the immediate sacrifice is likely to be small compared with the future benefits.[2]

But the critical issue is not so much whether the research is basic or applied; it is how far the research must be or can be compatible with the other objectives of the institution. Should all research be of the kind that enhances and strengthens the teaching or public service functions of the institution? What kinds of research are particularly appropriate for liberal arts colleges? Although Machlup's "opportunity cost" analysis would give strong preference to basic research because of society's long-term interests, it does not necessarily follow that basic research is appropriate for every discipline at every institution. Applied

[2] Machlup, *The Production and Distribution of Knowledge in the United States* (Princeton, N.J.: Princeton University Press, 1962), pp. 204–5.

research may conflict with teaching responsibilities, but then again, in many cases, it may not. One may well ask if classified research—whether basic or applied—is a legitimate aspect of the university's function of advancing knowledge, in view of the circumstance that the investigators are prohibited from publicly disseminating the results of such research.

The research function may differ from institution to institution and, within the institution, from department to department. If so, what criteria, rationalized in what fashion, define the appropriateness of research activity for particular institutions? Furthermore, who is to decide: the individual scholars, the faculty as a whole, administrators, trustees, or students? If institutions can find the proper means for determining that some kinds of research are more appropriate to them than other kinds, we may achieve greater coherence on our campuses.

PUBLIC SERVICE AND HIGHER EDUCATION: COMPATIBILITY OR CONFLICT?

Although both teaching and research, even "pure" research, ultimately benefit society, it is the public service function of the university that is today most commonly identified with the goals of the government and the community rather than with those of full-time students and faculty. The notion that colleges and universities have a duty to perform public service has changed the whole relationship between the university and society in the United States. While the academic community has struggled internally to adapt to the changing roles and goals of its students, faculty, and administrators, the external community has urged upon it new functions and different objectives. Many people regard the question of "whose goals?" as expressing primarily a conflict between the internal and the external worlds, with the internal being sharply divided.

Even if this oversimplified view were accurate, however, the question is not *whether* government should be involved in higher education, but in what ways and to what extent institutions must be responsive and responsible to society. In making an assessment, we may find it useful to compare our system with systems of several other countries.

In the Soviet Union, where national needs and higher education are tightly coordinated,

> Education is constantly and directly used both as an instrument of social policy and to manipulate the supply of trained manpower in a deliberate and detailed manner quite foreign to the Western way of thinking. Higher education is completely professional in aim. Each

course earns a qualification entitling the holder to practise in some branch of the economy. . . . The total enrollment of the universities and the colleges in the Soviet Union is determined by the requirements of the nation for specialists.[3]

The answer to "whose goals?" is clear: the state's.

Although the French government does not seem to regulate higher education in accord with national needs, its central control of the entire system would be objectionable to even the most enthusiastic advocate of coordinated higher education in this country. The Ministry of National Education controls practically all public educational establishments. As the Robbins Report says, "The dominance of the faculties, and their narrow range, is . . . one conspicuous feature of French higher education."[4] The high degree of centralization is illustrated by the fact that in 1960 more than one-third of the total number of students in France were at the University of Paris. Furthermore, even the details of staffing and of the university's budget are subject to close government supervision. Most academic appointments fall within the province of the Minister of National Education. At all levels of education, the state controls admissions policy, curricula, examinations, and academic awards. Scientific and technological research is directed by a ministerial committee under the chairmanship of the Prime Minister.

In postwar Germany, where the old traditions of *Lehrfreiheit* and *Lernfreiheit* have survived basically unchanged, the university is essentially divorced from the larger community, and the educational system has great difficulty responding to national needs. As a result, the obvious needs to expand the university, to develop the teaching function as well as scholarship, to plan a rational allocation of expensive research facilities—problems shared by most countries in recent years —have, in Germany, given rise to peculiar tensions. Although, as in France, institutions of higher education are publicly controlled, they are not controlled by the central government, and the organizational pattern of the school system varies considerably from one state to another. The constitution entrusts education to the governments of the states, leaving the federal government with no more than a general responsibility for learning and research.

England is encountering similar problems in its efforts to coordinate higher education with national needs. Robert Berdahl came to the conclusion that

---

[3] Committee on Higher Education, *Higher Education* (London: Her Majesty's Stationery Office, 1963), Cmnd. 2154-V, Appendix Five, p. 189.
[4] *Ibid.*, p. 66.

the universities, all privately founded and until recent years largely self-financed, formerly governed themselves in splendid isolation from one another and the state; now, however, they have become in effect part of an articulated national system of higher education, each still self-governing but strongly influenced by national policies in many of its decisions regarding curricula, faculty, student body, capital plant, and research, and each currently receiving an amount near the national average of three-fourths of its annual income from state funds.[5]

However different the systems of Germany, France, Russia, and England are from one another, they each contrast even more sharply with the system in the United States. Not that our government has avoided involvement in higher education: in its pragmatic wisdom, it has simply been careful not to run higher education.

Contemporary America is increasingly dependent upon the university for socially beneficial research and for innovation, as well as for the development of manpower. If present institutions of higher learning did not respond to these societal needs, the government would have to invent new institutions. But if Sir Eric Ashby is correct in stating that, in order to survive, educational institutions must be both sufficiently stable and sufficiently responsive,[6] then it is necessary that we determine whether the absorption of so many additional functions has endangered the stability of our institutions. American colleges and universities have not been ivory towers. They have played a decisive role in advancing American democracy, they have furnished the professional training needed by a growing nation, they have contributed to the efficiency of its economy by making possible the specialization required by a technological age, and they have helped advance man's knowledge of himself and his universe.

But are there no limits to the university's obligation to provide public service? Does society have no goals that may be regarded as over and beyond the duty and responsibility of higher education? Where is the critical divide between activities which are closely related to central academic functions and those which are at best peripheral? Must the separate functions of teaching and research always be justified by their contribution to public service? Lest higher education become too enmeshed in extraneous demands, we must continually ask ourselves the question: In what academic sense is this service important?

[5] Berdahl, *British Universities and the State* (Berkeley: University of California Press, 1959), p. 2.

[6] Ashby, *Universities: British, Indian, African* (Cambridge, Mass.: Harvard University Press, 1966), p. 3.

THE UNIVERSITY AS CRITIC:
OBJECTIVE OR PARTISAN?

In addition to pursuing their three main goals—teaching, research, and public service—colleges and universities play an important contemplative and critical role in society. Not only must they provide the atmosphere and opportunity for freedom of inquiry and debate as necessary conditions of the search for truth, but also they must serve as the main trustees of civilization. As such, institutions of higher learning have an obligation to lead. If they are to help create a greater society and a better world, they must be able to criticize as well as to comply, to shape as well as to serve.

In its role as critic, the university must maintain a delicate balance between propriety and strategy. It is expected to adhere to the rules of scholarship, to make no undignified noises. Many people would add that, if its stance is to be considered a responsible one, the university as critic must be objective. But does this mean that its criticism must be value-free? Can it lead without sometimes being partisan?

Is the university free to criticize all concerns of society, or are some areas to be regarded as sacrosanct? Does the critical function include, for instance, either endorsement of or attacks upon political positions, conventional middle-class mores, or traditional moral values? Must the university accept the world as it is and promote only those values that are currently honored by society? How does a university, in its function as critic, distinguish what is relevant to its enterprise from what is not? What guides are there, if any? Must the university conform to all the laws of Federal, state, and local governments? What if the laws are offensive to most constituents of the academic community, as, for instance, were those laws in some states which, until recently, required racial discrimination? Should the institution refrain from criticism when constituents of the academic community disagree, as in those questions of sexual morality where the students' view may be at odds with accepted norms?

What methods are appropriate to the university as critic? Should students, faculty, administrators, trustees, or government officials be allowed to force the university as an entity to take (or to refuse to take) a position as critic of society or even to be an agency for action in social reform? Is it ever proper for a university to act as such an agency, or does the contemplative role restrict its involvement, even though inaction implies tacit acceptance of the *status quo?*

Is it proper for an institution to be an implicit critic of the *status quo* through the administration of its internal policies? For example, should institutions decline to cooperate with local draft boards, refuse to permit their scientists to engage in research on biological warfare, openly defy traditional sex mores by authorizing their clinics to dispense contraceptives, permit Communists or other extremists the use of a campus forum, overlook the use of alcohol or drugs by students or faculty, or refuse to administer governmental scholarships and loans that require students to sign loyalty oaths?

Can institutions continue to serve such a contemplative and critical function as they and their destinies become increasingly entangled with the daily affairs of the community at large? Given the government's heavy involvement in the university and the professor's increased activity as consultant for both public and private agencies, can the members of the academic community still take a responsibly reflective view of our society? Delivering homilies on the virtues of democracy and freedom is easy. It is both more difficult and more important to maintain on our campuses the intellectual and moral climates that facilitate ethical and social growth. To help bring our moral and humane achievements to the level of our material and technological attainments is surely part of the mission of higher education.

THE ACADEMIC COMMUNITY: WHO DECIDES WHAT?

Recent shifts in the power centers of higher education—shifts attributable in part to the complexities created by increases in size and function and in part to the changing roles and activities of students and faculty—make it mandatory that we attempt to develop a viable decision-making process to replace the old and outdated pattern. We must consider which decisions should be made by (or with the advice and consent of) students, faculty, administrators, trustees, or outside agents. Who decides what about the curriculum, about the creation of new departments, about staffing? Who should participate in the decision-making process? And who should have final authority?

Legally, the power of the governing board is very broad; the board has sufficient power to make and enforce rules, and it often has authority to determine the policies of the institution, to elect its president, and to hire and fire its faculty members. In practice, however, this power is limited—or perhaps more accurately, self-limiting. An enlightened board which seeks to assure the integrity of education understands the need to respect the collective judgment of the community of scholars. As Robert MacIver says: "An institution cannot be well governed unless each of its components clearly recognizes its obligations as well as its rights in the promotion of the common end."[7]

If the board of trustees in both the public and the private institutions is "the protector of the public interest in higher education," as Millett says,[8] in what special types of decisions does the board enjoy a prerogative? Is it to decide on *all* matters which relate to the public interest? Do these include admissions standards, curriculum, course syllabi, decorum on the campus, and the extracurricular activities of faculty and students?

As to the faculty's role, "Traditionally, the university itself, not any outsider, sets its own goals, establishes its own standards, charts its own paths; and it does this most effectively by delegation to the professors—not even to the faculty as a group, but to the professors individually."[9] Is this tradition any longer functional? We scoff at the perennially sophomoric alumnus who tries to recreate the college as he remembers it, but do we ask our teacher-scholar-consultants whether they are viewing the world as it is today? Can we still say that the university sets its own goals, considering that most of its research funds come from the government, foundations, industry, and other outside sources? Should professors still establish and enforce their own standards when, like entrepreneurs, they seek research grants, publishing contracts, consultantships from industry, and recognition outside the university?

There has emerged in recent years a pattern of faculty behavior which has created new dilemmas for the governance of the academic community. At one time, a professor's commitment was to his campus: "The academic world was composed exclusively of 'locals' in contrast to 'cosmopolitans.' Characteristically, a man's status and his advancement depended far more upon what he was in the eyes of those immediately around him—colleagues, administration, and students— than upon whatever reputation he may have acquired in national or professional terms."[10] One wonders now if, in this new academic marketplace, the professor can be depended upon to take an interest and to participate in local campus concerns. Should the faculty be given full autonomy over all matters specifically relating to the curriculum, the content of courses, and the conduct of teaching and re-

---

[7] MacIver, *Academic Freedom in Our Time* (New York: Columbia University Press, 1955), p. 73.

[8] John Millett, *The Academic Community* (New York: McGraw-Hill Book Co., 1962), pp. 183-84.

[9] W. Allen Wallis, "Centripetal and Centrifugal Forces in University Organization," *Daedalus*, Fall 1964, p. 1073.

[10] Robert A. Nisbet, "The Permanent Professors: A Modest Proposal," *Public Interest*, Fall 1965, p. 43.

search? What role should students play? Who resolves the conflicts between the faculty and students over the curriculum or those between the administration and faculty over the kinds of research appropriate for an institution?

More and more, decisions about curricular development, research, specific projects, construction, and so forth are based on such external considerations as the prospects for foundation and government grants. Federal and state aid for scholarships, dormitories, student unions, and other facilities sometimes determines the dynamics of growth and the policies of an institution more than does its endowment or fund-raising potential or its stated objectives. It becomes increasingly difficult to distinguish the internal from the external. Publicly supported colleges and universities are coming more and more under the jurisdiction of state and regional coordinating councils or commissions. Public and private institutions are together evolving consortia and regional associations. National organizations and the Federal government, in their efforts to find solutions to common problems, emphasize the interdependence of institutions.

These trends have tended to erode the college administrator's freedom in making decisions. They have fragmented authority and responsibility both on and off campus, altering the power structure of American higher education. Thus, it is imperative that we reassess the decisional roles of the constituents of the academic community. Because decisions range from enforcing dormitory rules to expanding a college, from abolishing football to raising tuition charges, and from dropping a course in Greek to supporting a Free University, "who decides what?" may not be susceptible of a single answer; rather we may have to establish a new and broad theoretical framework for academic governance.

INSTITUTIONAL COHERENCE AND PRIORITIES

Virtually the entire panorama of human affairs is now the business of the American university; it performs valued services for students, unions, government, industry, and almost every other segment of society. The multiple goals of the university are compounded by the multiple goals of its faculty members, and the inevitable conflicts that arise from this multiplication have made the choice of priorities exceedingly difficult. It is imperative that we determine whether it is advisable for institutions of higher education to carry out so many tasks.

Is it possible to define the special concerns of a rapidly changing society that higher education is distinctively qualified to address itself to? Is it appropriate for higher education to reject certain tasks now pressed upon it? How much choice should society allow to its primary institutions of intellect? Should some of these tasks be channeled to profit-making and nonprofit enterprises or be performed, in-house, by the government?

The task of creating coherence and unity of purpose within our academic institutions is made more difficult by the extreme degree of individualism and decentralization which characterizes most of our colleges and universities. Even small liberal arts colleges are fragmented by departmental parochialism. Furthermore, many functions are interrelated with other important endeavors, as in the example of research that not only serves to advance knowledge but also has more immediate advantages, such as attracting to the institution, funds, well-known faculty, and good graduate students. Any ordering of priorities necessarily means that some vested interests will gain and some will lose.

Coherence within the campus is disrupted by centrifugal forces which cause institutions to lose control over activities within their own walls. The decision of whether to build first a student union, a library, a classroom, or a science building is determined more by the availability of Federal loans than by internal needs. Universities apply for, accept, and house research grants without adequately checking whether the research supports and enhances the purposes of the university or whether it diverts energies, space, time, and effort from more important institutional endeavors. In the academic game of grantsmanship, universities, by seeking the same prizes and badges of prestige, conform to values which have been determined by external forces. In doing so, they lose their individuality.

Although all colleges and universities share collective functions of teaching, research, and public service, each institution may have a distinctive role in the whole division of labor. The common goals of higher education may be almost infinite, but the local means to pursue them are always finite, and the nation may be better served if each institution pursues only those goals which are suitable to its requirements, needs, and abilities.

These questions we seek to answer are thorny and troublesome. They require a comprehensive reassessment of the mission and aims of colleges and universities, but they cannot be wished away. They provide the context within which our urgent theme of "whose goals?" is inevitably embedded.

PART I

The Basic Missions
Of Higher Education

PHILIP R. WERDELL

Teaching and Learning: Whose Goals Are Important Around Here?

College can contribute to the growth of student values only when it penetrates the core of his life and confronts him with fresh and often disturbing implications which are different from those he and his society have taken for granted.

Philip E. Jacob, in Changing Values in College [1]

You have to struggle with the nitty-gritty.

A student, at the National Conference on Student Stress in the College Experience, November 1965

If AMERICAN COLLEGES and universities are to take teaching seriously, they must provide space for student development, they must make the private needs and concerns of students a dominant thrust in their policy. This priority status for teaching calls for an alliance between educators and student innovators, more concern with how college graduates act as well as with how much they learn, and major innovations in the approach to student learning.

A highly developed democratic society is caught in the conflict of having to shape its educational institutions to meet both the needs of the individual members of a highly diverse student body and the needs of a society which allows individuality to flourish. I have limited this paper to a search for practical solutions that walk the razor's edge of these often competing needs. The first section sketches a setting for

[1] Jacob, *Changing Values in College: An Exploratory Study of the Impact of College Teaching* (New York: Harper & Bros., 1957).

an alliance between educators and student innovators and suggests the minimal conditions necessary for cooperation to begin. The second section outlines the goals of the alliance and suggests some general problems that might be discussed. The third section concentrates on three simple and practical learning models that could be initiated without any reforms to the present curriculum and that might themselves generate further improvements.

AN ALLIANCE FOR LEARNING

> *American colleges and universities are immunizing a generation of leaders.*
> John Gardner
> *Secretary of Health, Education, and Welfare*

> *Students are being had. Their education is not preparing them for the world in which they live.*
> *Editorial,* Moderator

Mass higher education is already upon us, and by 1970, the estimates predict, half the population between eighteen and twenty-one will be in degree-granting institutions. In 1940 there were 1.8 million college students; in 1970 they will number over 8.1 million. Along with the growth in numbers of students, there is already a shift from small, sectarian, residential colleges to vast, urban, commuter universities as the principal purveyors of higher education. It is expected that by 1970 over half of college students will be in major metropolitan centers and commute to campuses of institutions enrolling over 5,000 undergraduates. If these trends continue (this paper assumes that they will), the multiversity will become the chief means to higher education in the United States.

While the small liberal arts colleges are hustling for funds, facilities, and faculties (*and* regional alliances, so that they, too, can be multiversities), the multiversity is searching for an identity. Its growth has been rapid, and its direction and goals have been defined largely by those interests in American life large and powerful enough to command attention to their demands. Business expects the multiversity to train managers and technicians. Government expects the multiversity to supply consultants and to perform research. Labor expects the multiversity to provide a less expensive degree. Cities expect it to offer extension courses at the same time that it is the intellectual and cultural center of the city. The faculty expects an extension of the traditional curriculum for undergraduates and also more graduate assistants.

Administration of a multiversity is, almost by necessity, a holding action. In the face of conflicting demands and purposes, balance among the competing forces is reluctantly substituted for the more difficult task of molding an institution that best fosters diversity among its students.

The educator

During the 1950's educators began heroic acts of self-analysis and self-criticism. Three major collections of research at the end of the decade offered a resounding indictment of higher education. By this time the United States had become the most powerful country in the world and had committed itself to increasing involvement in international affairs. Yet Percy W. Bidwell's report on *Undergraduate Education in Foreign Affairs* stated that "seniors emerge from . . . college with hardly any more acquaintance with foreign affairs than when they entered as freshmen."[2] In the latter half of the decade it was becoming apparent that technological revolution was rapidly creating new societal environments. Yet Philip Jacob could shock the educational community with his finding that "the college student does not significantly change his view of himself or the society in which he lives as an undergraduate."[3] Finally, many of the most distinguished educators in the country offered well-documented findings, in Nevitt Sanford's *The American College,* that, in essence, intellectual development and personal development were inextricably intertwined, but higher education was not dealing adequately with the former because it was not dealing at all with the latter.[4] The verdict was clear: with regard to teaching and learning American higher education is provincial, structurally stagnant, and psychologically simplistic.

A wide range of experimental programs have successfully produced better models of teaching and learning, but for most students, undergraduate education continues to be an extension of the goals, the requirements, and the methods developed a century ago in response to the industrial revolution. Research demonstrates the great need to re-evaluate and reform the approach to student learning, but educators have not succeeded in translating results of research into broad-based reforms.

Students are themselves beginning to understand this problem,

[2] New York: Columbia University Press, 1962.
[3] Jacob, *Changing Values in College.*
[4] Sanford (ed.), *The American College: A Psychological and Social Interpretation of Higher Learning* (New York: John Wiley & Sons, 1962).

and they are quick to sense that it is they who have the most to lose. As Sanford recently put it,

> Only a few years ago, in *The American College,* I expressed the hope that public criticism of our colleges might induce the scholars and research men who run them to institute some reforms. It never occurred to me that students would soon organize protests against the education they were receiving or that leading citizens would join the academic establishment in support of the old way of doing things.[5]

Students cannot deal with the multiversity in the traditional and accepted manner employed by business, government, labor, and community leaders. Students do not have the money of businessmen, the legislative authority of government, the organization of labor, or the personal contacts of community leaders. More important, student expectations are more diverse and personal, always changing, and never satisfied by a simple plan or a slight accommodation. Yet students are a growing force with which the multiversity must reckon. Student veterans of the civil rights movement brought the skills of mass political organization back to campus, and students will not *un*learn the lesson that, beyond the power of their feelings and ideas, they now have a new power in their easily organized numbers.

The student innovator

Although the campus demonstration is the most visible indication of student discontent, it is *not* the major concern of most student activists. The similarity of the arguments of educators and the protests of students have been widely noted; equally, if not more, important, however, are the broad-based innovations and reforms initiated by these same students. Few of them have read *The American College;* yet through the student community tutorial movement more than 200,000 of them at over twelve hundred campuses are volunteering 7,000,000 hours a year to carry reforms into the primary and secondary schools of the ghetto that Sanford intended for higher education.[6] *Changing Values in College* is hardly a campus best-seller; yet thousands of student veterans of the civil rights movement took the Student Non-Violent Coordinating Committee's (SNCC) Robert Moses Paris seriously when he said, "Don't use Mississippi as a moral lightning rod.

[5] Nevitt Sanford, "The Development of Leadership in Higher Education," Address to the Association for Higher Education, March 17, 1967 (Mimeographed).

[6] Lowell Dodge, "The ABC's of Community Tutorial," *Moderator,* February 1967; also Tutorial Assistance Center, *Directory of Tutorial Projects* (Washington: United States National Student Association, 1966).

Use it as a looking glass. Look into it and see what it tells you about America—about yourself."[7] Hardly any undergraduates have read *Undergraduate Education in Foreign Affairs;* yet Paul Potter's challenge to create a social movement around the issue of Vietnam circulates widely on campus in mimeographed form. In a statement of the kind that attracts more student commitment than newspaper coverage, the former president of the Students for a Democratic Society (SDS) explained,

> By social movement, I mean more than marches, petitions and letters of protest or tacit support of dissident Congressmen; I mean people who are willing to change their lives, who are willing to challenge the system, to take the problem of change seriously. By social movement I mean an effort that is powerful enough to make the country understand that our problems are not in Vietnam or China or Brazil or outer space or at the bottom of the ocean, but here in the United States. What we must begin to do is build a democratic and humane society in which Vietnams are unthinkable.[8]

Note that veterans of student movements have the very qualities that educators would like to see in all college graduates—a fair degree of psychological sophistication, a high sensitivity to social change, and a deep personal concern for the role of the United States in the world.

A growing number of student veterans of the civil rights and other student movements have become conscious and critical of the inadequacies of their formal education. Many have led large demonstrations on campus, and many more are ready to do so if they deem it necessary. At the same time, students are little preoccupied with the tactics of confrontation, and, as innovators, they are attempting to create constructive, lasting reforms. An alliance between educators and student innovators could bring to bear a combination of professional expertise and student organizational ability on the task of reforming American higher education's approach to student learning. I have purposely left the labels "educator" and "student innovator" undefined; they would include those who provisionally accept the discussion above and are willing to enter into such an alliance.

The condition of the alliance

The condition that would foster an alliance between educators and student innovators is precisely the same condition necessary to a reform of higher education's approach to student learning—student academic

[7] Paris, untitled address at a Students for a Democratic Society march on Washington in protest of the war in Vietnam, April 17, 1965.

[8] Potter, untitled address at a Students for a Democratic Society march on Washington in protest of the war in Vietnam, April 17, 1965.

freedom. Charles Frankel's paper on "Rights and Responsibilities in the Student-College Relationship" prepared for the American Council on Education in 1965 contained as cogent and concise an argument for student academic freedom as any student has made:

> The right of students to present and to consider points of view of their own choice outside the classroom, and the right to do so as an intrinsic part of their collegiate experience, is a necessary condition for students' own free inquiries. The granting of this right cannot be construed as a matter of pedagogical policy, subject simply to the determination of the faculty. It is properly regarded as the recognition of a constitutional right of students, a right they require as a protection against pedagogical domination.
>
> The second reason the view is mistaken that students have no academic freedom in their own right is implicit in [the fact that] students are a part of the educational process, contributors to it and not merely beneficiaries of it. They do as much to educate one another as teachers do, and sometimes they educate teachers. . . . The college has an obligation, insofar as its resources permit, to make its facilities available to students for such inquiries. In doing so, the college does not grant students a privilege. It responds to their legitimate claim, as members of an academic community, to contribute to its activities.[9]

The need for a strong policy of student academic freedom is most urgent when, as educators would like and as student innovators could stimulate, students take responsibility for their own education. It is implicit here that a student must be allowed to make his own mistakes: lacking opportunity to build on his failures, he also lacks opportunity to develop his own successes.

Proposals have been made for a statement of student academic freedom by national organizations representing the three components of the educational community: the "Student Bill of Rights and Responsibilities"[10] of the United States National Student Association (USNSA), the draft "Statement on the Academic Freedom of Students,"[11] of Committee S, American Association of University Professors (AAUP), and the draft "Statement of Desirable Provisions for Student Freedom to Learn"[12] of the Association of American Colleges (AAC).

---

[9] Frankel, in *The College and the Student,* ed. Lawrence E. Dennis and Joseph F. Kauffman (Washington: American Council on Education, 1966), p. 242.

[10] Nineteenth National Student Congress, *Codification of Policy* (Washington: United States National Student Association, 1966).

[11] Committee S, American Association of University Professors, "Statement on the Academic Freedom of Students," *AAUP Bulletin,* Winter 1965, pp. 447–49.

[12] Commission on Students and Faculty of the Association of American Colleges, "Statement of Desirable Provisions for Student Freedom to Learn," May 3, 1966. (After this paper was prepared, the three organizations each approved a *Joint Statement on Student Academic Freedom.*)

Although the three statements differ somewhat in approach and emphasis, they are notable for their considerable agreement. Meetings of these and other national educational organizations have succeeded in arriving at a tentative draft of a common statement. Educators and student innovators on the campus may well begin their alliance by considering together these three documents and attempting to draw up a strong and effective policy for student academic freedom for their institution. From such meetings of students, faculty, and administrators on every campus, a cooperative effort might not only assert the rights of students but also start reform in higher education's approach to student learning. Without such an effort, confrontation remains imminent.

THE GOALS OF THE ALLIANCE

> *A great many college professors do not have extended interest in exploring the ultimate effect of college education. This lack of interest is so striking that it cannot be attributed merely to a hesitation to engage in self-study. It stems rather from a deep-lying philosophy—from the college teacher's conviction that the subject matter he teaches has absolute worth, quite aside from its effect on his students.*
>
> Joseph Katz, *in* The American College [13]

> *Higher education is confusing the teaching of subject matter with the learning of subjects that matter.*
>
> *Tom Hayden, Students for a Democratic Society (SDS)*

Colleges and universities, mankind as a whole, are growing knowledge-rich and understanding-poor. Oversimplified, curricula in most American colleges and universities are based solely on a search for knowledge and truth. A "problem" is solved when the "true," "correct," reasonable answer is discovered and verified. Knowledge is transmitted through organizing intellectual analysis of a problem into a lecture, paper, or book. The primary goals of teaching are to transmit an organized body of knowledge to the student and to help him develop the power of critical judgment. It is assumed that when a student has amassed a large body of knowledge and acquired a highly developed analytical ability, he is prepared to deal with the problems of society and to pursue further learning on his own. He is left to solve for himself the formidable problem of integrating learning and living.

[13] Katz, "The Classroom: Personality and Interpersonal Relations," *The American College.*

The goal of an alliance between educators and student innovators should be to develop teaching and learning models which help the student in this increasingly difficult and increasingly important task of integrating learning and living. While cognitive learning should have priority, the process of integrating learning and living clearly demands new emphasis on other kinds and styles of learning. Specifically, the curriculum must offer experiences in the creative and speculative uses of the intellect as well as analytical uses. Specifically, the curriculum must offer practice in dealing with people from diverse backgrounds, of various life styles, with differing goals, as well as practice in understanding their problems from a distance. Specifically, the curriculum must offer challenges to act on the basis of what one understands as well as theorizing about ideal solutions. In short, the curriculum must introduce students to a variety of styles of learning as well as a variety of bodies of knowledge. In no other way will a generation of students be prepared to use what they have learned to solve the problems of their society. In no other way will the student learn that the pursuit of knowledge and truth is personally relevant: before he can become a self-directed learner, he must understand that learning can be self-actualizing.

Until now, serious criticism of higher education has tended to be polarized. On the one hand are those, both educators and student innovators, who maintain that higher education must assume responsibility for meeting important social needs and that these needs have been deliberately or inadvertently misrepresented. On the other hand are those, both educators and student innovators, who maintain that higher education must pay first attention to the development of the individual student, and that it now does not do so. Ironically, one criticism cannot be met without meeting the other. Teaching and learning models which attempt to integrate learning and living must themselves be relevant to both.

The examples which follow are threefold in purpose: first, they demonstrate that some less analytical styles of learning are as necessary to develop citizens who can cope with major social problems as they more obviously are necessary to the development of the individual student; second, they show how these less analytical styles of learning call for risks, settings, attitudes, and rewards different from those in the traditional academic structure; third, they suggest where such teaching and learning models are being constructed today in multiversities by educators and by student innovators.

The problem of the future

All education is commonly thought of as education for the future
in the sense that the past and present are prologue. But this avoids a
crucial problem: many aspects of the future cannot now be anticipated.
Technology in this century is rapidly and radically reshaping the
entire society. In less than a half-century, the airplane has become
a means of transportation that has changed the rules of warfare,
politics, and business. The time span from Rutherford's basic discoveries about the atom to Los Alamos and Hiroshima was only
thirty-five years. The first landing on the moon was less than a decade
after the test run of solid-fuel missiles. How far away is the fusion
of man and machine, now that artificial organs, hormone producers,
transistorized brain supplements are reality in the laboratory?[14]

It is difficult even to anticipate scientific and technological advances, let alone understand their social implications. Yet, there is
probably no greater social need to which higher education must respond. Not that it will arrive at definitive predictions, much less solutions. Colleges and universities can, however, prepare students with
skills for such learning and encourage rigorous practice in their use.
A prime skill is that of creative speculation and synthesis.

Even the best-run academic seminar seldom encourages creative
speculation and synthesis; rather, it furthers analysis of existing information. The communication is discursive, the tone, argumentative;
the teacher is assumed to be an authority, for whose approval there
tends to be informal competition; the grading system reinforces informal sanctions against playing a hunch or speculating about the
implications of an observation. There is a strong, implicit assumption
that the student cannot be trusted.[15]

The challenge to higher education is to expose every student to
learning experiences more conducive to developing his creative capacities, including highly personal free association. If a group is involved,
the tone should often be open and gentle; the attitude should be cooperative and mutually reinforcing. There should be rewards for
daring articulation of experiences and theories. In short, the operating
principle should be that of suspended judgment.[16]

A variety of teaching and learning models to foster highly sophisticated creative thinking have been developed by educators and by

[14] Alvin Toffler, "The Future as a Way of Life," *Harper's*, June 1965.
[15] Carl Rogers, "A Passionate Statement" (Unpublished MS; Western Behavioral Science Institute).
[16] Alex F. Osborn, *Applied Imagination* (New York: Charles Scribner's Sons,
1957).

student innovators. The Institute for Creative Education at the University of Buffalo has developed a basic course, Applied Imagination, and the basic techniques have been applied to courses in a variety of subject fields including: aeronautics (San Jose State College), agriculture (Purdue), architecture (University of Illinois), business management (University of Illinois), chemistry (Graceland College), economics (University of Chattanooga), educational research (University of Colorado), English (Findlay College), engineering (University of Maryland), geography (University of Oregon), group discussion (University of Minnesota), human relations (University of Montreal), industrial design (Georgia Tech), journalism (University of Washington), marketing (Harvard University), physics (Long Beach State), teacher training (Reed College).[17] Major innovations have arisen from the Student-initiated Experimental College at San Francisco State College and from the Campus Dialogue program of the University Christian Movement: At San Francisco State, students were encouraged to design their own courses, and in doing so, they have produced some highly imaginative approaches to subject matter, to say nothing of a unique array of courses.[18] In the Campus Dialogue program, an essay, called a "dialogue focuser," is used to initiate free discussion about new approaches to the problems of education, poverty, and technology.[19]

The problem of a smaller world

American students today have lived since birth under the threat of the Bomb, have been continually bombarded by television coverage of world crises, and increasingly have been able to travel abroad while still in college. They should be gaining a new concern for, and knowledge of, world affairs. Yet, the complexity of international problems leads most students to believe that little they learn or do can matter. And they will gain little from their "educative experience" so long as they travel in the comfortable company of other Americans, limit their trips to Western Europe, and have little prolonged contact with natives of developing countries. A student may become highly involved in international crises through intimate, on-the-spot television coverage, but only frustration or indignation build when he can take no comparably involving action; thus resignation sets in. It is a source of con-

[17] *Ibid.*
[18] "A Declaration of Educational Independence," *Moderator*, November 1966.
[19] Richard Kean (ed.), *Dialogue on Education* (New York: Bobbs-Merrill Co., 1967).

cern to every student that a few people in positions of power could annihilate the world in a matter of hours. Yet because the individual student sees little that he can do to prevent this power play, he seldom even discusses the subject. Instead, he becomes fatalistic.[20]

The traditional curriculum, even if transplanted to another country, will not fulfill the need for exposure to people from other cultures and for practice in listening, even if not with empathy, to their opinions and aspirations.[21] Two elements would be missing: firsthand association with others; and opportunity for intense, personal encounters. Two teaching and learning models which might be adapted by colleges and universities are to be found in the work of the Human Relations Laboratories, developed by the National Training Laboratories, and the Training Program for volunteers to the Peace Corps. In the former, a heterogeneous group enters a two-week retreat to focus upon sensitivity training and interpersonal relations.[22] In the Peace Corps Training Program, volunteers are given intensive orientation to one country, using a variety of teaching and learning techniques but relying heavily on association with native instructors.[23]

The leading student innovation in intensive cross-culture experience is the community tutorial movement in which the new culture is, not that of another country, but the "other America," the culture of poverty. Students leading these programs have developed a sophisticated orientation to ghetto life, and have developed models for facilitating relationships between student tutors and the children and even with the children's parents.[24]

The problem of larger systems

Students today have more knowledge at their disposal, are pursuing education longer, and have more opportunities upon graduation than any previous generation, but the systems within which the students develop have become so vast, so imposing, and so awesome that most students feel only a profound sense of powerlessness. With 15,000

[20] W. Eugene Groves, "The New Plights and Pleas of Students," Address to the *Moderator* Drop-in, New York, June 15, 1967.

[21] Irwin Abrams, "The Student Abroad," *Higher Education: Some Newer Developments*, ed. Samuel Baskin (New York: McGraw-Hill Book Co., 1965).

[22] Leland Bradford, Jack R. Gibb, Kenneth D. Benne (eds.), *T-Group Theory and Laboratory Method: Innovation in Re-education* (New York: John Wiley & Sons, 1964).

[23] Michael Rossman, "Notes on the Implications of the Movement Regarding Educational Reform" (Mimeographed; Washington: United States National Student Association, 1966).

[24] A wide variety of publications describing and evaluating community tutorial programs are available in mimeographed form from the Tutorial Assistance Center, United States National Student Association, Washington, D.C.

significant journals being published every year, with the body of knowledge doubling every ten years, the student is at a loss to decide where he should begin, much less what he should pursue. With bureaucracies becoming larger and larger, with the prerequisites for advancement becoming longer and longer, the student often feels that he is locked into an inevitable pattern and that it is futile to attempt to pursue any new or unique direction. With material advancement no longer presenting a personal challenge for most students, with the number of possible roles one can adopt presenting a bewildering variety of options, the student often feels alienated and finds it difficult to discover his own identity. With society becoming so impacted in urban centers, with the growing necessity to relate on a superficial level to so many people, the student often feels lonely within the crowd.[25]

Today's is a mass society in which it is difficult to develop a sense of personal power. Yet, it is only through self-renewal of the individual that a mass society can develop social mechanisms for its self-renewal. Higher education cannot provide reform of the entire society, but its institutions can prepare students to deal with other institutions that can tackle large problems. Crucial to the undertaking is the ability to act from a sense of personal power and knowledge gained by practice in acting on the basis of what one understands, especially when it has been contrary to the formal and informal rules of society or of its institutions.

The traditional curriculum is itself an institutional system. It may prescribe rules and procedures that encourage passive learning but not action based on the student's own ideas.[26] The challenge to higher education is to offer every student an action curriculum, learning experiences in which he can test the consequences and practicalities of ideas, in which he can see for himself which subjects and styles of learning are relevant, in which he can generate his own ideas and select the concerns and problems he will pursue.

Models for action curricula are plentiful. In the Antioch College work-study program, the student alternates academic study with work every three or six months,[27] the Dearborn Program at the University of Michigan integrates internships in business with technical training;[28] the five-year B.A. at Yale allows a select group of students to under-

[25] Groves, "The New Plights and Pleas of Students."

[26] Rogers, "A Passionate Statement."

[27] W. Hugh Stickler (ed.), *Experimental Colleges: Their Role in American Higher Education* (Tallahassee: Florida State University, 1964).

[28] *Ibid.*

take an independent project abroad between their sophomore and junior years; Eastern Michigan University offers a broad program of work abroad in cooperation with the Peace Corps. Within a single course, an action component is possible: a model in which every student taking Introductory Psychology at the University of Michigan (as many as 1,300) has an opportunity to choose work "in the laboratory of everyday living" is a demonstration that an action curriculum on a mass scale is possible.[29] Student initiative in all of these is obvious. Student participation in the civil rights movement and in urban community action projects was an improvised action curriculum, and models to integrate action concerns of students with more cognitive learning are now being developed by the United States National Student Association.[30]

Research on these teaching and learning models indicates they do not disrupt or even displace the curriculum's traditional concern with developing analytical abilities in students. Every indication is that experience designed to help a student develop his creative ability, social skills, and ability to act on the basis of what he understands also supports and stimulates the cognitive learning of the traditional curriculum. The creative education models developed by the University of Buffalo Institute for Creative Education have been shown to produce large gains in practical problem solving and also to stimulate further reading and study.[31] The group dynamics and sensitivity training models of the National Training Laboratories and the Western Training Laboratories have been shown to facilitate dealings with others and understanding of oneself and also to further purely intellectual pursuits.[32] Students in action curricula have consistently fared at least as well on standard academic tests as those who have not participated in such programs. [33] In short, the introduction of new teaching and learning techniques in higher education would give students more opportunity to pursue their personal development, would help assure society of a supply of college-educated persons better able to cope with new and complex problems. But the new techniques would not for a moment

[29] Richard Mann, "Outreach—An Approach to Human Relationships in the Introductory Psychology Course" and "Some Notes on a Small Society: Psychology 101" (Mimeographed; Ann Arbor: Department of Psychology, University of Michigan).
[30] David Steinberg, "A Proposal for Action Curriculum" (Mimeographed; Washington: United States National Student Association, 1966).
[31] Osborn, *Applied Imagination.*
[32] William C. Schutz and Vernon L. Allen, "The Effects of a T-Group Laboratory on Interpersonal Behavior," *Journal of Applied Behavioral Science,* July-August-September 1966.
[33] Stickler, *Experimental Colleges.*

downgrade the quality of a student's traditional and important pursuit of knowledge and analytical skills.

THREE PRACTICAL AND FUNDAMENTAL
NEW TEACHING AND LEARNING MODELS

> *On at least two points, there seemed to be considerable consensus. First, although the defining lineaments of a good education were not made conceptually clear, there is a widely shared sense that very few colleges and universities offer programs which embody them; and, second, the lack of "really good education" is the central source of student stress.*
>
> Edward Joseph Shoben, Jr., Report of the National
> Conference on Student Stress in the College Experience [34]

> *The main problem with American higher education is that too many students come out of an institution without any understanding of learning. They don't know how to learn.*
>
> *The three main objectives for the student in this process should be to learn his own learning process, to learn what he wants to learn and to learn how to communicate this with other people.*
>
> *If this is accomplished, the student becomes an "autonomous" or "self-directed" learner as opposed to an "authority-centered" learner, dependent upon an external agent to determine how, what and if the student learns.*
>
> Michael Rossman, Free Speech Movement (FSM)

The greatest public service higher education can perform is to develop persons prepared to help solve society's problems—who can articulate new needs, develop new directions of learning and doing, and chart new goals. Only they will be able to assume new roles as old ones become obsolete. Only those who have gained confidence in their own identity and direction can chart new goals for society. The challenge is to develop self-directed learners.

Becoming a self-directed learner is a subjective process, not to be forced. Speeches about student apathy and the need for student responsibility in their own education may raise the issues, but they do not help the student discover what *he* is committed to learn. Nor can self-directed learning be cultivated in an atmosphere in which other thinking and working press; smaller classes may encourage better understanding of the subject matter, but they do not help the student decide what *he* wants to learn. It cannot be achieved for the student by someone else; students on educational policy committees may draw

[34] Washington: United States National Student Association, 1966.

attention to student problems and concerns, but committees do not help most students learn to articulate their own concerns. In short, the institution can develop self-directed learners only by innovating new teaching and learning models through which students can learn their own learning process, learn what they want to learn, and learn how to communicate this with other people.

Described below are three models. *Each could become fully operational without revisions or reforms in the traditional curriculum, with minimal financial commitment on the part of the university, and without adding new educational requirements for students.* Equally important, each is based on innovations that students have formulated in recent years and found successful,[35] and each stems from a longer experimentation by educators.[36] They have been adapted to a form appropriate for undergraduate education, and they are proposed as a practical, fundamental beginning for an alliance between educators and student innovators.

The Reference Group is designed to help a student focus on his own learning process. Nowhere else in the institution is he encouraged to work deliberately, nowhere else is he reinforced in this primary task of education.

The Experimental College is designed to help a student learn how he can best learn what he wants to learn. It encourages the student to formulate an intellectual framework for studying concerns that now lie outside the formal curriculum and to inquire into traditional subject matter in a manner immediately relevant to his interests. It is a focal point where he may attempt to learn what he chooses to learn through integrating learning and living.

The Individual Growth Program is designed to facilitate communication by placing the vast potentials of the computer at the service of the individual student. For the first time the computer would categorize information for the student rather than making him a category of information.

35 The Reference Group is most closely designed after the models of the Student Stress Program of the United States National Student Association. The major model for the Experimental College is the student program at San Francisco State College, 1965-67, although there are about fifty other student experimental colleges or free universities. The major model of the Individual Growth Program is the highly successful Computer Match Dating and the educational interpretations of this by Sherman B. Chickering in "The Student Impact on Educational Technology," Address to the Educational Realities Conference of the American Management Association, Aug. 10, 1966.

36 The experience and research most relevant to the Reference Group will be found at the National Training Laboratories, a division of the National Education Association. The experience and research most relevant to the Experimental College may be found in the Union for Social Science Teaching, temporarily based at the University of Denver, Thomas E. Drabek, secretary.

The Reference Group

At the beginning of the academic year, each student is assigned to a Reference Group that is fairly small (eight to fifteen, to facilitate participation in group discussions) and includes upper and lower classmen, one or two faculty members, and a mix of personalities and backgrounds. One upperclassman is trained in a group dynamics laboratory during the summer or the period immediately preceding the formation of the Reference Group. The group meets intensively the first week of school to become acquainted and to begin work. The task is not that of a traditional academic seminar but, rather, that of helping all members learn about themselves—how they learn, what they want to learn, and how to articulate their progress. Attendance is voluntary, and procedures are available to those who wish to change groups or pursue their goals in a different manner. Students who drop out are offered counseling. The group is encouraged to continue work together throughout the academic year, but must decide for itself how to do so. Alternative ideas and models for working together are fed to the group by the trained upperclassman, who himself meets regularly with other upperclassmen similarly engaged. The training program and the meetings of the upperclassmen are conducted by a small number of creative, skilled professionals.

The Reference Group may be started within a large section of a freshmen class, perhaps by being phased in through progressive reform of freshman orientation. Faculty should be involved from the beginning, for one goal is to have the group replace faculty advisers once work has got under way. The only financial investment is in salaries for the small professional staff that runs the program and possibly pay for the upperclassmen trained in group dynamics. The staff should be responsible to a board of faculty members, administrators, staff from the mental health services, and a diverse group of students. The over-all program may well be developed at a series of week-end retreats of the staff and the board.

It is worth speculating about the possible educational rewards:

· Intensive personal experiences that cut across normal social and friendship lines could lend a sense of community to an otherwise fragmented society. Students and faculty would meet on a basis meaningful to students.

· The training received in sensitivity to others and in group work would carry over to other relationships. Each participant would acquire experience in meaningful communication, and the experience gained in cultivating a group dynamic would facilitate organizing new, autonomous groups.

• As the group continued to meet throughout the year, it could constitute a focal point for students to bring up problems as they happen and explore solutions with others who may have the same problems; often students would have been party to a discussion of another student's problem before they themselves faced a similar situation.

• Upperclassmen would not only bring their own experience to underclassmen but also learn through teaching.

• The groups would provide an efficient and constant means for re-examination of the total educational experience. Students would be encouraged to bring new ideas, as well as personal problems to the group. Likely, many of the "cases" could be written up and made available to other groups. When a new idea was exciting, those interested in trying it out could cooperate in experimenting with reforms at a grass-roots level.

In short, the Reference Group could bring a personal excitement and relevance to abstract but basic elements of education.

The Experimental College

The Experimental College should be student-initiated, and is a logical outgrowth of high-quality student experience with Reference Groups. The philosophy of the Experimental College is best stated in the introduction to the Fall 1966 catalog of the Student Experimental College at San Francisco State College:

> The idea is that students ought to take responsibility for their own education. The assertion is that you can start learning anywhere, as long as you really care about the problem that you tackle and how well you tackle it. The method is one which asks you to learn how to learn, so that you can set the highest conceptual standards for yourself. The assumption is that you are capable of an open-ended contract with yourself to do some learning and capable of playing a major role in evaluating your own performance. The claim is that if people, students, faculty and administrators, work with each other in these ways, the finest quality of education will occur.

Students would participate in the Experimental College in addition to taking their formal course load. There would be no single experiment. Each participant would set the conditions for his or her learning, and each organizer would be free to set a different context for participants. There would be one central course in which those who wanted to participate could evaluate the different student experiments. These evaluations would be presented to the university through standing committees, departmental bodies, and the Reference Groups.

Students have had enough experience in Experimental Colleges that some thoughts about potential educational rewards are possible:

• The absence of grades would force a student to decide what he wants to learn. The necessity for self-evaluation would help him decide what subject matter was most relevant for him.

• Student-initiated courses would force the participant to consider not only what he wants to learn but how he can best learn it. Such reality testing would provide concrete experiences for discussions in Reference Groups and it would assure opportunity for the student to learn from his own mistakes.

• The absence of requirements would allow a student to begin learning at a point most interesting to him, and would give him time to relate his personal needs to the subject matter and the style of learning he chose. In this way he would likely become excited about, and committed to, the learning process.

• Student-initiated courses would allow students to structure an intellectual framework for studying concerns that normally fall outside the limits of the curriculum—including personal problems and extra-curricular concerns. The Experimental College would provide a focal point for the integration of learning and living.

• Students who accepted leadership in the Experimental College would be assets to the decision-making bodies of the institution because of their intimate knowledge of student concerns and abilities, their firsthand experience in educational organization, and the continually fresh fund of teaching and learning models, both those that work better and less well than does the formal curriculum.

The Experimental College would identify problems in the institution's curriculum through attempts to improve the relevance and effectiveness of learning. The number of students who might attend in addition to taking their normal course load is not less than the number whose educational needs remain unfulfilled by the institution. An Experimental College might develop new teaching content and learning styles which the institution could use as models in a process of individual and institutional self-renewal.

The Individual Growth Program

When a student comes to college, he takes a battery of tests designed to disclose his plans, interests, problems, and needs. A computer is programed to offer him direct feedback in the form of a print-out of organized lists: courses (in a variety of possible sequences); faculty members whose teaching styles are particularly suited to his learning styles; books or references to annotated bibliographies; students, faculty, and persons off campus with similar interests and concerns; work-study programs geared to his abilities; summer jobs; and other educational opportunities. If no information were available about a particular interest or concern, this would be noted, along with a standard explanation of how best to pursue independent study, organize a course in the Experimental College, or find assistance. When a student's interests or needs changed, he could reply to a shorter questionnaire and obtain new information. Students would be encouraged to participate in the development of new questionnaires whenever they felt the earlier questionnaires and information elicited were not relevant to their needs. The information questionnaires would not be kept on record unless a student asked that particular data be stored in the computer's memory banks to become available to others for information or personal contact.

The first computer programs would be very crude, yet worth university investment to employ a programer, a specialist in questionnaire design, and students to refine the program. Once established, the program could easily be hooked up with those in other institutions, and a student could test how his interests and needs might be better met by transfer to another institution.

The rationale for the Individual Growth Program goes far beyond mere information feedback. Creatively used, the program might produce a number of educational rewards:

• Faculty advisers would be relieved of the chore of helping students select courses and informing them about the intricacies of sequences of study, about which many of them have inadequate knowledge outside their own fields. At the same time students would be released from dependence upon perhaps inadequate information. Rather, the adviser's time would be available for the more difficult and important task of discussing students' approaches to learning in Reference Groups.

• The most valuable service of the Individual Growth Program would be to enable students to know of other students (or others registered) who have similar interests and needs but who have had no one with whom to work and learn. A student who had learned to organize his own learning experiences in the Experimental College could profit greatly from finding others with like interests.

• In larger institutions, a student is often wise to choose most of his courses by quality of teacher rather than subject matter. The Individual Growth Program could refine this process by offering information about teachers in terms of their effect on individual students.

• Listings of courses and teachers would become available for student perusal as soon as information was approved for listing. In fact, the Individual Growth Program could open the possibility of more flexible scheduling of courses.

• Students seldom think of summer jobs and activities outside the university community as intricately connected with their courses and extracurricular activities. The Individual Growth Program would not only offer the student such information especially suited to his needs but also would present a selection of educational experiences (courses, extracurricular activities, jobs, travel abroad, volunteer service) as a total group of alternatives.

The computer is invading education, and almost universally it is used to store information (memory banks full of student test scores), centralize (multiple IBM cards to be filled out at registration), and standardize (teaching machines) the individual student. Without analyzing the merits and the problems of this trend, it is long overdue that the computer be placed at the service of individuals. The Individual Growth Program would do just this.

In conclusion, it is clear that higher education can best be an effective critic of society by acting upon major criticisms it has been making of itself. Here, it is crucial that its institutions, especially the multiversities, begin by building teaching and learning models to reinforce and assist students in becoming self-directed learners. In doing so, the institution is at once developing a self-renewing mechanism both for itself and for those who are ready to participate actively in the process. Individual and institutional self-renewal becomes more than an educational slogan; it becomes a dynamic, working process central to the identity of the institution. With its new identity, the institution not only can be more responsive to the individual needs and concerns of its students but also can be more active and effective in the development of a freer world.

Teaching and Learning: Whose Goals Are Important Around Here?

JOSEPH P. COSAND, KENNETH EBLE,
JONATHAN E. RHOADS, HARRIS WOFFORD, JR.

The Professional Educator's Mandate

JOSEPH P. COSAND

MR. WERDELL STATES that "only those [students] who have gained confidence in their own identity and direction can chart new goals for society." I would like to add the word "humility" as a desirable attribute, for confidence by itself too often leads to little more than arbitrary action based on narrowness and channel vision. This statement, as qualified, could then well apply to the professional educator, who has a mandate to define new goals for higher education in keeping with the stresses placed upon it by increases in enrollment, knowledge, and social demands and by the resultant pressures from the thousands of frustrated and disenchanted students.

Mr. Werdell further states that "The challenge is to develop self-directed learners." I would question self-direction as an end if it is not combined with maturity and compassion and with an awareness of other individuals and of the various socioeconomic groups that make up our society. Too often, the self-directed learner is isolated in a world of his own, oblivious of other people, their interests, needs, and cultures.

Certainly, Mr. Werdell is correct in emphasizing that educational institutions must develop new teaching and learning models by which students can learn their own learning process. Just as important, however, colleges and universities need to foster climates of teaching in which all teachers in undergraduate and graduate schools are encouraged to develop methods which enable students to learn their own learning process.

Looking back on visits to college and university classrooms as a member of accreditation teams, I am forced to admit that a high percentage of the teaching being practiced is sterile, unimaginative, and, for the most part, a continuation of the long-established "chalk-talk" method. The student has a right to object to this type of dull force-feeding of facts, when both he and the teacher know that the vast increase of facts in today's world makes it almost impossible to choose those that can be taught with any degree of validity or reliability.

I find it difficult, however, to accept Mr. Werdell's statement that the second objective for the student is "to learn what he wants to learn." This goal may be justifiable for the mature student who is aware of the gaps in his development, and who has the ability to search for those areas of the college's offerings which would fill the gaps. But I doubt that the immature student would be able to cope with self-direction that comes too early; if he were persuaded to attempt it, he might very well wallow in a destructive morass of frustration and instability made worse by the lack of observable achievement.

All societies seem to swing from one extreme to the other: it is difficult to control the pendulum as it makes its way across the middle areas of common sense and responsibility. Not only have the colleges been found wanting, but also they have been irresponsible in their failure to acknowledge the need for change in curricula, course content, and teaching methods. All of those who make up the academic community—boards, presidents, deans, and faculty—have been and are at fault. Smugness, blindness, and our concern with bigness and bricks and mortars are a few of the villains. We have for too long, and in too many cases, forgotten or ignored our only real function, and that is, of course, teaching and learning. The student is paramount, not the board member, president, or faculty member. Pressures on the college from business, government, industry, labor, or the taxpayer, tend to befog the educational climate and to bias action away from students' needs, especially those of personal development. This bias must be recognized by all of us, and it is incumbent upon faculty senates, presidents, and boards to become personally involved and immersed in their only valid reason for being members of the education profession: a commitment to education.

The responsibilities for educational leadership should not be, by default, turned over to students, many of whom are already lost in the confusion of the multiversity. Enlightened leadership from the president and faculty is an obligation and a privilege, not a chore to be ignored or rejected. Anyone who expects to learn has a right to expect personal interest and expertise from the teacher. The teacher, then, must be more than a fountain of facts; these will be increasingly available from information retrieval equipment. Aware of his responsibility to develop open minds, and encouraged to do so by supportive administrators, the teacher will, in cooperation with the student eager to learn, bring about a reformation of American higher education.

Mr. Werdell is absolutely right in his argument that mere accumulation of knowledge and a highly developed analytical ability do *not* help the student solve his own immediate problem of integrating learning with living. The diminishing size of the world, the immediacy of today's crises, the closeness and yet apartness of our relationships with crowds of people, should impel all of us in higher education to examine our goals, our offerings, our teaching methods—in short, our educational climate. Students of widely divergent socioeconomic backgrounds enter our colleges in ever-increasing numbers; they must be better able to understand themselves and others, not just through reading and listening, but through actual confrontation and communication.

Equally important, faculty members should be aware of the many student subcultures within the college population. Splendid isolation within college departments or within the community housing areas generally selected by faculty members is not likely to generate sympathy for the personal needs of students. The faculty member must meet and know the affluent and the poor, the Caucasian and the colored races, the agnostic and the fundamentalist, for they are our students. They come to us with some hope, some cynicism, and some fear, but still with some faith that they will learn to live creatively and to be of benefit to their world. Most impressive was Mr. Werdell's comment that

> Today's is a mass society in which it is difficult to develop a sense of personal power. Yet, it is only through self-renewal of the individual that a mass society can develop social mechanisms for its self-renewal. Higher education cannot provide reform of the entire society, but its institutions can prepare students to deal with other institutions that can tackle large problems.

We teachers must teach students to learn their own learning processes if they are to realize their own creative potential. We can no longer gorge them with mere facts. This procedure is obsolete and has been for a long time. It cannot be condoned, rationalized away, or permitted in our more than 2,000 colleges and universities. I suggest that we, as educators, adopt the following statement as a positive approach to fulfilling our responsibilities: "Each student's achievement enriches me."

Subject, Teacher, Student: The Reality

KENNETH EBLE

READING MR. WERDELL's paper has been a somewhat unsettling experience. I am in complete sympathy with the needs and aspirations he expresses, but my agreement on specific points keeps wavering. Just as I am comfortably settled and being carried along by the force of his argument, I raise my hands to applaud and find myself bumped off his wagon. Perhaps a trip along "the razor's edge of . . . competing needs" (to quote Mr. Werdell) is bound to be a perilous one. And finding one's way in higher education or in this society is equally perilous despite the green lawns, polished stone, and shining glass and steel that grace our universities and our society.

Rather than chart my uneasy progress through the paper, I'll state my major areas of agreement and disagreement and speculate upon the reasons for them. I am in complete agreement with the paper's main points: the call for an alliance between educators and student innovators, for more concern with how college graduates act as well as with how much they learn, and for major innovations in the approach to student learning.

Most of my disagreements have to do with the means Mr. Werdell offers for bringing about these desired ends. Mr. Werdell does have a difficult task. As he states at the outset, educational institutions are caught in the conflict of meeting "the needs of the individual members of a highly diverse student body and the needs of a society which allows individuality to flourish." Our responses to this conflict differ, however; indeed, we seem to approach the problem from opposite directions. My own bent is to put individual development first: to seek means of developing the individual student and to assume that this development will be such as to meet many of the needs of society. His inclinations, I think, are to place social goals first, to pull the individual students into society, into reference groups, action curricula, student-initiated experimental colleges, and thus meet individual needs and social needs at the same time. His proposals, therefore, seem to me really do not struggle with the nitty-gritty, the reality of subject and teacher and student, of teaching and learning and thinking, of self—more than institutional or group—discipline. His concern is with structures, designs, ways of getting the individual into the proper "setting" so that he may act; my concern is with the means of somehow "educating" the student so that he may act decisively, effectively, and wisely. Both of us, I suspect, would agree that one does not do one thing—"educate" —separate from and prior to the other—"act." We agree, I think, that formal education suffers from the lack of engagement with actual doing, but we probably disagree about how much and in what ways the university should be either the ivory tower or the marketplace.

Let me give an example of a way in which my general disagreement with Mr. Werdell's approach manifests itself. His criticism of the curricula opposes mere accumulation of fact and preoccupation with analytical learning in favor of "creative and speculative uses of the intellect." At this point, I am in complete agreement, but when, in the next sentence he writes, "the curriculum must offer practice in dealing with people from diverse backgrounds, of various life styles, with differing goals, as well as practice in understanding their problems from a distance," he throws me off. It is not just that he uses "curriculum" where he might better have used "college and university," it is that he overleaps the nitty-gritty and asks both too much and too little of the curriculum. Too much, in making the curriculum the central means by which living and learning are integrated, whereas most of the objectives mentioned in the sentence might more effectively be achieved through other aspects of university organization and conduct. Too little in failing to acknowledge the hard, lonely discipline which justifies a curriculum, which is part of the creative and speculative act as well as the analytical one, and which must precede, accompany, and follow purposive action. His straw men, I fear, are the fact-grubber, the pedant-professor, and the insulated and isolated academic, as mine are the glib grouper, the airy creativitors, and the dropout activists. But for all that, I think we are not far apart in the discontent we feel for higher education as it is and in our somewhat shadowy hopes for what it might be.

I would make less of this conflict if I had more confidence in the proposals Mr. Werdell makes. Many of his specific reforms scant a consideration of teacher and learner or subject and learner, in favor of setting and learner. Somewhat paradoxically for one who opposes the analytic style of learning, he has great confidence in what research has demonstrated in the ways of better models of teaching and learning. I remain skeptical of both the "research" and the "creativity" which have given vogue to "brainstorming," "group dynamics," and institutes of applied imagination. Among my objections is one which I make to many of Mr. Werdell's proposals: the danger of institutionalizing aspects of learning which might flourish better for being noninstitutionalized. I am also suspicious of what groupy thinking seems to promise: that the difficult, sometimes irksome, and lonely tasks of self-development and of mastery of a skill or craft will become easy, pleasant, and convivial within the group. I am not posing monastic learning as an alternative. I think much more must be done to engage student and teacher in dialogue both inside and outside the institutional setting, just as I believe in more discourse between the academic minds —students and teachers—and the society outside. Being a professor, I suppose, I think there are some specific things I can teach, and the skill with which I do it has more to do with grouping my own and the student's scattered forces than with grouping the students. My gloomy strictures concerning group learning owe much to my thinking, of late, that the most valuable subject I teach is rhetoric, and rhetoric is a strongly personal, private discipline which develops into a public art only through hard individual application.

I will conclude my comments by mentioning two important topics raised by Mr. Werdell's paper: academic freedom for students and the changing of student values. Feeling as I do that helping the student develop a voice is a primary task of humanistic education, I am as insistent as Mr. Werdell in arguing the importance of student academic freedom. Because it is so important, should be insisted upon, and will be exercised whether students are given it or not, the need for giving them something to say, some sound basis for action, is that much more important. As regards changing student values, I am not so inclined as I once was to accept Philip Jacob's study as proof of the failure of the college. I am, however, troubled about the relationship of the colleges and universities to student values. Certainly, values are the concern of higher education, but how much responsibility must the colleges accept for shaping student values in face of the much larger forces acting upon students before, during, and after their college years? It strikes me that the university's values make their impress outside of the curriculum, somewhat apart from the basic function: teaching and learning. The individual reacts to the general impression of opulence, comfort, and busyness which marks both the campus and

American society, and to science, technology, power, and military necessity which are equally pervasive in both settings. "Higher education," Mr. Werdell writes, "cannot provide reform of the entire society." And yet, in regard to changing student values, is any lesser reform going to work much change? The wonder is that despite the society, despite higher education, strong dissatisfaction with existing values continues to be expressed by the young. Here is a reason Mr. Werdell doesn't mention for forging an alliance between student innovators and educators: the beneficial effects it might have upon the latter. Given Vietnam, riots in the cities, and the specters that haunt the world outside America, those values which are popularly attributed to student innovators today seem superior both to the values of most of society and to those of the official university community.

The Student's Freedom To Choose

JONATHAN E. RHOADS

IF I WERE TO STATE a single criticism of Mr. Werdell's paper, it would be the implication (unintentional, I presume) that we are trying to create one type of institution for one type of student, though it *is* clearly stated that this type is sufficiently broadly conceived to have many different disciplinary interests. I would contend that we need not strive for conformity or special standards of universal or near-universal applicability, but rather that it is quite appropriate for one institution to offer a curriculum based on the idea, expressed in the catalog of the Student Experimental College at San Francisco State, that students should assume responsibility for their own education, and for another institution to utilize the concept of a very formalized classical education requiring a number of years' study of Latin and Greek. Yet another institution could emphasize the work-study programs, as Antioch has done so well, and still another could do as Reed College has done: that is, create an environment with few restrictions, but with such high scholastic standards that at times fewer than one in three of an already self-selected freshman class emerges from it in four years with a bachelor's degree.

The reputation of a college precedes it, and rarely does a high school student enter college without some inkling of where it stands on the academic map. But many students cannot make a proper choice because they cannot bear to be tied down or because they do not yet have a secure sense of their identity. For them, the great problem is adaptation or, perhaps, simply maturing. Work-study programs, overseas study, working for a period with the unfortunate may be what they need most at this time in their lives. In an earlier era, these students often simply dropped out and worked for a year or two, or, if they could afford it, took a *Wanderjahr* to find out what other parts of the world could teach them. Today, the male student who ventures out of school is apt to be popped into the Army and sent to Vietnam. (Recognition that his freedom has been curtailed to this extent may lead him to analyze the freedom heralded throughout the elementary and secondary levels as the hallmark of America.)

For another student, however, the choice of a college or of a way of life may pose no problems. He may already know that his abilities are more than adequate, he may have a strong sense of whence he came and of the general direction in which he wants to go. His need, then, is for concrete tools to help him in his journey. For him, a well-structured curriculum which includes many facts and a fair amount of predigested information, gathered by older scholars from broad areas of learning and focused on his particular interests, may often be desirable.

We at Haverford College, proceeding on the assumption that many individuals are not secure in their goals, try to provide an environment where free inquiry is possible, where students are clearly stimulated to challenge the accepted. The college has not sought in recent years to impose many of the sanctions on those freedoms to which it is entitled under the law, nor do I think it the mission of an educational institution to take punitive measures against students who exercise their constitutional rights in unpopular ways.

The small residential college provides a community or, if you will, a microcosm of society, which has many innate advantages. Students who wish to write for a newspaper or to help to publish a literary magazine generally *can;* those who wish to design and present radio programs frequently have this opportunity. Others can develop themselves through athletics, community service, religious worship, research, debating, freewheeling discussions, friendships, campus politics, courtship of potential wives, or less commendable social activities.

The Russian breakthrough with Sputnik woke America up to an era in which it had lost a part of its technical leadership. The feverish race ever since to correct this relative failure has reached as far as our lower schools but has affected our colleges most. In general, the stronger the college academically, the deeper the effect, and the result has been to take the fun out of college. The emphasis on scholastic achievement has, in my opinion, unbalanced the lives of many college students, and I am convinced that the strong college is a poor environment for all but the highly motivated and very able student. The moderately strong student, in such a college, will be near the bottom of his class. In another day, he could have accepted this and had the option to excel in extracurricular activities, but now, if he takes the time to devote himself to other activities, he is likely to become a dropout. To my mind, freedom for students connotes freedom from having to follow a set pattern of progress through college. It should mean a far greater freedom to move about from institution to institution, at least within a fairly large group of institutions. This, the *Lernfreiheit* of German education, is a concept we have never really grasped in this country.

Finally, Mr. Werdell states that higher education is becoming mass education and that the small liberal arts colleges have been left struggling at the periphery. While I think there is no doubt that, if one looks at percentages, the small liberal arts colleges are playing a smaller and smaller role on the educational scene, if one looks at absolute enrollment figures, the small liberal arts colleges are still growing. (Indeed, as Mr. Werdell notes, this is perhaps what is the matter with them. Too many of them are no longer either small or liberal.) But, just as the private school has withstood more than a century of public education, so, I would predict, will small liberal arts colleges survive and serve a slowly growing clientele. These institutions are peculiarly adapted to serve, in varied ways, the needs of many different subcultures, and they should, in fact, be broadly encouraged to do so. I have no objection if some of them are so stodgy and conservative that they are generally unacceptable to many students who are, after all, at liberty to transfer to other institutions. Likewise, I am very happy that some institutions are so far in the avant-garde of educational thinking that they may seem to conservative thinkers to represent educational vacuity.

On Books and Other Common Things
Of a College

HARRIS WOFFORD, JR.

WHEN ASKED ABOUT how many people work in the Vatican, Pope John replied, "About half." How much of Philip Werdell's paper do I agree with? About half. I hope that is enough for the alliance between students and educational innovators which he proposes, because I believe that students are today the major force for educational reform.

But it will be an uneasy alliance at best, with tensions that will tend to polarize. For example, my response to his paper led one of the student planners at Old Westbury to say, "He finally smoked out the medieval mule in you." And an older colleague, who scoffs at the idea of students being partners in college-making, said: "Werdell forced you to see whose side you are really on and to accept Plato's advice, 'Don't trust anyone under thirty.'"

Denying both charges, I admit that his paper made clear how much I agree with him and our student planners in the dire diagnosis of what is wrong, and how much I disagree with part of the proposed prescription. We do need what Mr. Werdell calls an "action curriculum," and what Whitehead calls "the marriage of thought and action." As State University Chancellor Samuel Gould has said, higher education must become more relevant to our pressing public problems, must put itself in the middle of efforts to meet our urban and racial crises. And I agree with Mr. Werdell's three specific proposals, at least in modified form: we might call his small "reference groups" seminars or tutorials, but some such system for close and informal student-faculty communication is necessary; student-initiated experimental colleges or courses should be incorporated within the constitution and curriculum of a university; and an "individual growth program" that emphasizes independent study should be a large component of any college.

In part, Mr. Werdell's recommendations describe what we are trying to do in designing the new College of the State University of New York at Old Westbury. We are beginning next year with a work-study program that will offer students "risks, settings, attitudes, and rewards different from those in the traditional academic structure"; that will offer them "practice in dealing with people from diverse backgrounds of various life styles, with differing goals, as well as practice in understanding their problems from a distance"; that will "offer challenges to act on the basis of what one understands." We will provide a large opportunity for independent study that will include student-initiated seminars or workshops; in our central common seminar program, students will be able to determine about half of the readings and subjects to be discussed; in our field program, students will play a key part in shaping their assignments and following the problems where they lead. Out of the intense student participation in planning the college, there will no doubt emerge a strong student bill of rights and responsibilities, including the right and responsibility to continue to participate in the further development of the college. Old Westbury is being designed as a "college of colleges," which will comprise constituent colleges offering contrasting curriculums. So we also accept Mr. Werdell's prescription of diversity.

But we part company when he proposes making "the private needs and concerns of students a dominant thrust" in institutional policy; when he discounts the "search for knowledge and truth"; when he says that "even the best-run academic seminar seldom encourages creative speculation and synthesis"; when he primarily emphasizes pluralism and "space for student development." In elevating the seductive hippie proposition "Let everyone do his thing" into a new principle for American education, he seems to be compounding the faults of the elective system. This would be the anarchy of the elective system writ large.

THE TURNED-OFF

He defends his emphasis on sensitivity training, on "open and gentle" groups and "highly personal free association," and on other forms of pressure-cooking the emotional development of students, on the ground that higher education is not dealing adequately with students' intellectual development *because* it is not dealing at all with their personal development. The reverse seems to me closer to the truth: We will not deal adequately with students' personal development until we provide for far greater intellectual development. If we are to overcome "the profound sense of powerlessness" among Americans, we Americans will need to be more intellectual than we have ever been. Otherwise we will remain what a Long Island superintendent of schools recently taught me to call "the grease." It is not just inner-city black children who are being turned off by their education, the superintendent insisted in a seminar recently; the majority of suburban white children are also being turned off. These students (called, he said, "the grease") who are heading for mechanical, menial, or clerical work and not for college are, for all practical purposes, turned off anything intellectual or political as much as ghetto children. Isn't it also true that an anti-intellectual attitude is so widespread and strong among much of the college-bound half that a substantial proportion of college freshmen are already turned off higher education before they arrive; that only a small fraction of college students are ever really turned on to even a brief love of learning, let alone to a life of learning? And if we take C. P. Snow's "two culture" problem seriously, are not most of us who know little or nothing of the mathematics, science, and technology governing so much of our lives, in this sense "grease," too? In terms of intellectual capacity and confidence for self-government in a complex age, are not the great majority of Americans "grease"? Do not most Americans finish their education feeling intellectually impotent and incompetent?

Yet there is a paradox here. As automation, affluence, leisure, and higher education increase, we might expect not this feeling of intellectual impotence and incompetence, but instead the emergence of a new Renaissance man, a twentieth-century world citizen prepared to enjoy a life of many options—"prepared," as Mr. Werdell says, "to help solve society's problems" and "to assume new roles as old ones become obsolete." We might expect the appearance of a New Amateur, a new generation with a sense of mastery who take the knowledge of what they do not know as the first step in learning, who at least know how to avoid being locked in any one inevitable pattern, how to try a new direction, how to choose and keep choosing among possible roles and careers, how not to get hung up. We might see millions of modest latter-day versions of Benjamin Franklin, himself a somewhat hippie version of the eighteenth century's New Amateurs who settled this country.

But to produce such men today, we will need greater student goals than the three given us by Mr. Werdell: "To learn his own learning process, to learn what he wants to learn, and to learn how to communicate this with other people." What a self-centered inversion that statement is of the older questions: What can we know? What can we hope for? What ought we to do?

It seems that everywhere we go in the world we meet Protagoras coming back: the persuasive sophist who is able to help everyone do his thing, who concentrates on each student's own learning process, who enables a student to learn whatever *he* wants to learn and then to communicate *this* to other people. At this point Mr. Werdell seems to be proposing an education that will let everyone become his own sophist. The caricature of this notion is the computer in his proposed Individual Growth Program that "is programed to offer [the student] . . . a print-out of organized lists . . . [of] faculty members whose teaching styles are particularly suited to his learning styles." We could perhaps program the computer to print out lists of the faculty members who would most challenge the students to change their learning styles and to learn not just what they want to learn, but what they need to know. But can we expect from any computer a print-out of a liberal education?

One of our student planners kept crossing out the phrase "liberal education" every time we put it in the draft of our catalog or, as the students would prefer to call it, our "Non-catalog." Crossing "liberal education" out for the tenth time, she finally wrote, "What is it?"

That is a fair question. It is the primary question. It is the question Mr. Werdell does not seem to me to be asking. It is the question that takes a community of learning beyond a student's thing, or a teacher's thing, beyond even a president's thing, beyond your thing and my thing, beyond everyone doing his thing to everyone searching for the thing to do. Liberal education is the common thing of a college, and of any self-governing republic such as the United States of America; the thing that turns children into men, subjects into citizens, amateurs into liberal artists.

AT THE CENTER

There are indeed many different types of students and different styles of teaching and learning; but there is a common denominator; there are many possible paths to a liberal education, but there are some common things as essential to the mind and soul of man as water, bread, and wine are to the body. Our job is to search for them, to find and offer them, and to continue the search which by the nature of these things will always be incomplete.

Part of the search must indeed take us into the new realms of the psyche that Freud has opened. But this is an intellectual challenge of a high order, and the old prescription of finding oneself by losing oneself may have some application here, too. For the individual crisis of identity is inevitably part of a larger crisis of identity, the identity of the world. "Affective education"—designed to help us understand our feelings—is breaking out all over, along the lines Mr. Werdell proposes;

so is "experiential education," along the lines pioneered by Antioch and the Peace Corps. But where is the intellectual education we need? The training of specialists and professionals is under way on a scale that may be almost sufficient, but where is the general education— the education of generalists, of effective amateurs, of liberal artists— that the Republic and all its citizens need? For without liberal education the New Amateur will be amateurish in the worst way, a permanent—perhaps affective but not very effective—Peter Pan in an ever-ever land of adolescence.

As an alternative or antidote, I could present Plato's description and prescription of dialectic—the ultimate study in the curriculum for the Guardians of the Republic, the study that enables one to know a good life from a bad—to come after experience and public service and cross-cultural education in the Cave; after the affective education of the gymnasium and the drinking symposium; and after the learning of disciplines such as language and mathematics. But in reading *The Autobiography of Malcolm X* I found a more acceptable source for the radical proposition that we should put at the center of an education-in-action curriculum the ingredient Mr. Werdell does not mention, a very linear, medieval thing: books. Malcolm X, in his chapter entitled "Saved" says:

> I have often reflected upon the new vistas that reading opened to me. I knew right there in prison that reading had changed forever the course of my life. As I see it today, the ability to read awoke inside me some long dormant craving to be mentally alive. . . . My homemade education gave me, with every additional book that I read, a little bit more sensitivity to the deafness, dumbness, and blindness that was afflicting the black race in America. Not long ago, an English writer telephoned me from London, asking questions. One was, "What's your alma mater?" I told him. "Books." [1]

What is at the center of Mr. Werdell's model Alma Mater? The exploration of individual psyches, sensitivity in personal relations, experience beyond the classroom can be very intoxicating; but they are not enough. We may not know just what liberal education is, but we know what it is not: it is not adrenalin simply taking over, the imagination soaring beyond any intellectual base, interdisciplinary study that turns out to mean little study and no discipline, the hegemony of social action unseasoned by critical judgment and unsustained by professional skill. We will suffer many painful hangups if we think we can change the world without understanding it, or understand it without study, or study it without books.

[1] New York: Grove Press, 1964. P. 179.

Twenty years ago, at the University of Chicago, in those rare college years when I had a chance to read some great books regularly, I was so involved in social action that late one night a good friend came in and with some reticence delivered a warning to me from *The Brothers Karamazov*. Dostoevski was describing Alyosha, the young man of shining eyes with a "thirst for swift achievement" and for "self-mastery." Like many in his generation, he was (my friend read from the book) "honest in nature, desiring the truth . . . and seeking to serve it at once with all the strength of his soul, seeking for immediate action, and ready to sacrifice everything, life itself, for it." But Dostoevski added, "the sacrifice of life is, in many cases, the easiest of all sacrifices." But "to sacrifice, for instance, five or ten years of their seething youth to hard and tedious study, if only to multiply ten-fold their powers of serving the truth . . . such a sacrifice is utterly beyond the strength of many of them."

"Is this really beyond your strength?" my friend asked me.

With some reticence, I commend those lines to Philip Werdell and to the generation for whom he speaks; and I do it asking the question my friend asked me, confident that the liberal education all Guardians of the Republic need is not beyond his strength or theirs or ours.

LYLE M. SPENCER

The Research Function
And the Advancement
Of Knowledge

Not long ago, an article in the *New York Times Magazine* about the Rand Corporation, an institution ingeniously devised by our society to facilitate the conduct of research, reminded me that the Rand Corporation is sometimes called a "university without students." It is a pleasant slogan, one that I had never questioned. But, in putting my mind to the subject of this paper, I found it troubled me: either it was a logical contradiction, or there was something about university research programs that had previously eluded me.

In a search for parallels, I came up with "art without beauty," and had to acknowledge that there are some today who consider art possible without beauty. Then I tried "love without sex" but I found that a little complicated. Finally, at the risk of being judged old-fashioned, I had to state unequivocally that I could not conceive of a "university without students." It can be argued that an institution is so dedicated to research that it has no time for students—but it would not then be a university. This is not a mere game of semantics: students are fundamental to a university, just as the university is an institution fundamental to our society.

A university may be defined in many ways and, over the course of history, it has played many roles. But inherent in the nature of a university is the responsibility of one generation to impart its knowledge and its values and its wisdom to the next. The university is the guardian and preserver of all that is best in a society. It is a conduit through which culture is passed down through the ages. This function, in a word, is called *teaching*. If an institution does not perform this function, then, in my view, it is not a university.

This reasoning does not imply that a university is a static thing, a passive agent of cultural transmission. It is not that at all. Each generation, in passing its culture on to the next, has the responsibility to enrich it. This process is quantitative as well as qualitative. At several periods in world history, various generations defaulted on this responsibility, not only in failing to enrich the heritage they passed on but even in maintaining what already existed. It is no coincidence that there were no universities in the Dark Ages. About the tenth century, Europe awoke, to reacquire an appreciation of knowledge and culture, and the great universities of Italy, England, and France were founded. Since then, the universities have played an indispensable role, not only in preserving Western culture but in broadening and deepening it. In large measure, this enrichment comes about by a process that we call *research*.

THE ROLES OF TEACHING AND RESEARCH

The university in our society thus has two roles, one of preservation and one of creation. Call these roles, if you will, teaching and research. Both are fundamental to the university's nature. And any serious discussion of goals for higher education needs to include a re-examination of the relation of these two roles to each other. Currently, there is apprehension that the creativity function has tended to supersede the preservation function in the university. Some see in such a trend a threat to the university itself.

The source of the problem lies in the unprecedented creativity of our civilization in the last generation, a creativity that has released a passion for even more of the same. Over the course of eight or nine hundred years, each generation added just a little to what had been imparted to it by its predecessor. The accretions of knowledge were gradual and readily absorbed into the existing system. Both society and the university seemed content with the pace. As recently as 1870, Harvard, which has never been classified as a backward institution, turned down the request of a chemistry professor for a semester's leave and a small amount of money on the ground that the research planned would do the university no good. President Charles Eliot, who was no obscurantist, simply felt that the university's responsibility as creator was limited. He perceived no reason for shifting the balance between teaching and research. But the information explosion of our own day has changed all that.

The past half-century has propelled into our intellectual domain a quantity of data that have transformed our society and, necessarily, generated fundamental questions about the role of the university. As an institution, the university could scarcely remain unresponsive to the great transformation. In a general way, we know what has happened. Pressed onward by the demands of the exact sciences, the university has taken on a greater and greater responsibility for creativity, for our culture's original research. And most of this has happened without design.

No educator or team of educators sat down to issue a pronouncement on the duties of a university in a civilization thirsty for knowledge. It happened because society decreed there was a need and the university responded.

All this, of course, was not the product of spontaneous generation. To say that "society" decreed a need means that "government," the people's spokesman, made certain policy decisions. During World War II, the government found that it had to intensify, many times over, the amount of research it supported. It needed answers to specific questions, most of them in science and engineering. Naturally, it went for the answers to society's chief repositories of wisdom and talent—the universities. For reasons of patriotism or esteem or money or what have you, the universities proved eminently receptive to the call. This process of demand and response has multiplied and remultiplied since World War II. The government has come to dominate the university's research time and facilities. As the demands of the beast have grown, the universities have fed it, apparently with more and more willingness. We have now reached a point where, I believe, we must step back and look at what has happened. It is time to examine what we have done and what we ought to do in the future to fulfill our responsibilities for cultural enrichment.

Most administrators in higher education are familiar with the hearings on teaching and research conducted in 1965 by a congressional subcommittee under the chairmanship of Representative Henry S. Reuss of Wisconsin. Congressman Reuss, one of the more distinguished and thoughtful members of the House, was brought to his inquiry by the assertion that some 85 percent of all research currently conducted in universities is sponsored by the government. He decided to look into the allegation that government-sponsored research was impairing the teaching capacities of the university. His hearings were entitled "Conflicts between the Federal Research Programs and the Nation's Goals for Higher Education." Congressman Reuss had ample justification for his study and he found considerable evidence of both benefits and costs of the university research program.

The Reuss hearings, in my view, were fair and sober and yielded much significant information, and this paper leans heavily on data from those hearings. But the inquiry undertaken by Congressman Reuss can be regarded as unduly narrow, not in its premise so much as in its lack of comprehensiveness. It is my conviction that while research, in relation to the university's teaching function, is in many cases excessive, it is in other cases highly inadequate. The Reuss hearings failed to take into full account the degree to which research is fundamental to the university's mandate, just as researchers sometimes fail to take into account their obligations to students. The ideal is the university in which teaching and research—social preservation and social enrichment, if you will—complement and contribute to each other. Ideals, of course, are hard to achieve, but our present efforts can be improved.

CLASSIFIED RESEARCH, AN INAPPROPRIATE ROLE

Having stated that teaching and research should complement each other, I can point to the kinds of research in which the university should not engage. Except in times of major national emergencies, it is a serious mistake for universities to lend themselves and their facilities to classified research. This is not stated as a value judgment on the kinds of projects that must be kept secret but as a condemnation of secrecy itself. A secret project is one done in isolation. It usually contributes little to our culture. Its results cannot be transmitted to others. It neither enriches nor helps to preserve our culture, except perhaps in some narrow military sense.

Historically, universities became involved in secret research during World War II, when the reasons for it may have been excellent. Today we can legitimately question whether universities ought to continue the practice. If our society were so organized that the university was the only institution available for this sort of work, then the belief that classified research is not the university's business would require re-evaluation. But the Rand Corporation and other similar organizations, to say nothing of private industry and facilities the government itself possesses, provide an ample institutional foundation for the research of a secret nature that must necessarily be conducted. The university deals in knowledge for dissemination, not in knowledge for concealment.

There are at least some in university life who share my view. Last spring, New York University announced a new policy to discourage its faculty members from engaging in classified research. If NYU did not go quite far enough, it took a big step in the right direction. It will be enlightening to quote from NYU's brief policy statement on this matter:

> The university is concerned with the preservation and enrichment of human life rather than its destruction and will enter into classified, sponsored research projects when the nature of the inquiry is deemed consistent with these concerns and when our faculty has a special competence to perform a national service.
>
> The need for this university's involvement must demonstrably outweigh the disadvantages of having to subject the project to security requirements and possible publication restrictions.

There may be instances when secret undertakings are justified on a university campus, though I am not sure what they are and am not passing moral judgment on the subject matter of classified research. From the perspective of the university, classified work in chemical warfare is no more or less defensible than a secret study of Vietnamese mountain people. I disapprove as strongly of projects in nuclear weaponry for the Atomic Energy Commission as in policy training for the Central Intelligence Agency: as a nation, we may need our nuclear weapons and we might well have the obligation to train Vietnamese policemen. But, in my view, the university is not the appropriate institution to perform these functions.

I do not quarrel with the motives of the institutions which agree to conduct classified research. For a university that is not affluent, a secret project may represent an important source of income. It is understandable if some administrators regard this money, which so few universities see fit to refuse, as a step toward solvency, even if not toward academic excellence. To these administrators I would declare: Proceed at your own risk. Lincoln said of the Union that it cannot exist half-slave and half-free. Neither can the university exist half in darkness, half in light. I feel compassion for the well-meaning professor who possesses the burden of keeping sorted out in his mind his classified from his unclassified knowledge when he lectures to his students or chats with his colleagues. I am poorly disposed to campuses that have intimidating off-limits buildings and a corps of personnel who often display the titles of academic professionalism without ever emerging from behind the locked doors of their laboratories into the broad daylight of intellectual interchange. I am not so cavalier as to propose that a university abandon an important segment of its revenue in a year, perhaps even in five. But I would propose that universities currently saddled with classified responsibilities begin, as we say, to "phase out" this work, turn it over to institutions to which it is more appropriate, and find other sources of support.

But secrecy is far from the only issue in dispute in the question of government-sponsored research. In recent years, the government has passed on to the universities about $1.8 billion annually in research funding. There has been complaint, noted above, that the money diverts attention from teaching. It has been charged that the constantly increasing emphasis on research intensifies the evils of the publish-or-perish obsession in academic advancement. There has been grumbling that the government's research funds have been concentrated in too few institutions and limited to a few geographical areas. Many object to the government's calling the tune in research direction. Over-all, the critics charge that the government has run roughshod over education in order to achieve its goals in development and research. As it is put in Washington officialese, the government's research and development efforts may be "counterproductive" to the national interest.

I shall not dwell unduly on these complaints, not because they are unimportant but because the arguments, on both sides, are familiar to faculty and administrators. The Reuss Committee went into them in considerable detail.

IMBALANCES IN UNIVERSITY RESEARCH

Still, some of the criticism of government funding of university research demands further attention. It would, after all, be unusual if there were not some disapproval of a system in which 85 percent of the funds came from a single all-powerful source. Many academic administrators think that life was better in the old days, when government research occupied a less strategic place in the university, when it was regarded more as a pleasant diversion than a prime responsibility. (But life in many other ways was more pleasant in the old days.) We can be nostalgic about a more casual era in the university's history but we cannot push back the clock. The government's concerns are currently the chief factor in university research, and for the foreseeable future they are likely to remain so. It is appropriate, then, to take that factor into account and make the best of it.

Although government funding means that the government will frequently direct the course of research, it does not mean that the government can force on the university assignments that are incompatible with its integrity or its own responsibilities to society. One can criticize government policy, but in a free country the university is responsible for preserving its own virtue. As we are frequently told, we live in a pluralistic society where power is diffused. In the government-university relationship, the government is admittedly the stronger partner, but I have never heard that it applied coercion to get a research project under way. The universities can say "no" whenever they want. Obviously, they ought to have done so more often. I question the judgment of many universities for undertaking secret research, for diverting resources excessively from the teaching function, for giving the dignity of their name to enterprises that at best have a doubtful place in the university community, for concealing activities which, when made public, have sometimes created scandal. I think it would be perfectly proper to complete a reorganization of the structure for financing research in the United States. At the same time, I am not willing to absolve the universities of the duty, in their relationship with the government, to safeguard their own integrity.

The time has come for the university community to set some new rules, to establish better self-discipline, regarding the acceptance of the government funds for the financing of research. Although I would not presume to suggest procedures for going about such an undertaking, the difficulties of organizing it do not seem great. Far more difficult would be to find a basis for an agreement on rules. I have made my own proposals for the lines I believe those rules should follow and recognize that there are important interests at stake. If universities have accepted limitations on their freedom of action in the controversial area of recruiting football players, then it should not be impossible for them to reach agreement on a similar discipline for building research structures. The objective is the same in both cases: the preservation of the integrity of the university as a social institution. Such rules, in pursuit of this objective, would by no means be anti-government or run counter to the national interest. But they would serve as guidelines to the government on what research the universities feel it is within their capacity to conduct. Such rules, by making clear what the university community regards as legitimate in government-financed research, will be useful to both partners in the relationship.

Having established rules in the field of government-sponsored research, the universities should then sit down and give some hard thought to the nature of the research projects they are fitted to undertake. Put as a question: Are the universities enriching our society as much as they ought to and can? I noted with dismay the figures submitted to the Reuss Committee on the distribution, by subject field, of government research and development funds to all recipients. The figures show that 26 to 28 percent go to the life sciences. Of the $16 billion spent for Federal research generally, more than $14 billion is spent for the projects of three agencies: the Department of Defense, the National Aeronautics and Space Administration, and the Atomic Energy Commission. Only 2 percent of Federal research funds go into the social sciences. Surely the universities ought to be asking themselves whether it is in the national interest for research funds to be allocated as they are. The research conducted outside the domain of the exact sciences is peanuts. Is it enough to spend peanuts for research on our social problems?

Obviously, research in the exact sciences is not evil. It is necessary and proper. Nor is there reason to doubt that the government is getting its money's worth for the work in these fields. We have the strongest military establishment in the world. Our space program is stupendous. Our atomic weapons are deadly. We are making remarkable advances in medical sciences. For these achievements, the universities deserve much of the credit. University science and technology have made fundamental contributions to the enrichment of our society. It is not my purpose here to question the size of the funds for this research. In fact, it is their success that leads us to look for opportunities in other areas.

But, the very single-minded intensity of Federal sponsorship of research in these sciences is, in my view, at the core of many of the criticisms of the current system made by the Reuss Committee. There is persuasive evidence that the university community is severely strained by the ratio in which Federal research funds are allocated. Research in the exact sciences is very expensive. It requires not only talented personnel but elaborate physical facilities. It is quite natural for the government to go for its scientific research to those institutions that are already well organized for the calibre of work it demands. It is understandable that most Federal money goes to a relatively few institutions, enhancing facilities that are already first-class and reputations that are already excellent. Small wonder that the "have-not" institutions complain of discrimination that deprives them not only of money but also of the talent that is lured away from them. Meanwhile, the "have" universities which remain the beneficiaries of Federal funds become transformed into research institutions, in which faculty and administration become oriented more and more toward research and less and less toward teaching. In this sense, I share the Reuss Committee's concern over the way government research money is now passed around.

What chiefly worried the Reuss Committee was that the system might be gradually reducing the level of science education generally. The have universities were paying less attention to teaching; the have-nots could not get good teachers because they could not compete in offers of money and exciting projects. The committee made a set of recommendations to correct some of the inequities. It recommended, for instance, that project awards be more diffused, both among geographical areas and institutions. It also proposed that boards of judges be more widely representative of American higher education, so that the tendency toward self-perpetuation of the concentration of research would be reduced.

I have no particular quarrel with the Reuss Committee recommendations. As far as they go, they are unexceptionable. But they fail to get at the heart of the matter, and are a palliative when what is needed is thoroughgoing reform. For what is at stake here is not simply science education but better education generally.

DESIRABLE NEW POLICIES IN
GOVERNMENT-SPONSORED RESEARCH

The government deserves to get the best results possible for its research expenditures. Obviously we should offer to our young people education of the highest possible quality. But I am willing to presume that the government undertakes programs of research to get answers to certain unknowns, solutions to certain problems. It is fair to assume that it measures the effectiveness of its expenditures by the product of the research that it sponsors—a quite proper measure. I do not agree with those who maintain the government should try to improve science education by spreading around the research funds, unless it were clearly established that there is no better way to spend money to improve science education. In other words, we ought to spend whatever money is necessary to improve science education on the university level, but we ought not to confuse the goal of such expenditures with that of expenditures for research. We spend for research to get answers to questions; we spend for education to develop the capacities of our young people.

This view does not, of course, argue that teaching and research are unrelated. The thrust of my entire argument is that they necessarily complement each other. If a university aspires to excellence and has the potential to achieve it, then the government should grant it the means to realize its capacities. Excellence will not be attained simply by a university's obtaining some scattered research grants; furthermore, that would be a poor way to conduct a research program. Certainly it would be well to build more universities capable of conducting first-rate research. When they are built, research funding will be diffused by a natural, not a contrived, process. Hand in hand, research and teaching will grow and improve.

But inasmuch as research funds now go, for all practical purposes, almost entirely to the exact sciences, the argument above scarcely applies to the large segment of the university community that is preoccupied with other intellectual disciplines. I am troubled that when talk focuses on the problems of university research, it focuses almost exclusively on the sciences. The Reuss Committee said almost nothing about other fields. What I found significant about the Reuss Committee report was not only the criticism of procedures related to the 96 or 97 percent of government research funds that go to the sciences, but also the absence of concern about the remaining 2 or 3 percent.

That only 2 percent of public research funds are directed to the social sciences is shocking and seems to suggest that our country has few, if any, social problems. Goodness knows that in addition to our military, space, atomic, and medical shortcomings, we have social shortcomings of a monumental nature. It seems clear that both the government and the universities are to blame for the failure of the social sciences to realize the contribution they potentially can make to the national interest. To me, the social sciences are a great untapped resource, not only for the enrichment of our culture but for resolving many of the inequities generated by the unbalanced distribution of Federal research funds.

Every day we are confronted with glaring evidence of inadequate social research, with opportunities missed, with troubles that might have been averted. An example is readily found in our own back yards. Why, for instance, was the nation caught unawares by the disruption at the University of California? We know now that it was not some unique, arbitrary outburst, however irrational some of its manifestations seemed to be, but a profound cry of pain. There are excellent social scientists at Berkeley. What were they doing when all this was developing?

Surely there was a fertile subject for study in the attitudes of the University of California student body. Perhaps there still is. We know by what has transpired in universities around the country that, whatever the germ, it was not isolated on the Berkeley campus. Perceptive social scientists have probably known for some time that something is amiss among American college students. Perhaps if they had taken the trouble to find out what it was, the conditions that gave rise to it might have been corrected—well before the outbursts at Berkeley and many other colleges. By its nature, research in the social sciences admittedly rarely produces the direct and certain results that government administrators and congressmen like to get for their money. But even in the exact sciences, there is much energy wasted in pursuing knowledge down blind alleys. In my view, the social sciences need not be apologetic. It is tragic that their potential for useful research is used so little.

The element of social utility needs to be emphasized. In the academic community, especially on the side not oriented toward technology, there is a strong residue of a conviction that research should somehow remain "pure"—untainted, that is, by practical social considerations. Like Voltaire, I defend vigorously a researcher's right to seek truth in the habits of New Zealand aborigines, Okinawan poetry, commerce in the Federal period, or the relationship of hair color to sexual potency. Funds should always be available, from one source or another, for a competent researcher to follow his intellectual inclinations, no matter how eclectic they may appear to most of us. It is not, however, inappropriate for the government to require that the research it finances—at least most of it—be socially useful at least in the long run, and it is reasonable for it to decide what kind of research it wants and then pay to have it done. What is objectionable is the government's failure to use the skills of researchers in the social sciences, who can acquire information as instruments to help solve our social problems. Without disturbing the system that permits a man to do research of his own choosing, the government should do much more to encourage in the social sciences, as it does in the exact sciences, the kind of research that will be socially useful.

All of us can think of fundamental social problems in which there is a serious deficiency of information. The few proposed here can each readily be matched by a dozen more.

The nation's Negro minority is still imperfectly understood. The Civil Rights Commission, a government agency, did the pioneer work on discrimination. The Moynihan Report, which came out of the Department of Labor, remains a challenging work on the pathology of the Negro family. We still know very little about how to teach educationally deprived Negro children, to say nothing of their parents.

There have been social criticism, analyses, reminiscences, and poetry—much of it excellent—but there has been far too little research.

The impact of television on our society is anyone's guess. Everyone has a theory. Many of us complain bitterly about what it is doing to our children and our culture. We all have the feeling, which Mr. McLuhan has perhaps quickened, that television is having a revolutionary impact on us. But since none of us knows what that impact is, we hardly know whether to try modifying it or how to go about it if we do try.

Crime, statistics tell us, is increasing at an alarming rate. Juveniles seem to represent the worst problem. A Federal Crime Commission recently collected the available information and came up with a good report that emphasized the inadequacy of the data and the lack of knowledge. We should be able to explain why crime, both juvenile and adult, is getting out of hand before we undertake a major effort to reverse the trend. We seem to be faced with a qualitative social change, about which we know almost nothing and seem to be doing far too little research.

Our cities are well into a period of protracted agony. We are at last engaged in modest research programs, federally financed, in air and water pollution, mass transit, and social welfare services. A few hesitant steps are being taken, but not enough by the universities, to learn to improve the design and construction of housing and the quality of urban living generally. There have been limited experiments with new theories for modifying the urban environment, but much, much more research is needed.

Social scientists are not seers any more than physical scientists are alchemists. This essay perhaps pays insufficient tribute to the few social scientists who have, on their own, done remarkable work in socially useful fields, and also perhaps makes insufficient reference to some modest improvements in the Federal research budget in the past year or so. It may be wrong in its contention that much of the disruption in our society in recent years could have been avoided if we were richer in knowledge about ourselves and our culture. But if our society can, through its government, spend some $16 billion annually for research, then surely it must allocate more than 2 percent to find its own soul.

It is my contention that the government should forthwith announce: "In the next five years, we are going to devote X billion dollars to acquiring a maximum of understanding of the nation's twenty-five most serious social problems." Then it should call upon the academic community to define those problems. Having done this, it should solicit projects from social scientists—including historians and anthropologists, political scientists and sociologists, psychologists and philosophers, and indeed, natural scientists and engineers as well—in colleges and universities everywhere, who feel they can open some door that will admit a glimmer of light. The undertaking would be a kind of IGY of social research.

An undertaking of this nature will have far-reaching consequences, quite apart from the cultural enrichment that emerges. I believe it will attain the objectives of the Reuss Committee by diffusing research funds, not only to a variety of institutions but to a great number of scholars. It will help restore the institutional and geographical balance that the committee seeks in disbursing funds. It will give new prestige to many more universities and many more teachers. It will bring new stimulation to college campuses, large and small. And it will prove to be an important asset to education generally.

And so this paper comes full circle. It began by saying that the university has the obligation both to preserve and to enrich our culture. It suggested that in the exact sciences we are doing too much enriching and not enough preserving, while in the social sciences we are doing just the opposite. We have been excessively zealous in one area of our domain as educators and a little slothful—let us say "unimaginative"—in the other. For it is not in the exact sciences alone, or in the social sciences, that we, as a society, will succeed or fail. It is by giving our attention to our needs seen "as a whole." I am stern about the university's duties and optimistic about its potential. We have made mistakes. I believe we must now devote much energy to correcting them.

The Research Function and
The Advancement of Knowledge

KEITH SPALDING, W. EUGENE GROVES,
KERMIT GORDON, E. PETER VOLPE

The Role of the Social Sciences

KEITH SPALDING

IN ANY DISCUSSION of the "conflict" between teaching and research, it is easy to get bogged down in the matter of definitions. Nowadays, the word "research" is used in a much broader and looser way than it was when the nation first realized that basic research was essential to its survival. The fact is that colleges as well as universities are preoccupied with research. In a number of leading colleges, it is believed that introducing students to research is one of the most effective teaching methods. Curricula are being devised which avoid cookbook laboratory experiments and engage the student in original approaches to old questions, if not in original research.

Unfortunately, the term "research" is seldom used with precision. It is often employed interchangeably with "scholarship" or even with "publication." Research has come to be indiscriminately acclaimed and rewarded. But, if by the terms "research" and "scholarship" we still refer to the practice of wide and tireless reading and writing by a faculty member, to his continuous re-examination of the content and methodology of his subject, to his relentless effort to extend and deepen its meaning, then certainly every instructor in a college must engage in research. Indeed, the college or university faculty that permits its members to prosper on "research" without also demanding "scholarship" is making a serious error.

There are some who argue that synthesis and generalization—so often lacking in specialized research—is more readily accomplished in a college than in a university. While research can be narrow if it is carried out by specialists with tunnel vision, it is equally a means of breaking down barriers for those who seek to generalize and synthesize. In these terms, the performance of research may become an essential part of the dynamics of a college. The problem remains to determine the nature and extent of the commitment a college should make to research activity.

As Mr. Spencer points out, because the Federal government is the largest purchaser of research, there is an inevitable temptation to suggest that the government has the responsibility to equalize support, to spread the benefits around among all types of institutions in all parts of the country, without regard to whether these institutions can perform the function well. More recently, it has been suggested that the government should give as much support to research in the humanities and social sciences as to research in the sciences.

It is not acceptable for a society to be able to preserve foods and to produce more food and fiber than it can use (now possible because of technological advances) and yet to have poverty and even starvation (because of its inability to construct a distribution and market system that will use those products). Every thinking person perceives that our technology has outdistanced our ability to provide all the members of our society with the full advantages of that technology. Such a state of affairs is not tolerable if our society is to continue to be healthy and vigorous. Clearly, we must develop new knowledge in the social sciences, knowledge that will lead to improved social practices.

According to one popular proposition, because there is a National Science Foundation, and now, though modestly funded, a National Foundation for the Arts and Humanities, there should also be a National Foundation for the Social Sciences. Mr. Spencer ably extends this proposition to incorporate the argument that the social sciences have much to offer in solving such national problems as the treatment of the Negro minority, the impact of television, the rising crime rate, and urban blight. Nobody can doubt the importance of these problems, nor the significant role that research will play in solving them.

There is room for reasonable doubt, however, that the Federal granting agencies, under their present system of operation or under any appropriations procedure that can easily be projected, are the most effective sources of funding for these significant endeavors. Research in all of the problems mentioned is a sensitive matter because all men and women have views about them, because they directly affect vested interests and long-established business practices, and because they are major political issues. Although research in the behavioral and social sciences is becoming more and more quantitative, it is a fact that valid conclusions on important matters still depend upon mature reflection, taste, and discriminating judgment. It is a fact, too, that the solutions to some of the urgent social problems of the day are being solved by action rather than by research.

If one accepts the axiom that power, influence, and intrusion follow the granting of money, then one must admit that the social sciences could be hurt rather than helped by the establishment of a Federal grants program, particularly if it should be subject to the close scrutiny of the Congress. And what other way is there? The point is simply that it is not yet clear whether the social sciences should be federally funded in the same way as the "hard" sciences and the currently less volatile humanities and fine arts are. Whatever the Federal decision may be, however, it is clear that research in the social sciences is an important area, deserving wide support from private philanthropy.

For What Is All This Knowledge?

W. EUGENE GROVES

"Graduate departments exist," Robert Maynard Hutchins once remarked, "to teach people to teach in graduate departments." The same criticism is appropriate to the model of a university Lyle Spencer has constructed. For him, the university embodies almost objective truth. It is a repository, transmitter, and occasional enricher of the wisdom, values, and knowledge of the ages. Upon this faltering Athena, he bestows the major problems of the twentieth century, trusting that a few more million, or billion, dollars funneled into academic research will magically produce solutions to relieve us of crime, urban ghettos, racial discontent, and the bothersome dislocations and uncertainties that stem from the technological revolution of this century. But his analysis of the university does not fully accommodate the enormous social problems he justifiably poses to its faculty and students.

Emphasis upon knowledge per se rather than upon the human problems and questions that are more properly the *raison d'être* of knowledge, unnecessarily introduces the stark dichotomy between preservation of old knowledge and solutions, on the one hand, and creation of new facts, concepts, and solutions on the other. The revolutionary pace of technological and social change precludes us from thinking of the university as a compendium of knowledge passed down to the young, and occasionally enriched. Existing knowledge and theory are of little relevance when taught for their own sake; they are important only as they assist in answering questions and solving problems with which we are now faced. Most importantly, each younger generation must continually develop its capabilities to prepare for realities virtually unrecognized by the previous generation.

Not only is the nature of knowledge rapidly changing from generation to generation, but the social cleavages and human misunderstandings created by such changes also stimulate us to probe deeper, asking the age-old question: for what purpose is all this knowledge? It is not trivial to acknowledge that man is continually searching for meaning, and for power. Each individual, as he grows, wants to act effectively with those around him; and he searches for a conceptual thread with which to tie together all the disparate events and objects he perceives and feels. Individuals, interest groups, and leaders in a society provoke probing questions when the distribution of physical and ideal resources is not consonant with the various aspirations of the people.

Numerous institutions help to resolve these questions and problems, either by instilling traditional answers and habits or by providing an environment in which new solutions may be conceived, tried, and disseminated. The university could claim the role of a total institution embodying "all that is best in a society": analytical tools, moral values, verbal expertise, social graces, and political skills. But I strongly believe that the unique function of the modern pluralistic, secular university is the intellectual enterprise of independent, critical analysis and action. Students and faculty raise questions and attempt to answer them in productive and challenging ways. The advanced scholars should propose more complex answers, and ask questions more articulately and profoundly. All participants should engage in a mutual intellectual investigation, conducted at differing levels, conceived in terms of problems troubling them and others to whom they feel an obligation to respond.

THE TEACHING VS. RESEARCH DELUSION

The "information explosion," to which Lyle Spencer refers, signifies a shift in the emphasis of the intellectual enterprise away from preservation, toward creation. This shift, however, has not so much increased the preoccupation with research at the expense of teaching, as it has changed the notion of what learning is all about. Learning can take place just as well, sometimes better, in a research setting as in a classroom. Because we are all trying to solve our own and others' problems, teaching should contribute toward that process of critical investigation. In a broad sense, such critical investigation is research; it is creation. Typically, research is narrowly defined only to include investigations—no matter how mundane—that are well funded. Teaching, in its narrow definition, includes the time spent helping others to ask and answer questions at a level on which the teacher already feels fully competent. The danger in the modern university is that the narrow definitions can become pervasive. When that happens, a conflict arises between "teaching" and "research."

The critical difference is not between teaching and research but between an intellectual enterprise funded for goals specified by external agencies, and one that is generated by the internal demands of the intellectual community as its members search for answers to broad questions about human life. Given these two sets of demands, we must ask whose questions are most important. We must ask what kind of questions are permitted by the university, and what the rewards are for devoting time to questions raised by individuals and groups both within and outside the university walls. Who determines the priorities, whose interests are at stake, and how can the balance change? The real conflicts are political and normative, not intellectual.

The proficient researcher acquires prestige from his colleagues by his contribution to the literature of the profession, wins praise from his university for bringing research money to the institution, but receives only indirect, delayed rewards for producing others who can contribute to the same area of knowledge. I detect four rewards that accrue to him from time spent attending to students' needs: (1) financial, teachers get paid for carrying a teaching load; (2) professional, they groom protégés to assist in research, to promote the instructor's methodology and pet theories, and to extol the virtues of the teacher as the graduates move on across the country; (3) aesthetic, there is a certain self-satisfying beauty in formulating ideas in communicable terms and getting across a point to others; and (4) interpersonal, the intellectual and personal interchange, especially in small group discussions, can be emotionally rewarding.

To improve the quality of the classroom experience, allocation of additional Federal funds earmarked for this purpose may be a necessary condition but certainly not a sufficient one. If more attention is to be paid to questions that are interesting and relevant to the intellectual, political, psychological, and moral needs perceived by the entire academic community, the students should have more power, especially over the financial and professional rewards to the faculty. In the last few years, students often have demonstrated that they are effective house cleaning agents. They demanded the right of free political expression and organization on the Berkeley campus. They forced the University of Pennsylvania to abandon a secret bacteriological warfare project. They have forced several universities to retain excellent teachers who had published less than was acceptable to their colleagues. They have embarrassed numerous faculty members with public evaluations of poor teaching practices. And when education has been intolerable, students have set up counter institutions, usually called experimental colleges.

An economist should be shocked that students, as consumers of even an admittedly intangible product, have so little quality control over purchasing in the academic "supermarket." Because the university is not a community of scholars with totally identical interests, students need enough independence to protect their learning interests. One way to give the student more control over the rewards offered the faculty, and hence over his own education, would be to make him financially independent of his particular departments; he would have a guaranteed fellowship paid directly to him by the government agency, foundation, and so forth that supports him. He would then have a great deal more flexibility regarding the use of tuition money. As an example, students might pay tuition in proportion to the amount and quality of instruction purchased, with students contracting for teaching services more or less directly with individual faculty members or with outside experts. Besides individualizing and improving the students' learning, this greater independence might force faculty to engage in more interesting research, for fear of not being able to impress students into doing their routine chores.

Another power over professional rewards, already potentially in the hands of students, is a national evaluation of graduate departments and instructors based on the criteria most important to the prospective graduate student. Faculty rank graduate students, and the American Council on Education has conducted surveys of leading faculty in each discipline in order to assess departments. But already, through the grapevine communication system, some of the "better" departments are losing good students because of their dissatisfaction with internal policies. It is time to force departments to respond to students. By these proposals, many of the traditional feudal powers of the faculty would be undermined.

THE BIASES OF RESEARCH

So far, I have discussed research only in the context of competing demands within the institution. Mr. Spencer contends that the extensive government-sponsored "research" is impairing the teaching function of the university; but nowhere does he ask if this "research" is impairing the creative function of the university. This, to me, is a more central question. The present sterility of much of academia arises from a plethora of rote scientific investigations divorced both from interesting and challenging questions and from power and political realities. Lyle Spencer admirably upholds libertarian values in reproaching institutions for accepting secret research. But beyond that, he does not develop criteria for discriminating among the purposes, methods, biases, and conditions of research.

The key question is: Where is the source of pressure to keep the analysis of social problems comprehensive and critical? I am not certain I have the answer, but will make a few suggestions. Agencies and foundations which fund research usually have narrow interests, begin with strong biases, and sometimes are cautious about personal considerations irrelevant to the actual research. This caution is reflected even by the National Science Foundation, which recently failed to renew a grant to a leading mathematician, allegedly because he had received a prize in Moscow and had voiced opposition to the war in Vietnam. In the conduct of the actual research projects, some investigators have the integrity or the curiosity or perhaps the prestige to convince a client to broaden his interests. Writing in Robert S. Morrison's *The Contemporary University: USA*, Peter Rossi tells how research centers sometimes play Robin Hood, by advising clients to include questions in their studies that are not directly relevant to their topic.

Research for a client often is limited by the value bias with which the questions must be asked and the sample for investigation drawn. This bias may be explicit or implicit in that the investigator is aware of the general nature of the conclusions desired in order to get additional research funded, particularly research on controversial topics. Studies of drug use, when funded by Federal agencies, especially when they require the cooperation of the Federal Narcotics Bureau, are oriented toward discovering the epidemiology of use, building a predictive model of who uses pot or LSD so that more effective social controls may be devised to stop such use. Joel Forte, a respected doctor in San Francisco, for example, had a license to investigate the effects of marijuana on users. But when he began to advocate, though mildly, the

legalization of the use and possession of pot, his license was soon re-
voked by the State of California and the Federal Narcotics Bureau.

The myth of objectivity, which may have some validity in the
hard sciences, is untenable in the social sciences. Most studies are conducted to justify predetermined theories, prejudices, and habits. Conclusions are constrained by the way in which questions are formulated,
by the exact methods of research, by the principles used in the interpretation of the data, and by the vehicle and context of communication
of the results. Occasionally, a controversial study will slip into the
hands of dissident investigators, as when Havighurst and Hauser at
the University of Chicago were asked to conduct studies of the Chicago
public school system or James Coleman was asked by the Office of
Education to study desegregation in American education. When documents which threaten many power interests gain wide circulation,
counter studies soon emerge to justify postponing action. Philip Hauser
recently commented that not one of his recommendations has been
implemented by the Chicago School Board since he reported his results
about three years ago. The problem of whose answers are listened to
is as important as whose questions are asked. When faced with critical
problems, the legislator's hope in proposing a study is usually to post-
pone the problem through a socially acceptable delaying ritual or to
buy time in order to find a political solution that requires less sacrifice
of the ideal and material interests of the major power blocs. Only
occasionally does genuine inability to solve a problem arise from a lack
of knowledge. The important decisions, in the beginning and in the
end, are political and normative, not scientific.

Hence, I must conclude that Lyle Spencer is too optimistic in his
contention that "much of the disruption in our society in recent years
could have been avoided if we were richer in knowledge about ourselves and our culture." Berkeley still would have happened, the
inner city would remain a slum, crime would not have decreased significantly, and scientists would still be clamoring for more research. I
do not say that we should not have research or that it should not have
social utility, a point emphasized by Lyle Spencer. But I challenge
him to define whose social utility research should serve, and I feel that
research is not the key to social change (it may either assist or delay
social amelioration).

COMBINING RESEARCH AND ACTION

I fear that the university, as a research institution, has become too
subservient to traditional, and sometimes rather trivial, social values

and priorities. It is conceivable that some of the studies resulting from Lyle Spencer's proposed IGY for social problems would be counterproductive. As an increasing number of researchers ask questions and give answers in a manner appealing to funding sources, a study often is merely an examination of our social fabric for the seams that are about to split; it implies that more data will enable us better to patch those seams, to preserve the culture, wisdom, and heritage of our past, and perhaps to stabilize the patterns of human relations now set by those classes and groups who control the resources of our society.

Many of the problems are already quite clear. Lyle Spencer grants that there now exist social criticism, analyses, reminiscences, and poetry—some of it excellent—but let us have more solid research, he pleads. I submit that the recently published polemic by Jonathan Kozol, *Death at an Early Age—The Destruction of the Hearts and Minds of Negro Children in the Boston Public Schools,* more clearly portrays that problem, and probably will have more effect on the attitudes of the average citizen, and hence on the legislator, than most of the studies any academician or government agency could construct.

Do we really need much more "understanding" of the Negro minority, in any other than a patronizing way, to increase our social control? A few weeks ago Kenneth Clark told the national convention of Negro elected officials meeting in Chicago that they soon may be the prime target of racial strife, especially if, with more Negroes in government and public office, the ghetto Negro finds his condition continuing to deteriorate. The unemployment rate in the urban ghettos is upwards of 20 percent—a low estimate based on inadequate census records—and some say we need more studies about what causes urban unrest. The world has been lulled into a slumber by the lyres of its ivory-towered researchers who concern themselves with the advancement of formal systems of knowledge rather than with the solution of human problems: solutions usually requiring substantial sacrifice by wealthy suburbanites. The important questions raised by our attempt to reduce crime in America will also not be resolvable solely by academic studies. One basic prerequisite is to improve the living conditions of at least 20 percent of the American people. But even more basic to law enforcement is that we make a normative decision between justice based on retribution and deterence, and justice that emphasizes prevention and reform.

Further, criminal behavior is both encouraged and defined in a socioeconomically biased way by a legal structure that reflects upper-middle-class white Anglo-Saxon Protestant values. According to a

Southern Maryland judge's ruling in an Aid to Dependent Children case, for example, welfare is an act of grace on the part of the state, not a right, and punishment is meted out to those not observing proper standards of personal conduct, regardless of the harm done to others and of personal needs for decent human subsistence. Studies can begin to clarify our factual thinking about these conditions of civil disorder and defiance, but they cannot change the political and moral realities that create the problems.

Social questions receive attention more by political choice than by academic interest. Intellectuals must get their heads out of the sand, emphasize the important questions, and study them in a manner that will have impact. Studies can be important when they are politically relevant: that is, when there is a power block that has a stake in the answer. Gunnar Myrdal's *American Dilemma* and other studies of the American Negro in the late 1940's and early 1950's were a factor in the 1954 *Brown vs. Board of Education* decision of the Supreme Court. When there was publicly acceptable evidence around which to organize their demands, the people whose interests were at stake were no longer willing to accept the myth that separate Negro educational facilities were, in any sense, equal to the white schools.

The human relevance and critical perspective of research might be served by combining research with action programing. The participant investigator in the social sciences builds empathy with and understanding of the internal feelings, needs, and actions of the subgroup or phenomenon he is describing, and for whom he often is prescribing solutions. Community organizing, tutoring in deprived areas, organizing political campaigns, working overseas in the Peace Corps, and setting up a college might make the life of the mind more relevant to human feelings and social action. Such tests against reality continually pose the question: for what is all this knowledge? They force the researcher to think about the human impact of his studies, and ideally to organize action himself. The disembodied intellect has reigned too long. It is time that the university be more than a spur to the intellect and a servant to the society; it must, itself, begin to create political problems.

Advance Knowledge Or Perish

KERMIT GORDON

MR. SPENCER COMES TO HIS SHARPEST FOCUS in considering the conduct of social science research in the university and the inevitable question of Federal support. I will address my comments to some of the issues that he raises in this connection.

As the principal officer of an independent institution engaged in social science research—an institution which I will refrain from characterizing as a "university without students" out of respect for Mr. Spencer's aversion to the phrase—I will startle absolutely no one by concurring in Mr. Spencer's judgment that such research is relatively underfinanced and possesses a strong claim for more generous public support. And since my own institution addresses its research efforts to public policy problems, it will not come as a shock that I share Mr. Spencer's view that the Federal government has a perfect right to limit its support to research which is, at least potentially, socially useful.

But lest these seem to be simply the views of an interested mendicant, I hasten to point out that I held them at least as strongly at an earlier time when I was in a position—within the Federal government —to observe and lament the flimsiness of understanding on which the government must base decisions of incalculable importance to American society. One cannot fault the government for doing what the government has to do, which is to decide, but one can lament the fact that even the most conscientious efforts to reach informed decisions by drawing on accumulated knowledge were so often unavailing.

Moreover, I shall point out, somewhat reluctantly, that Mr. Spencer's indictment concerning the inadequacy of Federal support of social science research—though essentially correct—is somewhat overdrawn. Federal support for social science research may indeed be "peanuts," as Mr. Spencer asserts, but it is larger in relation to the total research budget than the 2 percent figure he cites. This miscalculation arises from the very common mistake of confusing total Federal expenditure on research and development (about $16.5 billion last year) with total Federal expenditures for research alone (about $5.3 billion). (The term "development" covers expenditures for designing, building and testing prototypes of complex government hardware, such as weapons systems, space vehicles, and nuclear reactors.) Thus the correct figure for the share of the Federal research budget which goes to the social sciences is closer to 6 percent than to 2 percent. Even 6 percent might fairly be described as "peanuts," but the goobers are a bit huskier than Mr. Spencer's figure suggests.

There are a few other considerations which tend to temper severe judgments about the degree of malnutrition of the social sciences. First, though the Federal government has many fewer dollars to pass out to social scientists than to investigators in the harder sciences, the social science queue is a good deal shorter; of the approximately 240,000 scientists of all kinds employed in colleges and universities, only about 44,000—or 18 percent—were in the social sciences and psychology. Second, the dollar goes a bit further in supporting the research efforts of the social scientist, for on the average he requires less equipment than does his opposite number in the exact sciences. Third, Federal expenditures for research in the social sciences have been growing rapidly, and have increased about fivefold in the last decade.

But when all is said and done, Mr. Spencer's central point stands as essentially correct. A study three years ago showed that 62 percent of all the physicists in the United States received Federal government support for their work, but only 38 percent of the psychologists had such assistance; 59 percent of those in the biological sciences benefitted, but only 36 percent of the sociologists; 45 percent of the mathematicians were supported, but only 30 percent of the economists. These are not huge discrepancies, but they bespeak a significantly more restrictive policy of support for social science research than for research in the exact sciences.

Mr. Spencer urges greater government support for that kind of research that is "socially useful at least in the long run." I can accept this formulation without difficulty, though I would not read it as expressing a strong preference for the support of applied as opposed to basic research. It is hard to see how *good* social science research—that is, research which focuses existing knowledge effectively on current problems or which advances understanding of human behavior—can *fail* to be useful. Public policy problems must be addressed as they arise, and it is the role of applied research to inform decision making by bringing to bear such scientific knowledge as is relevant to the problem. But such research is no more useful than is the basic research which augments the knowledge available to aid in the solution of the public policy problems of the future. I would suggest that the species of social science research that flunks the test of usefulness is not pure research, but poor research.

I have no way of judging the incidence of poor research in other fields of knowledge, but I know it to be distressingly high in the social sciences. It may well be harder for a pedestrian talent to make a modestly useful contribution in the social sciences than in the exact sciences: controlled experiments are rarely possible, reliable data are harder to come by, the disciplines are less cumulative, methodology is less clearly defined. However that may be, one all too frequently encounters social science research which builds uncritically on data of questionable accuracy, which is slipshod in method, or which is simply discursive and unfocused. A scholar who chooses to treat a two-page idea in two pages is frequently regarded as an eccentric. And one who works for two years on a single article is often regarded as hopelessly old-fashioned.

Part of the blame, I am sure, must be assigned to the publish-or-perish rule as it appears to be administered at some institutions. If the rule were advance-knowledge-or-perish, a strong argument could be made in its defense. But with the proliferation of outlets for the products of scholarship, one need not advance knowledge to find a publisher. Not a few young scholars behave as though they had been led to believe that their professional advancement would rest on the volume of their output, not its quality, as though they expected that their research output would be weighed, not read. Our habits of speech tend to confirm these views. We mean to flatter a scholar when we say "He's a producer"; we say "He has an impressive bibliography," meaning a long one; we say "He got an article out of it," suggesting that building a bibliography is what research is all about.

I would suggest that the kind of motivation which is implicit in these attitudes is not the kind of motivation best designed to enlist social science research in the cause of social amelioration.

Finally, let me note at least briefly some of the special problems which arise in conducting social science research with Federal financial support. Applied research intended to raise the quality of government decision making must be timely to be useful; but the process of decision making in government is often so compressed in time and so headlong in pace that it is impossible for outside investigators to produce their research findings before the issue is settled. Major improvements are needed in the government program planning process to make room for the orderly marshaling of knowledge in advance of decision making.

Second, it is unreasonable to expect government operating agencies that support external social science research to maintain an objective and indulgent attitude toward research findings that call into question the validity of the agency's program. We have come to expect a great deal of our public servants, but this is asking too much. Accordingly, if social science research is to ask the hard questions and follow the evidence wherever it leads, it cannot afford to be too dependent for financing on the government agencies which have a direct interest in the findings. Some Federal support for research of this type should come from an agency which is remote from the firing line of program controversy, but more important, nongovernment financing should be available on a more generous scale to support this kind of research.

Teaching, Research, and Service: Union or Coexistence?

E. PETER VOLPE

I CONFESS TO A VAST IMPATIENCE with the point of view that ascribes the inadequacy of teaching on our nation's campuses to overemphasis on research. I submit that the highest form of teaching is being practiced today by our research scholars. My thesis, simply stated, is as follows: A professor in any discipline stays alive when he is engaged in creative work, however modest. He stays alive when he carries his enthusiasm for discovery into the classroom. The professor is academically dead when the spark of inquiry is extinguished within him. It is then that he betrays his student. The student becomes merely an acquirer of knowledge rather than an inquirer into knowledge.

Perhaps I oversimplify, but I have known too many professors who have stirred too few imaginations. The research scholar creates an atmosphere in which the student becomes genuinely interested in learning on his own. Research is founded in human curiosity. As Edward Teller aptly remarked, research "is a game, is play, led by curiosity, by taste, style, judgment, intangibles." Teaching is also a game directed by curiosity. Teaching and research are as inseparable as the two faces of the same coin. I may be belaboring the obvious, but it bears emphasizing that the dedicated research scholar shares the inner excitement of creativity with his student. He infuses the student with the spirit of inquiry. The student derives the esthetic pleasure of witnessing how seemingly unrelated observations are woven into a meaningful, comprehensible pattern.

Our fundamental goal in education is, or should be, to broaden and intensify the student's innate curiosity so that he may experience the deepest kind of intellectual enjoyment. This, of course, is not a new educational principle. But it is the neglect of this principle that has led to the ossification of instruction, particularly at the undergraduate level. As stated by Commissioner Harold Howe II, the basic ill of American higher education is "the failure to probe for the intellectual curiosity in every student and guide it in those directions that we have found over the centuries to be most important to a civilized and fulfilling life." To this I might add that the research scholar, in the vanguard of new approaches, techniques, and rapidly expanding knowledge, is best prepared to present new discoveries with understanding and enthusiasm.

If undergraduate education seems to have deteriorated, it is not because we have too much research, but because we have too little of it in most institutions. And, far too often, the research scholar is subjected to a rigidly structured, unimaginative undergraduate curriculum, monopolized by formal lecture courses, when he would prefer to teach in the manner he knows best: by intellectual contagion and lengthy discussion. We must take the bold step of largely replacing formal discourse by informal seminars and independent study programs. The students will then learn to think for themselves again. We will learn to talk to the students again.

We are hopeful that the student, once he sheds his cap and gown, can express the creative force which has been nurtured in him, not only that he may gain enduring self-satisfaction but also that he may contribute to the society of which he is a part. We expect this dual role on the part of our former students. But how are we to view our role as professors? Do we fulfill our obligation to society solely by equipping others to meet the pressing problems of our times? In the last two decades, the proverbial ivy-covered walls of our campuses have cracked almost beyond repair. The boundaries between university activities and those on the outside have become increasingly vague. In particular, with the vast infusion of Federal funds for scientific activities, the ivory tower position on the separation of science and politics is a thing of the past. Should we now become teacher, researcher, administrator, moralizer, adviser, and politician? How much involvement and commitment can we shoulder as professors? How much of society's burden can we bear? Thousands of professor-hours of thought and conversation on these vital questions have produced no consensus.

Few would deny that the research scholar must have complete freedom in his choice of field of inquiry. This limitless freedom carries with it, I firmly believe, an obligation that the scholar make the results of his inquiry freely available to students, colleagues, and the public, a principle in accord with the thesis that teaching and research are interlocked. If the research program does not contribute to the education of undergraduates and graduates, then the program does not properly belong in a university. A university should address itself primarily to the community of scholars and secondarily to the community at large.

It has been said that science in the colleges and universities left the "horse-and-buggy" period when the Federal government courted the academic scientist during and after World War II. Federal support provided unprecedented opportunities for the stimulation of creativity in both basic (undirected) science and applied (directed) science. At present, given the government's increasing preoccupation with quick-fix results and the overstrained financial resources of universities, there is a grave danger that the programs of many academic scientists involved in basic research may have to be cut back to the "horse-and-buggy" days. This is tantamount to producing the collapse of many elaborate, imaginative research programs.

If the members of Congress cannot fully understand the concept that the long-range national welfare depends upon the vigorous support and growth of basic research, then, perhaps, it would be easier for them to comprehend the notion that to dampen the spark of creativity in present-day academic scientists is also to harness the creativity of the immediate generation of young minds. The continued excellence of American science depends upon the proper training of many young scientists. In a similar vein, we defraud students when the research endeavors of scholars in the humanities and social sciences are shackled by the dearth of funds. If it views the argument in this light, Congress should move to devise a means of funding research programs that are related to the education function. Undergraduates and graduates must be made the beneficiaries of Federal grants for basic academic research. The present "project-oriented" grant system, which contributes only tangentially to education, should be supplemented by a broad "research-instruction" grant system. Awards of "research-instruction" grants should be based principally on the number of Ph.D. candidates or undergraduates engaged in independent study under the direction of the research scholar. The student is thus afforded a genuine opportunity to share in the satisfaction of exploring the frontiers for new knowledge. The student must have this opportunity as a right, not as a privilege.

JOHN J. CORSON

Public Service
And Higher Education:
Compatibility or Conflict?[1]

$\mathbf{D}$AVID HENRY HAS SAID that ". . . a great current challenge is to gear up the public service role of the universities to meet social demands, while insuring that such service is related to main institutional educational activities and conducted at the highest possible professional level."

The evidence of social demands to which President Henry refers is illustrated on many campuses. On one campus the faculty of physical education works continually with the Bureau of Alcoholism in a state department of mental health. A distinguished Harvard professor designed a garbage disposal ship for the city of Boston. The Yale Medical School provides health services for many in the New Haven community. The faculty of a liberal arts college, at the request of a large private employer, trains foremen in the employer's plant. A school of education faculty developed programs, at the behest of the U.S. Office of Education, for the social and economic rehabilitation of the unemployed. Key faculty members are absent from a number of campuses while they help to establish or strengthen colleges in other lands or aid with still other functions. The medical school faculty on another campus has contracted to provide medical care for a whole neighborhood that has been racked by race riots.

The list might be lengthened, but there is no need. The contents

[1] A revision, in the light of reactions from several university presidents, of remarks made before the National Association of State Universities and Land-Grant Colleges, Washington, D.C., Nov. 16, 1966.

would not be new to you. My only purpose in presenting this list is to provide the basis for assessing:

Why this demand upon the university exists, and
What the university is to expect in the future.

WHY THE UNIVERSITY?

Why turn to the university? Why should not private enterprise resolve these new problems, even as historically we looked to private enterprise to build the railroads, invent the gadgets that made life simpler, discover the new drugs that would save our lives, and create the new textbooks that would better the education to be offered? Why has not government expanded its own staff and geared itself up to handle the new facets of international relations, or to invent and develop the new fighting weapons, or to provide the medical and social services needed to combat racial tension?

There are, I believe, five reasons why the American society increasingly turns to the universities to aid with the vitally important problems of building a great society, and let me emphasize that the words "great" and "society" are here intended to convey their literal, not their political, meaning.

First, the university provides unique institutional strengths. It has a staff, buildings and grounds, and endowment, and it has more. The university has a climate within and a prestige without that constitute unique institutional strengths for resolving the problems of a society.

I sat on a panel a year ago to review the accomplishments of one of the regional educational laboratories, created and supported by the Office of Education to diagnose the ills of our schools and to do the research that will produce solutions. This laboratory, like others, is a new, independent, nonprofit institution. Its accomplishments to date have been despite the lack of the institutional strengths that a good university could have provided. That laboratory lacks the libraries, the laboratories, and the administrative structure that serve the faculties of a university. But it also lacks the capacity to attract the ablest of researchers; it lacks the collegial-interdisciplinary approach to inquiry that makes some universities truly great; and it lacks the reputation for objective, independent fact-finding that the term "university" carries with it. That laboratory struggles feebly along because it lacks all the institutional strengths it requires to do its highly important job.

Second, the universities, as they have grown, have acquired a substantial monopoly of the particular kind of human talent required for dealing with the problems of a society as distinguished from the problems of an enterprise.

The universities have no corner on superior intellects. Indeed, having spent almost equal thirds of my adult life in university faculties, as an executive in business, and as an official in government, I am concerned that neither government nor the universities attract and hold their share of truly superior intellects. The rewards offered by the profit-making world—be it as a businessman or a professional man—are relatively so much greater that government and the universities (as I have seen them) suffer. But private enterprise focuses many of our ablest minds on the problems of making, selling, promoting, and accounting for their products—from diapers to tombstones. It seldom focuses their minds and energies on the formulation of foreign policy, the design of educational programs, or the eradication of urban blight —be it slums or smog. The university, I repeat, has a substantial monopoly of the particular kind of human talent that is capable of seeing the shortcomings in our foreign policy, in our educational programs, and in our cities, and capable of bringing knowledge to bear on the finding of solutions.

Third, the universities possess a discipline of objectivity.

That asset is scarce—and infinitely valuable—in a competitive, tension-packed society. The sales manager, the Negro leader, the union leader, the corporate labor relations negotiator, or the political executive in government cannot afford (nor has he the time for) objectivity. Moreover, the organization—the corporation, the union, the government department, the political party, or even the church—demands, perhaps requires, for its survival, acceptance and conformity with its policies. Hence, after a decade or two at plying their trades, most businessmen, public officials, union leaders, and preachers are so habituated to one way of thought that they cannot attack a problem with the fresh, detached objectivity that is required. William James was surely right when he wrote of the scarcity and "infinite value" of "the capacity for nonhabitual perception."

Fourth, the universities are committed to the search for new knowledge. They are not the only institutions committed to this end (for example, a few business enterprises engage in basic research) but they are the major social institutions pursuing this objective.

The consequence of this fact was well stated by Harold Stoke in these words:

> The more nearly society is operated on the basis of knowledge carefully gathered and impersonally applied, the more nearly the processes

of higher education and of social action coincide, and the more nearly the processes of public administration and of legislation become those of the academic community.[2]

It is the business of university faculties to pursue the curiosity that yields new knowledge. And we live in the time of what Robert Solo has dubbed "the science-based society."[3] This means, as I understand Solo, that we live in a time when advance in many (or most) fields depends upon the creation of new knowledge. Paraphrasing Emerson, let me suggest that, in a science-based society, he who would have the world beat a path to his door will find the idea for his improved mouse-trap in a university laboratory. The day when advance is based on tinkering and improvisation has passed. The solutions for not only our physical ills (cancer and heart disease, for example) and for our scientific needs (such as are illustrated in space exploration), but as well the solutions for our international problems, and, yes, even our racial difficulties will most likely be found in the minds of those who have the capacity, time, and inclination for rigorous, detached, creative thought.

Fifth, a university possesses values; it stands for something; indeed it stands for the most civilizing values of which we know—freedom, for example.

Thus, Merrimon Cuninggim aptly suggests that university people must "say their piece . . . must proclaim their values, that by their very nature they believe and accept, not for society's salvation alone but for their own."[4] His prescription poses these conscience-shaking questions: Can a university be true to itself—let alone to the society that supports it—if it could, with the knowledge at its command or within the reach of research, alter the lives of crippled children, but not accept responsibility for administering, through its medical school, programs that would apply that knowledge to their care? Or can a university be true to what it stands for if it has access to or can create knowledge that would lighten the social problems of our cities, if it does not collaborate with regional and municipal authorities in efforts to combat juvenile delinquency, to reduce racial conflict, or to renovate obsolete forms of local government? Or can a university stand by when it has the know-how to "make the world safe for democracy," in 1967 terms, by under-

[2] Stoke, *Viewpoints for the Study of the Administration of Higher Education* (Eugene: Center for the Advanced Study of Educational Administration, University of Oregon, 1966), pp. 30-31.

[3] "The University in a Science-based Society" (Unpublished MS).

[4] Cuninggim, "A Campus Without Limit," Address to the Danforth Associates Conference, Aug. 29, 1966.

taking responsibility for building the educational, governmental, agricultural, or health institutions of underdeveloped countries? Or can a university choose to have no part in the national struggle for stable economic growth? Can it refuse to accept the requests it receives (even as Governor Connolly requested three Texas institutions a year ago) to investigate surging prices, or rising unemployment, even though its findings will create some enemies at the same time they identify solutions?

It is these qualities that the real university *uniquely* possesses. And it is the possession of these qualities that makes it inevitable that society will turn to the university with increasing frequency. Thus Daniel Bell declares that "the university is taking on a vastly different role. It is becoming one of the active shapers of the society, taking over, perhaps, the role which the business firm played in the past hundred years." [5]

THE NEW PLURALISM

What I see emerging in the American society is a new form of pluralism. Even while the Federal government grows larger in function and in expenditures, it tends to diminish in size, if size is measured by the conventional yardstick of employment. It achieves this by contracting for assistance in the solution of problems, from the sweeping of floors to the determination of how to explore, under the seas, the very core of the earth.

Consider the magnitude of this trend. The Department of Health, Education, and Welfare made contracts during the past fiscal year with more than seven hundred nonprofit institutions throughout the country. The National Aeronautics and Space Administration used more than 80 percent of its total appropriation to finance contracts for services of nongovernmental agencies—business enterprises, universities and other nonprofit institutions. And, as observers have noted, government has gone very far in asking or permitting nongovernment agencies—business enterprises, nonprofit research institutions such as Rand, SRI, and Battelle, and the universities—to participate in decisions which elsewhere are made only by government. [6]

The reason seems clear. A science-based society is an aggregate of increasingly specialized institutions and individuals. For the solution of new problems, in both public policy and individual enterprise,

[5] Bell, *The Reforming of General Education* (New York: Columbia University Press, 1966), p. 106.
[6] Edward S. Mason, "Interests, Ideologies and the Problem of Stability and Growth," *American Economic Review*, March 1963, pp. 1-18.

the society seeks the specialized talent that can create new knowledge or apply it to new problems. Hence, government as well as business increasingly contracts for assistance.

Looked at in the large, we are abandoning an old system of organization and creating a new one. We are abandoning, because it is obsolete, a system in which agencies of government, business corporations, and universities each conducted its affairs as if it were an island unto itself. We are building a system of organization, which cumulates the capabilities of each in an integrated effort, to accomplish tasks that are too big (the building of a supersonic transport) or too important (the development of an artificial heart) for any one organization alone. In this new organization, the university—with the unique capabilities it possesses—will be expected to play a large part.

Indeed, philosophers of the twenty-first century may say that this was the way we preserved political and economic democracy in the American society: the rigor of specialization prevented big government and big business from becoming all-encompassing consumers of scarce talent and the only centers of power. A measure of freedom and dignity was preserved for the individual and for the individual enterprise by the need for utilizing talent wherever it was to be found. And, fortunately, many creative minds were found, because they flourished best there, in nongovernmental and in nongigantic corporate units—a significant proportion in the universities.

THE FUTURE ROLE OF THE UNIVERSITY

Some may ask: What's new in all this? The land-grant college accepted this obligation for the dissemination or application of new knowledge a century ago. What is new is simply this: The American society now avidly and hungrily seeks talent for the solution of many more problems than those of increasing agricultural productivity. It seeks talent with a high order of specialized skill, the capacity for objectivity, and an unquenchable curiosity. That need poses for the university vastly greater demands than it has confronted to date.

These demands are to be seen in the pleas for assistance from two-score urban centers, in the seduction by business firms—through consulting contracts—of the mobile members of university faculties, in the provisions of titles i and iii of the Higher Education Act of 1965, of title ii of the Economic Opportunity Act of 1964, of the State Technical Services Act of 1965, the Law Enforcement Assistance Act of 1965, and the Cancer, Heart, and Stroke Program enacted by Congress in 1965. And it is to be seen in the launching of a study, by the National

Association of State Universities and Land-Grant Colleges, of The State University and Public Affairs.

Can the university accept these added responsibilities? Can it modify a value system that tends to discourage the scholar who would apply his knowledge to the society's problems? [7] There are those who would remind me that the university's responsibilities are, first and foremost, the discovery of knowledge (research) and, second, the transmission of knowledge (teaching). They who emphasize this view will rightfully inquire: Who is going to do the teaching? Will faculty members who become involved in overseas and underseas projects maintain their detachment? Can the institution accept such responsibilities and maintain its autonomy? Where is the money coming from?

The ablest statement of the dilemma faced by the university president who would have his university meet demands upon it for public service and simultaneously its obligation to educate students was made by Homer D. Babbidge, an alumnus of a great private university and the president of a rapidly advancing state university. At the dedication of the Yale–New Haven Mental Health Center, he commented that: "It is no longer enough to educate the men who will, in turn, serve society; the American university itself has now become an instrument for direct social action," and then went on to plead for the discriminating use of the university by society and to specify six guidelines by which the university and the society may well determine the "uses" to which it will put the university.

For myself, I do not know the answers to the questions I have posed. But this I do know. Our society is desperately seeking the talent that will better our cities, improve our schools, lengthen our lives, overcome racial tensions, and find solutions to international ills. John Gardner aptly put his intellectual finger on the point when he wrote that this society is plagued by the fact that most of those able to help on such problems

> are simply tending the machinery of that part of the society to which they belong. The machinery may be a great corporation or a great law practice or a great university. These people tend it very well indeed, but they are not pursuing a vision of what the total society needs. [8]

[7] Edward Teller, a university scientist, has lamented the neglect of applied science and of the development of applied scientists by the universities, in a stimulating paper "The Education of the Modern Inventor," in *Science and the University* (New York: Columbia University Press, 1966). The volume also includes a relevant paper by Frederick Seitz, "The University: Independent Institution or Federal Satellite."

[8] Gardner, "The Anti-Leadership Vaccine," Essay included in the *Annual Report*, Carnegie Corporation of New York, 1965.

"On a clear day," the title of a current musical comedy says, "you can see forever." It is presumptuous for one to suggest that he can see forever, but such presumptuousness was bred in me by five years' early service as a newspaper editorial writer. Mencken, you will recall, lambasted his own trade, as the only breed of men that would presume to express profound and certain judgments on any problem on each succeeding day. That early training helps me to envision what this society needs. It needs a university that is willing to accept increasing responsibility for moving ideas along the road to action, to accept the responsibility for learning how to develop the knowledge needed and how to apply useful knowledge in the solution of society's major ills.

Acceptance of these responsibilities may make of the university an intellectual holding company. Even as it has subsidiaries, known as colleges, concerned with teaching and research, it may also have subsidiaries, known as institutes, laboratories, or centers, engaged in research and in the application of new knowledge to current problems. Within this holding company structure may exist many nonprofit institutions. Now, many of these valuable institutions float in unproductive space, lacking the umbilical cord to an institutional setting.

Failure to accept these responsibilities—and the inability of universities effectively to modify their procedures and their structure in the past suggests they may fail—will likely result in the proliferation of nonprofit, independent research agencies unrelated to the pools of talent that make up university faculties.

Some will doubt this vision for the future. I insist my vision differs little from that described by the more experienced observers Clark Kerr and James Perkins.[9] For these doubters, I leave this question: If not the university, what agency will accept the responsibility for seeking out and *applying* the new knowledge that will shape the society in which our grandchildren live?

[9] Kerr, *The Uses of the University* (Cambridge, Mass.: Harvard University Press, 1963), and Perkins, *The University in Transition* (Princeton, N.J.: Princeton University Press, 1966).

Public Service and Higher Education: Compatibility or Conflict?

EDWARD D. RE, ALBERT N. WHITING,
ROGER LEHECKA, HAROLD W. CHASE

Education in the Nation's Service

EDWARD D. RE

CALVIN LEE'S PAPER on the central theme "Whose Goals for American Higher Education?" identifies, at the very outset, what he regards as the five constituents of higher education: students, faculty, administrators, trustees, and public officials. Although I find it difficult to limit myself exclusively to any one of the five categories, I shall nevertheless choose the constituency of the trustee, defined by John Millett as "the protector of the public interest in higher education."

In Mr. Lee's discussion of "Public Service and Higher Education: Compatibility or Conflict?," he poses a question that goes to the heart of the matter: "The question is not *whether* government should be involved in higher education, but in what ways and to what extent institutions must be responsive and responsible to society?" Differently stated: Have our institutions made their maximum contribution in attempting to solve the massive problems confronting our society? Or, as institutions, have they remained isolated, adhering to the traditional notion of an academic community existing within, but apart from, the larger community? Clearly, as I view the matter, the question is not one of "compatibility" or "conflict" between public service and higher education; it pertains more to the priority that must be ascribed to public service as a goal of higher education.

The university has a vital role to play in helping to solve national problems and I urge that we give new meaning to "education in the nation's service," a phrase which Woodrow Wilson made the subject of some of his earliest and most notable educational contributions. Our inquiry pertains to the general contribution that all institutions should make within the limits of their capabilities, and the special contribution that particular institutions can best make. Not only do I fail to see any conflict with traditional goals of teaching and research in this mission, but I believe that a contribution to the public service would strengthen them.

John J. Corson gives five valid reasons why the nation has called upon the university to help build a better society. They are: "unique institutional strengths," a "substantial monopoly" of human talent, a "discipline of objectivity," a commitment to the "search for new knowledge," and "values." As Mr. Corson describes these qualities, it becomes apparent that the university has not made a contribution to society commensurate with its vast material and intellectual resources. The magnitude of the expansion of the Federal government's involvement in higher education may be gleaned from the fact that 46 or more agencies of the executive branch are now administering programs that are significant to higher education. Thus, the question is no longer whether the relationship exists or is substantial, but rather what its nature and goals are to be. There seems to be universal agreement that Federal support has greatly aided the universities, and serious studies attest to the fact that its effect on the quality of higher education has "been decidedly beneficial." [1] Although the extensive Federal involvement in higher education has been good, it is, nevertheless, a subject of constant re-evaluation. What is now required is an assessment of the public service mission of higher education in relation to the Federal support that it has received. The concept of "public service" envisaged here is broad and all-encompassing. It embraces the totality of services required to meet the needs of an incredibly complex society. This responsibility is not limited to the obligation to supply public service personnel, although in this area the university can play a major role in the public interest.

What I envisage and strongly recommend is a dedication of the university, *as an institution*, to massive social problems such as the urban ghetto, housing, unemployment, education, social welfare, race relations, organized crime, water and air pollution, population control and food supply, the conquest of space, and the resources of and under the sea. I also urge that this public service mission be accepted on a level of priority with teaching and research, a move that will require an

[1] Harold Orlans, *The Effects of Federal Programs on Higher Education* (Washington: Brookings Institution, 1962), p. 133.

adjustment of traditional academic roles and a realignment of the hierarchy of values. The new scale of values must reflect a *commitment* to public service, not merely an acknowledgment of or course of study on the problems of society, but a dedication by the *institution* to the responsibility of helping to solve them. The issues are too large, complex, and pressing to be left to the social agencies, church, or government. It is the duty of all segments of society, including the university, to contribute toward their solution.

It may be fairly charged that the university has not been a good institutional citizen. Like other institutions and individuals, it has not made its maximum contribution to society. I submit that, like the church, the university has done more preaching than practicing. In short, it has not been a "vehicle for social action." The concept that is urged here does not seek to diminish the role of the corporation, foundation, church, social agency, or government. But it suggests that, because universities claim almost a monopoly on talent and intellectual power, society is justified in demanding that higher education contribute in proportion to this professed ability.

If we agree that knowledge must be related to concrete problems, then we have added a new dimension to higher education. In fulfilling this mission, we would do well to ponder the admonition of Harry Gideonse:

> We should avoid like the plague the temptation to camouflage the protection of cherished routine and vulgar vested interests as the preservation of academic standards.[2]

I submit that, once we reach agreement upon the public service mission of higher education and are genuinely committed to its fulfillment, the internal institutional problems of organization and administration will be easily and rapidly solved. Indeed, we are told by as distinguished a college president and economist as Gideonse that, once we accept a moral challenge, even "the budgets will take care of themselves."[3]

[2] Harry D. Gideonse, *On the Educational Statesmanship of a Free Society* (New York: Woodrow Wilson Foundation, 1959), p. 39.
[3] *Ibid.*, p. 40.

A Proposal for Colleges of Applied Sciences And Public Service

ALBERT N. WHITING

MR. CORSON'S PAPER presents a strong and tight argument for a functional expansion of the role of the American university. As one reads his paper, it is difficult to disagree with the distinguishing qualities which he attributes to the university that make it uniquely suited to play a central role in resolving the problems of society. In addition, his descriptions of the "contracting out" system employed by the Federal government and the emerging pluralistic approach necessitated by the scope and intricacies of today's social issues seem indisputably supportive of the idea that the university in this country must now become an instrument for direct social action. And finally, if such a function is accepted, one easily visualizes with Corson the university's ultimately becoming an "intellectual holding company" with subsidiary institutes, laboratories and research centers of various descriptions related to research and practical application of knowledge on the one hand, and subsidiaries known as colleges, on the other hand, concerned only with teaching and research.

The question which hovers hauntingly over the projection of the "Corson vision," however, is one which he himself poses, and, rather significantly, does not answer, namely: Can the university accept these added responsibilities? Or differently phrased: Can a university involved in direct social action retain those distinguishing characteristics (climate of objectivity, freedom, academic prestige, its monopoly of scholars)—which are its strength and uniqueness—if its sociological form is altered and if its dominant axis of interest is extended to include active public service?

Even though Corson says his vision differs little from that of Clark Kerr and James A. Perkins, the latter's answer to the above question seems unequivocally clear in the passage below:

> But the unique contribution of the university in all of this is knowledge, not operating skills, and this should be a limiting factor of great importance. The government and particularly the corporation have been organized in our society to get things done, and it is to these institutions that society normally looks for operational responsibility. The university social scientists can provide the economic case for a state sales tax, for example,

but they should not be expected to collect the money. It is legitimate for a university engineer to design a bridge but not to involve the university in building it and it is often to the university's credit that its agronomists are called upon to discuss the corn-hog price ratio, but it makes no sense for the university to participate in the mechanics of that complicated business. The fact that lines can be and are drawn between advice on how to do something and assistance in doing it thus constitutes a limiting force which aids the university in its need to preserve its balance and its unity.[1]

I believe that the university cannot accept the added responsibilities outlined by Corson because involvement of any segment of an institution in a cause or an action precludes, or at least reduces, neutrality and objectivity. Similarly, direct action, it seems to me, could jeopardize the university climate, the freedom, and even the retention of talented specialists. But this is in the realm of speculation. Let us look for a moment at some of the strains which have already emerged in and are a result of "multiversity" situations with multivaried functions.

In many high-budget universities, the diversion of top professors from teaching to applied research and other types of government-, foundation-, and industry-supported projects has created internal tension. This is evidenced not only in the depreciation of teaching (e.g., at UCLA in 1962-63, less than one-third of an approximate one-half billion dollar budget went for items related to teaching),[2] but in the question of how status and tenure should be handled for the large number of research and special project employees. This general problem divides into a number of interrelated irritants which work against the educational effort. Teaching schedules must constantly be reduced to accommodate the obligations of prestige professors to special university projects; graduate course assignments must displace undergraduate teaching assignments because of the relation of the former to the professor's research or project interest. In both instances, the effect on the educational function is obvious.

Over and above this, in the "intellectual holding company" milieu, the tendency of professors—in higher education generally, but particularly in the multiversities—to emphasize standing in one's discipline rather than service to the school will be even more vigorous, because reward systems will inevitably be based on stature in discipline rather than in local campus affairs. Further, it is abundantly clear that expansion of the university function can only occur as money is available

[1] James Perkins, *The University in Transition* (Princeton, N.J.: Princeton University Press, 1966), pp. 37-38.
[2] Daniel Bell, *Reforming of General Education* (New York: Columbia University Press, 1966), p. 96.

and that if the present distribution pattern of Federal and foundation project and research monies is at all indicative, then "intellectual holding company" status will only be possible for a relatively small number of universities. In 1962, for example, less than 10 percent of the 2,000 accredited institutions of higher learning received 97 percent of all government research funds.[3]

Because this imbalance was related primarily to the urgencies with which solutions to problems were required by the government and because the leading researchers were located at the major universities, a self-reinforcing circle was almost inevitable. The effect, however, has been to widen the distance between the elite and the other universities and, of equal importance, to place a great strain on the independent liberal arts colleges. This process would be even more greatly magnified if universities of the future were transformed into multivaried "intellectual holding companies."

While Corson refers only to the university in his discussion, it should be noted that there is an observed tendency in the United States for colleges to aspire to university status. In North Carolina, for example, we now have a new phenomenon known as the regional university, which embraces most of the colleges offering five-year programs. The point here, obviously, is that the "intellectual holding company" status would likewise be sought by colleges, often without reference to institutional capability or the impact upon standard educational and collegiate research programs.

In my view, much of the thinking which has led to the increasing management of government and foundation projects by universities, and ultimately to the "Corson projection," has been based on the premise that the university structure or collegiate setting provides a condition of "dispensability." Provisions for academic leaves, the emphasis upon research, and the high mobility rates in the academic world support this view. From within the collegiate administrative orbit, however, I strongly feel that adherence to this concept of "dispensability" creates an increasingly troublesome state of affairs in that the superior professors who are on leave are seldom, if ever, replaced by equally qualified persons; the ramifications of this are varied with regard to damage to the academic program, continuity of supervised research and advanced degree programs, and institutional prestige. Furthermore, the shuttling from regular academic programs to the various government- and foundation-sponsored institutes and applied research projects makes the planning and staffing of regular school year instructional programs

[3] *Ibid.*, p. 98.

a difficult, if not impossible, task. In other words, I believe that university and college teaching today is not an occupation with the same degree of "dispensability" that is possible, for example, in the practice of law and which probably accounts for the large number of lawyers in active politics. With rapidly increasing enrollments and a shrinking supply of qualified persons in almost all disciplines, universities and colleges will have to devise ways to heighten recognition of the relative "indispensability" of university and college personnel, particularly at the top levels, in the interest of preserving quality in education.

Because I am one of those who share doubts about the "Corson vision," I am obligated, in closing, to address myself to the question posed at the end of his paper: "If not the University, what agency will accept the responsibility for seeking out and applying the new knowledge that will shape the society in which our grandchildren live?" I suggest, for exactly the kind of public service purposes suggested by Corson, that thought be given to the development of a new type of institution, staffed by academicians, organized around research and public service rather than teaching and research, and financed by the Federal government, industry, and the foundations. For purposes of discussion only, I suggest further that these institutions be called Colleges of Applied Science and Public Service. *College*, as used here, would refer to a society of scholars incorporated for study in the higher branches of knowledge for the purpose of: (1) moving ideas along the road to action; (2) learning how to develop the knowledge needed in society; (3) applying useful knowledge in the solution of society's major ills. Such institutions, I believe, could amass the talent required for the tasks, devote themselves exclusively to the delineated functions, and provide, ultimately, even more unique institutional strengths for resolving the problems of society than a multivaried "intellectual holding company" university.

No University Should Become "A Happening"

ROGER LEHECKA

THERE IS NO DOUBT that universities are being asked more and more to perform public service, nor is there any doubt that these demands will further increase. Mr. Corson, in his paper, outlined the reasons why it is natural to expect institutions of higher education to do so much and why it is convenient for society to turn to them for help.

The important question today, however, is what benefits and what harm come to universities from engaging in public service? A university cannot say "Yes" to every request that comes its way, however worthy the purposes. Rather, it must consider what resources it has available (and these are always finite) and then establish priorities for their use. It must weigh the consequences of any added function it assumes. Clark Kerr has said that no one created or planned the multiversity. It just happened. A university should not become a "happening." If it cannot plan or control its own development, how can it help a city or a nation plan its future?

Let me more specifically examine some different kinds of public service and their consequences for universities. Some things that we would label public service may fit in extremely well with, and even enhance, a university's other activities. Take Mr. Corson's example of faculty members of a school of education developing a program for the social and economic rehabilitation of the unemployed. If the faculty followed through with the program, they would probably gain as much from it as the unemployed they were rehabilitating, not socially or financially, but in increased knowledge and understanding of their own field. In fact, in a field like education, it is absolutely necessary for some faculty members to go out and try some of the measures they propose. Some services which a medical school performs could be beneficial to both faculty and students. Although action itself is not the aim of the university, action sometimes promotes both teaching and research.

Another kind of public service which accords well with other university activities is a student volunteer program. While such a program may not have the immediate impact on society of faculty research, it offers other benefits. First, it is an extracurricular activity which appeals to a large number of students as a channel of constructive involvement. Second, at its best, a student service program is more than just volunteers doing clerical work for a charitable organization; it is students using their imaginations and energies to find creative solutions to problems. Thirty Columbia students running a study club for second graders is not going to solve New York City's educational problems, but for the people involved, it is as educational an experience as there can be. Third, the *involvement* is something that many undergraduates feel is as vital to their education as their classes. It is a time for students to test themselves in ways that are important to *them*, rather than in ways important to their parents and teachers. Any college interested in more than the strictly academic success of its students can support this type of activity without hesitation.

Mr. Corson's paper also provides an example of the kind of service a university should not perform. With the many demands made on faculty for research, consulting, publishing, and conferences, and with the rapidly increasing number of undergraduates, the faculty's time should not be wasted by sending them to factories to train foremen. When good teachers (even merely adequate ones) are scarce, they must be used very carefully, not cajoled or pressured into taking on more tasks without good justification.

Universities must also be wary of grafting on completely new branches to perform some further service. No school should feel that it can or should do everything. Even though it might be doing an extraordinary public service by beginning, for instance, an adult education program, it should ask itself many questions first. Among them are: What will it cost, and are the present activities of the institution sufficiently financed and otherwise supported now? (Adult education programs are easily made financially self-sufficient, but other problems could arise.) How will the total size of the institution be affected? Will this lead to a slighting of other, more central, activities of the institution? Will a separate faculty be hired? If not, how will the intellectual quality of the new students compare with the present students? Can the time of the present faculty be better spent? Each institution must reach its own decision, but there are many more questions to be asked than merely "Is it good for society?"

I would like to note that I am not trying to encourage universities to resist all change. I feel that changes in approach are sorely needed in the standard teaching and learning processes, in undergraduate education especially. Many changes in an outward-looking direction are called for in universities. These changes are important for the enhancement of teaching and research as much as for any direct service they may provide to society.

Let me give a specific example of a public service that many universities perform for very sound reasons. This past summer, over 200 colleges and universities participated in the Office of Economic Opportunity's "Upward Bound" Program. The program recruits high school students who have been identified as potential college students and who come from low-income families, to live on college campuses during the summer. Through classes and other activities, the program attempts to spark the students' interest in learning, and in eventually attending college. If the colleges merely made their facilities available to OEO, for the enterprise, the service would be an empty one. But an Upward Bound Program involves the staff as well as the students of an institution. The faculty and administration thus gain more understanding of the high school students they are admitting to or rejecting from their colleges; they may discover that they have made a few mistakes. They learn what adjustments colleges must make in order to accommodate this kind of student, who will be showing up in colleges in greater numbers soon. In short, the program stimulates faculty and administrators to work for the improvement of college education in this country. Such a program is an appropriate activity for a university, as well as being beneficial to society.

Much of what I have said about such careful use of resources may apply more to private than to state universities. Because private institutions are becoming a smaller and smaller proportion of the universities in America, they must see to it that they continue to do what state universities cannot. When they make a decision about whether to perform a public service, they must consider their own purposes and priorities. Indeed, preserving themselves may be the greatest public service these universities could perform.

Indifference, Smugness, and Rigidity In Academia

HAROLD W. CHASE

I CANNOT CLAIM to give a representative view of the faculty member on these questions, for I believe I am in a distinct minority with respect to the issues to which I shall address myself. Perhaps I should have explained my position and bowed out of the discussion. But, believing that the point of view which I hold most strongly ought to be put into the hopper, I rejected such a course of action.

For all the reasons that Mr. Corson offers, colleges and universities should "gear up the public service role . . . to meet social demands." I daresay that most faculty would agree with the principle, *in principle*. But, as Mr. Corson so clearly points out, the difficulty comes in moving from principle to application. In his polite and restrained language, he says that "the inability of universities effectively to modify their procedures and their structure in the past suggests that they may fail [to accept their responsibility of adopting a public service role]." The truth of the matter is that—notwithstanding all the stereotypes about the radicalism of academics—when it comes to running colleges, universities, and academic programs, we are most conservative in our attitudes, unbelievably rigid in our ideas, and unbecomingly smug about our knowledge of the "truth." Such an indictment demands a bill of particulars to be credible. Perhaps, the illustration of one situation—itself substantively important in a discussion of the public service role of higher education—will suffice.

Several years ago, I had the enjoyable and stimulating experience of being a civilian faculty member at the National War College for one year. That year convinced me (if, indeed, I needed convincing) that providing a mid-career education to people with talent, character, and promise as leaders was a highly desirable enterprise. I was consequently delighted to learn that there was to be a conference sponsored by the Woodrow Wilson School of Princeton University on Mid-Career Education for Public Officials. Excellent background papers were prepared and circulated. Such worthies of the Federal bureaucracy as John W. Macy, Jr., chairman of the Civil Service Commission, Roger W. Jones of the Bureau of the Budget, and Elmer B. Staats, now the comptroller general, came to speak on the crucial need that mid-career training programs for Federal officials be established on a scale far exceeding programs then available at the universities.

One might have assumed that the academicians would have responded affirmatively and enthusiastically to this expression of confidence in them and their work. Instead, one after another, university administrators and faculty used this opportunity to caution against large-scale efforts to accept the challenging assignment of educating our Federal officials. We were told of the many dangers which lurked in the shadows of any attempt by universities to tailor programs for such a clientele. It would mean, among other things, that the faculty would have to be considerably increased. And horror of horrors, for such tailored programs, people of experience rather than those with Ph.D.'s might be needed. We were warned that the whole character of a university might be warped by the different set of demands that such a program would make on the faculty; they might, for instance, become less research-oriented. In short, the Conference was a bitter lesson for those who had come in high hopes that the meeting would result in our leading universities embarking on large-scale programs for mid-career government officials. True, all were eager to allow a very select few to come and, as they so colorfully put it, to "take off the shelves" the education that they already offered. True, a few universities have even been willing to provide small, individualized programs, and they have done well at it. But in view of the enormous need for such programs on a widespread scale, the colleges and universities have not come close to meeting their responsibilities. It is no wonder, then, that the Civil Service Commission has felt that it must rely on its own resources, if the job is to be done. Nor would I, for one, accept the premise that it is better done that way, in any event. Just as Mr. Corson has reasoned, I would argue that the universities have the personnel and resources to do a much better job, if they were willing, first, to do it and, second, to seek whatever help they need from the outside.

In retrospect, one of the most disappointing aspects of the Princeton Conference was the failure of the academics to see that large-scale, mid-career programs would be a two-way street. If we accept the axiom that the basic function of a university is to seek knowledge, then there can be no question that the experience and understanding of mature men who have had vast responsibilities would contribute something to those who truly seek knowledge, as anyone who has ever taught in such a program can attest. In the academic community, there is a strong element of arrogance manifested by the notion that only Ph.D.'s can be "experts." Academics cling to this concept despite the evidence that the nation's leading experts in many fields are people who have gained expertise through experience. One could hypothesize that the quality of research and of undergraduate and graduate teaching would markedly improve in any university in which a large-scale, mid-career training program existed.

One can hardly take seriously the argument that the basic character of a university would change if it introduced such a program. Harvard has not suffered noticeably as a university from its Business School's first-rate program for advanced management.

In sum, Mr. Corson is right on all scores. Higher education *does* have an obligation to serve, and in the broadest sense of that word, it is well-equipped to do so. Furthermore, to do so is not incompatible with the main mission of colleges and universities. On the contrary, these missions are mutually supporting and reinforcing. We in academia need only shed the blinders of indifference, smugness, and rigidity in order to see.

PART II

Forces That Shape
Institutions

DAVID FELLMAN

The Academic Community: Who Decides What?

T<small>HE</small> <small>INTRIGUING</small> and important question of who decides what in the academic community is a difficult one to answer because of the diverse character of American higher education. If all or most of our educational institutions conformed to a substantially similar pattern, the task would be relatively easy. But one of the few generalizations that one can safely make about the American system of higher education is that it is not a system at all. Variety, not uniformity, is its leading characteristic. In this country, there are some 2,000 institutions of higher learning: private and public, large and small, rich and poor, excellent and mediocre. Every state of the union has one or more public institutions. A few states have single governing boards, others have several governing boards, and most states now have some sort of superboard or coordinating authority at the apex of the pyramid. These governing boards vary tremendously in almost every important respect: size, organization, methods of recruitment, powers, customs, and patterns of behavior. Nor is there a single pattern for private institutions. For one thing, church affiliation or the lack of it makes for great differences,[1] and even church-related institutions have many different patterns of authority, since the nature of the affiliation varies a great deal. In short, even among schools of the same character—such as large state universities—internal governing patterns are extremely diverse, mainly, I suppose, as a consequence of fortuitous historical factors.

The issue is further complicated by the very rapid change and

[1] See Edward Manier and John Houck (eds.), *Academic Freedom and the Catholic University* (Notre Dame, Ind.: Fides Publishers, 1967).

growth that characterizes the period in which we live. It is hardly necessary to document here the well-known facts about the rise in student enrollments since the end of the last world war and the consequent expansion of faculties. New institutions, particularly junior colleges and community colleges, are being established at a rapid pace. Furthermore, junior colleges are becoming colleges, teachers colleges are becoming liberal arts colleges, and many liberal arts colleges are leapfrogging their way to the lofty status of universities, some a bit prematurely. Many of our big universities are expanding into multiversities, and these sprawling state-wide systems have given rise to new problems of organization, management, and faculty control.

Another factor that makes it difficult to analyze the decision-making processes in our colleges and universities is the paucity of reliable objective research in this area—an ironic situation, considering the great amount of research activity in other areas of education. The few general studies available are based on data collected from a limited number of institutions.[2] A few essays on faculty organization at particular institutions have been written,[3] but on the whole, the body of published information on institutional government is not substantial. Further, research scholars have done very little work on the politics of higher education.[4] It follows that, without the solid foundation of a large body of orderly and reliable data, I must speak rather impressionistically, and my impressions are based mainly upon personal experiences and observations in large public institutions. My contacts with small schools and with private institutions have been limited.

Finally, a discussion of who decides what in the academic community is rendered difficult by the fact that there are few clear-cut divisions of authority among the main elements of that community—

[2] See John J. Corson, *Governance of Colleges and Universities* (New York: McGraw-Hill Book Co., 1960); E. C. Elliott, M. M. Chambers, and W. A. Ashbrook, *The Government of Higher Education* (New York: American Book Co., 1935); Charles P. Dennison, *Faculty Rights and Obligations in Eight Independent Liberal Arts Colleges* (New York: Bureau of Publications, Teachers College, Columbia University, 1955).

[3] For a recent series, in the *AAUP Bulletin,* on faculty participation in university government, see: Glenn R. Morrow, "The University of Pennsylvania," Winter 1962, pp. 114-22; Richard P. Adams, "Tulane University," Autumn 1963, pp. 221-25; Lynn W. Eley, "The University of California at Berkeley," Spring 1964, pp. 5-13; Howard V. Jones, "The State College of Iowa," Winter 1966, pp. 437-41; Philip Denenfeld, "Western Michigan University," Winter 1966, pp. 390-97.

[4] Nicholas A. Masters, Robert H. Salisbury, and Thomas H. Eliot, *State Politics and the Public Schools* (New York: Alfred A. Knopf, 1964); James B. Conant, *Shaping Educational Policy* (New York: McGraw-Hill Book Co., 1964).

governing board, administration, and faculty.[5] At some point or other, each has its hand in most of the decisions which ultimately emerge as policy. In addition, decisions are often strongly influenced by groups outside the academic community—parents, alumni, donors, legislators and other politicians, professional societies, accrediting associations, professorial associations, church bodies, and business groups, to cite but a few.[6] For example, a university that has a school of pharmacy must give the title of dean to its director—even though it might prefer to give him some other, less exalted title—because the association of schools of pharmacy insists upon it. A law school must have a full-time librarian because that is a condition for accreditation by the association of law schools. Many institutions have a maximum probationary period of seven years for faculty—and all of them should have such a rule—because the American Association of University Professors, the Association of American Colleges, and some fifty professional societies regard that as an essential element of a proper tenure system. In short, a final decision in the academic community may well be the result of the influence of many different people both in and outside that community.

THE AGE OF THE PROFESSOR

Higher education in America has gone through several stages. From the point of view of who decides what in the academic community, the period in which we now live may be characterized as the Age of the Professor. At least at present, the professor is in a very strong position. He has a great deal to say about his role in higher education. The rapid growth of tenure systems[7] and the widespread recognition of the professor's right to academic freedom testify to

[5] I have deliberately avoided discussing the role of the students in the decision-making processes of the institution. The whole subject is presently in a state of flux and requires separate treatment. Clearly, American students are getting into the picture more and more, and they are now demanding, with increasing effectiveness, an opportunity to participate in at least some of the institution's decision-making processes. Institutions with forward-looking and imaginative leadership are beginning to recognize that students are in a position to make valuable contributions to the shaping of educational policy, through student government and journalism, through student membership on faculty committees, and through improved channels of communication. These changes are occurring not because it is expedient to yield to people who can make trouble if they are ignored or rejected, but because students have something to offer that will improve the quality of our colleges and universities.

[6] See Robert M. MacIver, *Academic Freedom in Our Time* (New York: Columbia University Press, 1955), Part I, "The Climate of Opinion," pp. 21-63.

[7] Clark Byse and Louis Joughin, *Tenure in American Higher Education* (Ithaca, N.Y.: Cornell University Press, 1959).

his strong position in the academic community. The supply-demand ratio in the academic marketplace has also given him mobility, and the availability of alternatives adds to his independence.[8] He functions with special effectiveness in the department, and this is significant because the department has become the most viable unit of the educational community, at least in the larger institutions. Departmental decisions, which constitute many of the institution's most important decisions, are made by professors acting mainly in a collegial capacity.

The notion that the professor is a mere employee, a hired hand, was once widely held in this country. As late as the mid-1920's, William Jennings Bryan gave classic expression to this view in the course of his argument in the famous Tennessee "monkey" trial,[9] when he declared that "the hand that writes the teacher's paycheck is the hand that runs the schools. . . . Otherwise, a teacher might teach anything!"[10] A similar position was taken by a trustee of a great Midwestern private university, who asserted that "in social and political science," professors "are only a little less qualified to be the final arbiters as to what shall be taught than they are concerning financial problems. In all things they should promptly and gracefully submit to the final determination of the trustees. A professor must be an advocate, but his advocacy must be in harmony with the conclusions of the powers that be."[11]

Such views are rarely expressed today, at least in public. They are totally rejected by the teaching profession. The position taken by the eminent scholars who organized the American Association of University Professors and who enunciated their views in the 1915 Declaration of Principles [12] represents a turning point in the concept of the faculty's status. They pointed out that, although professors are the appointees of the university's trustees, they are not in any proper sense the trustees' employees, just as Federal judges are appointed by the President without becoming, as a consequence, his employees. "For, once appointed," the association's founding fathers declared,

---

[8] Theodore Caplow and Reece J. McGee, *The Academic Marketplace* (New York: Basic Books, 1958).

[9] Scopes v. State, 154 Tenn. 105, 289 S.W. 363 (1927).

[10] Howard K. Beale, *Are American Teachers Free?* (New York: Charles Scribner's Sons, 1936), pp. 256, 656.

[11] Ulysses G. Weatherly, "Freedom of Teaching in the United States," *Proceedings: American Sociological Society*, IX (1915), 141.

[12] "The 1915 Declaration of Principles," reprinted in *AAUP Bulletin*, Spring 1954, pp. 90-112.

"the scholar has professional functions to perform in which the appointing authorities have neither competency nor moral right to intervene." And they added, "A university is a great and indispensable organ of the higher life of a civilized community, in the work of which the trustees hold an essential and highly honorable place, but in which the faculties hold an independent place, with quite equal responsibilities—and in relation to purely scientific and educational questions, the primary responsibility." Running through this notable document was an emphasis upon the nature of the academic calling. "If education is the cornerstone of the structure of society," they wrote, "and if progress in scientific knowledge is essential to civilization, few things can be more important than to enhance the dignity of the scholar's profession, with a view to attracting into its ranks men of the highest ability, of sound learning, and of strong and independent character."[18]

Any self-respecting faculty will demand the right to participate fully in institutional policy making. The current attitude is illustrated by the story of the president of a large and eminent Midwestern university, who, in a moment of pique, told his faculty that if only the tenure principle were abandoned, professors would as a consequence be on their toes. A famous scientist on the faculty promptly responded. "Mr. President, you have made a mistake in anatomy; you mean the knees, not the toes."

The American Association of University Professors gave succinct expression to this view in its 1960 statement of principles on "Faculty Participation in College and University Government."[14] The statement rests on the assumption that "the basic functions of a college or university are to augment, preserve, criticize and transmit knowledge and to foster creative capacities." If this is a fair summary of what our colleges and universities are designed to accomplish, then the association's answer to the question of how this mission can best be fulfilled is that "these functions are performed by a community of scholars who must be free to exercise independent judgment in the planning and execution of their educational responsibilities."[15]

A joint "Statement on Government of Colleges and Universities," adopted in 1966 by the American Association of University Professors, the American Council on Education, and the Association of Governing Boards of Universities and Colleges, recognizes that only through joint

[18] *Ibid.*, pp. 98, 99, 97.
[14] *AAUP Bulletin,* June 1960, pp. 203-4.
[15] *Ibid.*, p. 203.

action can we hope to develop an "increased capacity to solve educational problems." [16] For, it is pointed out, there is an "inescapable interdependence" among the major constituents of the academic community, an interdependence produced by "the variety and complexity of the tasks performed by institutions of higher education." The definition and execution of long-range goals requires effective planning and communication by all components of the academic community. Joint efforts are required in making decisions about the use of physical facilities, about budgeting, and about the selection of the chief academic officers, including the president.

More particularly, the tripartite statement recognizes that the faculty has "primary responsibility" with respect to curriculum, subject matter and methods of instruction, research, faculty status, and those elements of student life which relate to the educational process.[17] The faculty determines the requirements for the degrees offered in course and decides when and how these degree requirements have been met. The faculty has primary responsibility with respect to academic appointments, reappointments, decisions not to reappoint, promotions, the granting of tenure, and dismissals. This responsibility derives from the circumstance that scholars in a particular field have the chief competence for making such judgments. Of course, administrative review and board approval are part of the complicated procedures involved in making decisions on questions of faculty status, but faculty judgment on these matters should normally be decisive, and should not be overruled except for very compelling reasons, and then in conformity with procedures spelled out in detail ahead of time. The faculty should be consulted in the selection of department chairmen, deans, and presidents. There should be meaningful faculty participation in the making of budget decisions, including policy on salary increases. Finally, if faculty participation is to mean anything, the institution must provide suitable agencies for such participation through scheduled meetings of faculties, through representative assemblies, and through faculty committees, the most important of which, at least, ought to be elected directly by the faculty.

Speaking to the annual meeting of AAUP in 1959, the then Secretary of Health, Education, and Welfare, Arthur S. Flemming, summarized this point of view:

> I believe that our institutions of higher education should be organized so as to make the faculty the most influential group in the governing

16 *AAUP Bulletin,* December 1966, p. 376.
17 *Ibid.,* p. 378.

of our colleges and universities. I believe that this is also essential if our institutions of higher education are to be communities of scholars engaged in the search of truth. I feel that if this objective is to be achieved, then there are certain responsibilities that must be discharged by the faculty. It seems to me that the faculty must be placed in a position where it has the primary responsibility for the development of the objectives of the educational community. Not only do I believe that this should be the faculty's primary responsibility, but I also think that the faculty must be in a position where it can insist on adherence to these objectives.[18]

THE PRESIDENT

This conception of the faculty is a fairly modern phenomenon. Historically, the faculty got off to a bad start in American higher education. Early faculties were very small, and were made up not of professional, full-time teachers, but of preachers and lawyers who occasionally did some part-time teaching for limited periods. Rarely was the typical professor genuinely committed to the teaching profession. It was not until around the turn of the century, with the rise of graduate education and the growth of the Ph.D. degree, that a solid cadre of professionally trained, specialized scholar-professors, dedicated to the concept of objective research and scholarship, appeared on the scene.

Prior to their appearance, the key figure was the president. In part, his primacy prevailed because he had no serious competition within the educational community itself; he was not only the leading spokesman for the college, but in a very real sense its only spokesman.[19] The president alone was permanent enough and strong enough to be able to raise his voice in defense of the college and in the promotion of its interests. The president alone had enough prestige and authority to protect the college against its enemies, to recruit such faculty as the colleges were then able to assemble, and to secure outside support for the institution. Viewed in this perspective, the great change that has come about in the patterns of decision making in American institutions of higher learning has been the consequence of the steady growth in the number of highly skilled, specialized, research-minded professors. Our professors today have a permanent stake in their institutions and a sufficient feeling of self-confidence and dignity, nurtured by profes-

---

[18] Address to the Forty-fifth Annual Meeting, *AAUP Bulletin*, Autumn 1959, p. 407.

[19] Richard Hofstadter and Walter P. Metzger, *The Development of Academic Freedom in the United States* (New York: Columbia University Press, 1955), pp. 125-26; Laurence R. Veysey, *The Emergence of the American University* (Chicago: University of Chicago Press, 1965), pp. 302-17.

sional competence and commitment, to make their voices heard in the councils of the academic community.

I do not mean to suggest, however, that the American college or university president is without power.[20] He not only remains in a very strong position, but he still is a rather special characteristic of the American system of higher education as compared with most other systems in the world today. It is unquestionable that the president still makes many significant decisions in the life of the institution, and it follows, therefore, that his character, ability, and purposes make a great deal of difference. He is by no means a fifth wheel. Nevertheless, he shares power—the power that was once exclusively his—with the faculties. Indeed, it is no exaggeration to say that to a considerable extent the power of the president persists because of the inability of the faculty to exert its own influence efficiently, effectively, and consistently. Presidents are strong because faculties fail, for a variety of reasons, to exercise the authority that is within their grasp if they wish to take it. When a faculty is uninformed or indifferent or divided, the president has added scope within which to operate.

A great deal of administrative power rests upon little more than access to the necessary facts that constitute the indispensable content for making decisions. In cases where an administration withholds essential information from the faculty or where professors are too preoccupied with their own immediate affairs to acquire knowledge of the underlying facts, there the door is open for the president to exclude the faculty from sharing the authority: the faculty simply doesn't know enough to participate in making the decision.

Furthermore, in a considerable measure, administrative authority in our colleges and universities results from faculty indifference. I doubt very much, for example, whether many professors really care to have a hand in the planning of dormitories, or in the athletic program, or in the letting of building contracts, or in many other decisions of this nature. It is unfortunate, from the faculty point of view, that so many professors are inclined to leave campus planning to the administrators, since campus planning carries within it the seeds for many significant aspects of the academic program of the institution. The familiar phrase "the sleeping giant" is a useful description of the faculty whose potential power is vitiated because of lack of information, lack of interest, or lack of unity, all of which conspire to give the president a freedom which he would not otherwise enjoy. To the extent

[20] See MacIver, *Academic Freedom in Our Time,* chap. 6; Corson, *Governance of Colleges and Universities,* chap. 3.

that administrative power is exercised because of these inadequacies on the part of the faculty, presidential authority may well be described as interstitial in character.

The tripartite "Statement on Government of Colleges and Universities" declares that the president "has a special obligation to innovate and initiate" in respect to the institution's educational programs.[21] While this is a laudable ideal, it is very doubtful whether contemporary conditions permit the president to perform the innovative function very effectively or very extensively. In this age of bigness, complexity, rapid expansion, and strong departments, he has many other things to do which generally take priority in his busy day. The president must devote considerable attention to financial matters, and indeed, the budget is probably his most important weapon. The president is the institution's chief public relations officer, a role that commits him to almost ceaseless speech making and much traveling. He must deal with, and placate, parents, alumni, and politicians. He must be alert to secure gifts and other donations, and thus he must invest a great deal of his time and energy in cultivating possible donors and other sources of new funds. He is deeply involved in the upkeep and expansion of the physical plant; accordingly, he must deal with architects and campus planners; he must examine and approve blueprints and specifications; he must negotiate contracts; he must operate parking facilities, and even sometimes supervise campus bus systems; he must worry about buildings and grounds; usually he must act as the over-all manager of a substantial entertainment industry; he supervises a large hotel and restaurant business, and so must concern himself with the price of bedsheets, hamburger, and chamber maids; in short, he is a very busy and harassed academic entrepreneur.[22]

It follows that the president does not have much time or energy to devote to educational innovations; he is much too deeply involved in problems of general administration. In our larger institutions, the president has little to do with faculty selection, which is now chiefly controlled by the faculty itself. (He does, however, have authority to select deans and, occasionally, department heads, a power which gives him indirect control since these men do have a hand in the process of selecting new personnel.) Furthermore, the president has few contacts with the students, except in relation to the athletic program or in cases where unusually serious disciplinary problems arise or

---

[21] *AAUP Bulletin*, December 1966, p. 378.
[22] See Harold W. Stoke, *The American College President* (New York: Harper & Bros., 1959).

where students demand the right to hear controversial speakers or insist on more power in shaping institutional decisions. In addition, the president is the chief channel of communication between the institution and the governing board, in some cases, the only channel. One of his most significant functions is to educate the members of the board, who are usually laymen without specialized knowledge in the field of education, and to recommend courses of action to them for their approval. As the chief link between the faculty and the board, he must interpret each to the other. In short, as the tripartite statement puts it, the president operates "the communications system which links the components of the academic community." [23]

THE GOVERNING BOARD

The tripartite statement declares that "the governing board has a special obligation to assure that the history of the college or university shall serve as a prelude and inspiration to the future." [24] It notes that the board must relate the institution to its chief constituency and that it exercises "final institutional authority." In addition, the statement declares that "the board has a central role in relating the likely needs of the future to predictable resources," and that it must concern itself with endowment, the obtaining of adequate funds, and long-range planning. Finally, "in grave crises it will be expected to serve as a champion."

Although the language of the charters or parent statutes implies that the boards are theoretically all-powerful, normally this is not descriptive of the realities in the educational world.[25] Most boards are rather large and function mainly through committees, the most influential of which is usually the executive committee. Boards do not meet very often, rarely more than once a month, and then for relatively short periods of time. It is absolutely essential that the board delegate most of its legal powers to those who are permanently on the job, especially the president, although there is no single pattern of delegation in the country. The board usually acts on the recommendations of the president, and probably the most important single function of the board is the appointment of the president, who invariably serves at the board's

[23] "Statement on Government of Colleges and Universities," *AAUP Bulletin*, December 1966, p. 378.

[24] *Ibid.*, p. 377.

[25] Morton A. Rauh, *College and University Trusteeship* (Yellow Springs, Ohio: Antioch Press, 1959). For an argument that trustees ought to take back from the faculty authority over the design and administration of the curriculum, see Beardsley Ruml and Donald H. Morrison, *Memo to a College Trustee* (New York: McGraw-Hill Book Co., 1959), p. 13.

pleasure. In addition, the governing board is deeply involved with money matters and property management and with public relations. It has the ultimate responsibility for general supervision of academic standards in the institution, but except in unusual circumstances, this responsibility actually rests in other hands.

PROFESSORIAL PAROCHIALISM: THE DEPARTMENTAL SYNDROME

The pattern of decision making in the contemporary American institution of higher learning is shaped by the professor's conception of his place in the institution. In our country, one of the characteristics central to this conception is what I would call the professor's parochialism. That we live in an age of intense and growing academic parochialism is the source of some of our most serious unresolved or emerging problems. Parochialism is rooted in the primacy of the department, for it is hardly an exaggeration to assert that we in higher education live today not only in the Age of the Professor but also in the Age of the Department.[26]

The department has become the most active, the most significant, and the most intelligible unit of the contemporary university. My own institution, for example, may be safely described as comprising a collection of more or less autonomous departments loosely held together by a central administration for purposes which may be important, but which are not perceived to be so by the vast majority of faculty members. The departments are not, of course, entirely autonomous, but they do enjoy a considerable amount of self-determination, and the general drift is in the direction of more and more departmental self-determination. For a variety of reasons, they have become the most vital units of the university.

To illustrate this generalization, I use a very simple test: that of faculty participation. People participate in those activities which they think are important. And like the nonvoter in the body politic, the

---

[26] See the remarks of Winfred T. Root, "The Teacher and Liberal Education," *AAUP Bulletin,* Autumn 1947, p. 514: "Specialism carried from graduate training to teaching bears with it undesirable consequences. The teacher, having fallen victim to his success in his narrow field, becomes a prisoner of specialism. Moving within the confines of a little segment of knowledge and within a closed academic department, his vision is limited by a parochial existence. Bred in the inertia of isolation, he cannot see his subject as a single element in a balanced whole of liberal education. Mental myopia destroys the centrality of knowledge and breeds separatism within the faculty. Departmentalism is a cult deep of root and strong of fiber. Each group moves in the spirit that we belong to ourselves and not to others."

nonparticipating professor is almost wholly impervious to moralistic preachment about where his duties lie. Just as "get-out-and-vote" campaigns have very little to do with actual turnout at the polls, so do professors respond negatively to mere appeals to their sense of obligation. Like most other people, professors respond to the push and pull of their interests, not to mere exhortation.

This is reflected in attendance at department meetings as compared with attendance at general college- or university-wide faculty meetings. I do not have figures for faculty attendance at various institutions, nor are such figures available, so far as I know. But I do have firsthand knowledge about attendance at faculty meetings in my own institution, and I have good reason to believe that our experience at Wisconsin is not at all unusual. In any event, it is worth noting that in my institution the attendance at general college or university faculty meetings is very small, and that attendance at departmental faculty meetings is very large. (It should be pointed out that attendance at any sort of meeting is altogether voluntary.) General university faculty meetings, to which all people of professorial rank are invited, are held regularly once each month throughout the academic year. In addition, each college or school in the university has faculty meetings of its own, though usually at the call of the dean; with some exceptions such meetings are held only at irregular and very long intervals. At the monthly general faculty meetings, it is most unusual if as many as 10 percent of the faculty attend, and the customary turnout is around 5 or 6 percent. Only when some unusually exciting or vital issue is involved will more faculty come to a meeting. During my twenty years at Wisconsin I doubt whether the very largest meeting included more than about a third of those eligible to attend. (I hasten to add, however, that when a third of our faculty comes to a meeting, we have a very large crowd of professors, much too large to serve as a deliberative body. All it can do is register simple "yes" or "no" responses to propositions framed in advance by faculty committees.) Attendance at college or school faculty meetings is likely to be even smaller than the attendance at the regularly scheduled university faculty meetings. I recall that one of the most important decisions ever made by our graduate school faculty was carried by a vote of thirteen to eleven. About three thousand faculty members had been invited to attend.

I do not comment on the poor attendance at general college or university faculty meetings in any spirit of criticism, though of course it is inevitable that I should have some thoughts about the quality of academic citizenship reflected in these figures. I merely report these facts in order to give due emphasis to the power of the departments. For faculty attendance at departmental meetings is about 100 percent all the time, even though these meetings are usually held fairly often, certainly much more frequently than general college or university faculty meetings, and usually last longer. Only when a professor is ill or out of the city does he fail to attend departmental meetings.

The explanation for the poor attendance at general faculty meetings and the almost perfect attendance at departmental meetings is that the professor senses that the general meetings settle few matters which concern him deeply. He understands that the business of the departmental meeting, on the other hand, is genuinely important to him. He knows very well indeed that many decisions which affect him directly and vitally are made at the departmental level. The department is the main unit for the recruitment of new personnel and for decisions on promotion of staff. Budgets, including salary recommendations, are made initially at least at the departmental level. The department is the chief initiator of new courses and programs and makes decisions with respect to such vital matters as teaching load, and assignment of courses, sections, and facilities. Basic questions involving graduate students, teaching assistants, research assistants, office help, recipients of fellowships and scholarships, and undergraduate majors are handled for the most part within the department.

Just as water will always find its own proper level, so will a professor find the point at which his participation is important to him. Therefore, the department is apt to be the main center of attraction for most members of the faculty. Fortunately there are always some professors who, for one reason or another, concern themselves with the larger interests and problems of the institution and take an active part in general faculty affairs. But they are few in number, and except for the most unusual occasions, one does not anticipate that many professors will give much attention to affairs above the departmental level. Like other rational people, professors know where the buttered bread is to be found.

Another index to the centrality of the position of the department in the world of higher education is the stature of the department chairman.[27] As the head of the institution's most vital unit, he is bound to be important. My involvement in the affairs of the AAUP has impressed upon me that questions relating to the selection, tenure, and authority of the departmental chairman are of first-rate concern. Therefore, the

[27] See Charles H. Heimler, "The College Departmental Chairman," *Educational Record*, Spring 1967, pp. 158-63.

administrative officer who is most frequently discussed and criticized, and who is most widely resented, is the departmental chairman, or worse yet and more obviously, the departmental head. By a departmental head, I mean someone who is imposed upon a department by administrative fiat alone and who holds indefinite tenure in his position. The complaints I have listened to regarding the behavior of departmental chairmen greatly outnumber those directed against all other administrative officials at all levels of authority. When most professors complain about administrative tyranny, they are talking about their departmental chairmen.

The explanation for this is obvious: it is largely a matter of size and complexity. In all but the smallest institutions the distance between the professors and the dean is very great. In our big institutions, professors literally have no direct dealings at all with their president. Those who do not bother to attend general faculty meetings may not even see the president from one year to another. Even in a major subdivision of a big university, such as my own College of Letters and Science, which has a faculty of some nine hundred, there are many professors who have no meaningful personal relationship with the dean. On the other hand, because distances within the department are small, the closer relationships are easily understandable. The chairman is never very far away from the individual professor. He is always visible, always immediately accessible, and in a position to exert great authority in the most direct ways. The professor cannot possibly avoid dealing with him. That is why I think that the most careful attention must be given to the dimensions of the office of the departmental chairman in organizing a college or university.

In an age when the department has become the source of most educational innovation, as well as the most intelligible and manageable unit of the big institutions we now have, it is understandable that the horizon of most professors is the departmental horizon and that the department absorbs their expendable time, energy, and loyalty. Within its ambit will be found the arena in which the professor's dreams and aspirations flourish or wither away. Most academic rewards and punishments are meted out in the department. Status is usually determined by the judgment of departmental colleagues. To paraphrase a certain facile Canadian writer, in our time the department is the message.

Like other people, professors care about things worth caring for, and they have compelling reasons for caring a great deal about what goes on in the department. The things that go on at the higher levels of institutional authority do not concern most professors very much, nor very often, certainly not nearly as much or as often as those matters which transpire within the department. It is the luxury of the elder statesman, who has already arrived professionally and whose departmental and professional position is unassailable, to be able to participate regularly in the larger affairs of the institution.

Academic life is full of insecurity, anxiety, and the fiercest sort of competition. Because the unrelenting pressures of academic life are sharpest in the department, most professors are quite unable to be concerned with interdepartmental, college, or institutionwide matters. There is very little reason to be surprised, therefore, at the typical professor's almost total indifference to what goes on in neighboring institutions. He is not very much interested in what goes on in the neighboring departments of his own institution.

The increasing amount of support that comes from sources wholly outside the institution is another factor that dilutes the professor's loyalty to the institution—particularly the professor who is engaged in serious research and publication activities. His professional opportunities may depend almost entirely upon his ability to secure support from various Federal agencies, foundations, professional societies and organizations, and other private sources completely outside the sphere of influence of the institution itself. Here, too, the professor will find his buttered bread. His loyalty to his institution shrinks as his reliance upon outside sources for support, and indeed for recognition as well, grows. It is commonplace today that the loyalty of many a professor to his particular specialty is far greater than his loyalty to his institution. Furthermore, since he enjoys solid support, he is quite free, if at all miffed by the officials of his institution, to pick up his punch cards and assistants and, together with his money, go elsewhere. His mobility makes him independent of his institution and encourages him to stay within the confines of his immediate professional discipline. This phenomenon may be called the parochialism of professional specialization. In the perspective of the institution as a whole, and certainly in the perspective of neighboring institutions, the pursuit of professional success through outside support breeds an intense parochialism which tends to shut out of the professor's mind a great many institutional problems that by any rational calculus ought to concern him a great deal.

Professors, like other people, do the things that pay off, whatever the payoff may be: salary, status, prestige, satisfaction, or anything else for which men in our culture strive. The research specialty and unremitting preoccupation with departmental affairs pay off in our present educational system. Participation in larger faculty affairs or in interfaculty affairs does not.

The departmental and specialist orientation of the American college professor gives the president some room for independent maneuver, while at the same time it sets severe limits to his authority. I doubt whether the president has much power of initiation so far as the old-line programs, which are firmly rooted in the traditional departments, are concerned. In our time, few departments look to the president for new educational ideas; rather, they themselves develop their own programs and engineer their own changes. Indeed, I suspect that presidential interest in their programs would merely generate resentment and resistance. In this sense, the president is always in peril of being regarded by the departments as an outsider. In our mature, high-quality institutions, I suspect that there are firm understandings as to jurisdiction so far as the departmental faculties and the president are concerned. Each tends to his own knitting.

That leads us to the question, what does the president knit? I think the answer is that he finds scope for taking the initiative and exercising power outside the old-line departments and their well-entrenched programs. An active president, or a president who seeks for activity, must roam outside the departmental area. He still has a great deal of initiative and a chance to be responsible for new developments in the area of interdepartmental programs operated by faculty committees which cut across departmental lines. The establishment of specialized institutes, centers, bureaus, and the like is well within the range of presidential initiative. He is also the institution's chief negotiator with the Federal government, the foundations, and private donors, the principal sources of fresh funds outside the normal channels available to the institution. Missions, and not the established disciplines, are grist to his mill. I do not wish to minimize the significance of this sort of presidential activity, for it involves many of the most vital growth points in contemporary higher education. Nevertheless, it is true that a vast area of university activity is firmly rooted in well-established departments, and in this area a wise president knows that he must proceed with great caution and with special regard for faculty sensibilities.

THE PROCESS OF DECISION MAKING

I do not believe that there is any quick and easy way to work out a wholly satisfactory and efficient system of college or university government which will function without strain. Where administrative officials have long been in the habit of making policy decisions without considering faculty opinion, the transition to a partnership with the teaching staff will not be accomplished without resistance and without pain. And where faculties have been passive and uninvolved, the process of involvement will make large demands upon them. There are no rights without duties, and if professors want to enjoy the right of participation in institutional government, then they must be prepared to give as well as to receive. But even in those institutions where faculty involvement is accepted as both desirable and normal, one should not expect a life of easy and peaceful relaxation. Institutional government in which all major elements of the educational community participate meaningfully does not hold out the promise of a life without friction. It is government the hard way. It is much easier to give orders to inferiors than to discuss them with respected equals. Where the circle of decision making is large, the variety of opinions and desires is all the greater, and the task of finding a consensus from clashing views and competing wills is never easy or simple.

Furthermore, it is worth repeating that wise decisions rest upon adequate awareness of the facts from which the decisions emerge. This means that if faculty members are to play a meaningful role in the process of making policy decisions, the administrators—who are more apt to have command of the underlying facts because they have initial access to them—must make those facts available to the faculty so that they may be able to take informed positions. Without a steady flow of information from those who have it to those who need it, cooperative decision making can never amount to much.

Decision making is not a final state of rest, but an ongoing process which moves from problem to problem as they appear. Responsible participation in decision making is neither a counsel of perfection nor a formula for the elimination of tensions. It does not promise that all of our problems will be solved properly, but it does offer us some assurance that at the very least the problems will be faced up to in a responsible, informed, and intelligent manner. In an imperfect society of imperfect people, this is no mean objective.

The Academic Community: Who Decides What?

ARNOLD M. GRANT, JOHN W. OSWALD,
EDWARD N. ROBINSON, J. BROWARD CULPEPPER

Men Whose Primary Concern Is the Institution

ARNOLD M. GRANT

AFTER EXAMINING the views, demands, and performance of students, faculty, administrators, and governing board, President Rosemary Park observed several years ago:

> In this extraordinary conglomerate of prerogatives not exercised, of usurpations by default, the ship moves! And more extraordinary still this fundamental structure of movable parts has not totally disintegrated. Something holds it together, but for how long?

Because the answer to her question may well be "Not very long," a consideration of "Whose Goals For American Higher Education?" is extremely pertinent.

It is significant that, in Professor Fellman's seventeen-page paper, the role of the governing board is presented in exactly one page, and that page is made up largely of generalizations. This may be a Freudian, as well as an intellectual, assessment of the significance of the governing board.

The paper contends that decision making should basically rest with the faculty and cites Flemming's statement that "the faculty [should be] the most influential group in the governing of our colleges and universities." But to discuss decision making in general terms blurs the problem. Granted that the problem is complex, if we could be more exact in defining the different kinds of decisions that must be made, the discussion would be clearer. Obviously, decisions differ in nature. No one would suggest, for instance, that trustees should decide how to teach a subject. On the other hand, can it be successfully argued that faculties should select the president or fix their own salaries?

A more precise distinction between influence upon a decision and responsibility for the final decision is needed too. For example, when Mr. Fellman states that there should be administrative review and board approval of questions regarding faculty status, but that faculty judgment should normally be decisive, he is pointing out that, in a particular area, the greatest weight should be given to faculty judgment because in this area the faculty is best informed and has the most significant experience. But surely Mr. Fellman does not argue that the function of a governing board is merely to rubber-stamp. No man of integrity and ability would be content to serve in a capacity which consisted only of paper responsibility, of automatically affixing his signature to unreviewed programs. If this is to be the role of trustees, then we must search for an entirely different pattern of governance in higher education. And, perhaps the day has come when this should be done. If so, it should be decided directly and forthrightly. It should not happen by masked erosion.

We have always recognized the special problems of educating the physically handicapped, the emotionally disturbed, and the mentally retarded. We do not depart from that philosophy when we recognize that the most important domestic crisis in our country is that of coping with the needs and hopes of those who are disadvantaged economically, environmentally, socially, and culturally. Surely, education is at the core of this complex problem. We live in what has been described as "the era of rising expectations." Our colleges and universities have a significant responsibility to help solve this massive problem. They cannot ignore it and live on isolated, intellectual islands, separated from and indifferent to the greatest domestic problem of our age.

If higher education recognizes its new obligations, vital institutional decisions must be made. Shall the institution set up programs to accommodate students who do not meet academic entrance requirements, who come from minority groups which have not had the benefits of a white, middle-class life? Shall institutional funds be appropriated for programs specifically designed to enable these young people to "catch up," or shall the particular institution insist upon maintaining tight requirements for admission? The decisions in these critical areas are not departmental ones. They require an institutional judgment, to be made in the light of our responsibilities and goals. Students and faculty have been on the front lines in behalf of civil rights, but neither group has yet been heard to suggest a policy decision to further integration by refusing applicants from nonintegrated schools, or by any other method which the university could apply at the point of origin to attain the desired social end.

Because the problems confronting educational institutions today are not merely pedagogical, but also social, the training and professional background of a professor is often no more adequate than the experience of an intelligent, concerned, and informed layman. Mr. Fellman, indeed, concedes the obvious fact that there are many decisions which are institutional ones. But are there not men in industry, in finance, and in the general professions whose judgment on behalf of the institution is quite as informed, intelligent, and statesmanlike as the opinions of those who serve on the various faculties?

Throughout, Mr. Fellman emphasizes that, in his opinion, professors are motivated by self-interest: the department is all-important to him because "most academic rewards and punishments are meted out in the department," "most professors are quite unable to be concerned with interdepartmental, college, or institutionwide matters," "professors, like other people, do the things that pay off, whatever the payoff may be."

Does not a major institution need the service and judgment of men who have no self-interest in the decisions? Does it not need the responsibility of men whose primary concern is with the institution, rather than the kind of man whose devotion "to his particular specialty is far greater than his loyalty to his institution"?

To solve the problem of usurpation by default of prerogatives not exercised, there must be the fullest communication among faculty, administration, trustees, and students. Through dialogue, a determination can evolve as to which decisions are institutional and which are departmental. From there, we may reach a clear understanding as to which groups should influence which decision and which has final responsibility for decision-making. Therein lies the answer to "Whose goals?" and to whether the ship will hold together.

The Inherent Authority of the President

JOHN W. OSWALD

As a faculty member, Dr. Fellman has developed a thoughtful and thorough presentation for other members of the academic community to consider in regard to decision making. In my comment on the paper from the view of a college president, I have selected six points.

Beginning with the premise of the "professor's parochialism," we are faced with the situation in which one department's decisions come into conflict with another's. Obviously, an institution must have an over-all decision-making procedure which resolves such conflicts in order to function as a college or university and to have what Mr. Lee calls "institutional coherence and priorities." It is true that, in a day-to-day program, the departmental rulings on classrooms, research, equipment, or books are effective and necessary and, perhaps, as Dr. Fellman states, "constitute many of the institution's most important decisions." However, even this autonomy may be harmful if the department is mediocre, or is interested only in its own preservation and freedom of action. Unless it refers to wider interests, even a strong department can make decisions which conflict with other departments' needs. It is often at this point that persons or structures outside the department, including the president, function in promoting the formulation of a resolution.

Indeed, in contrast to the Age of the Department phenomenon, some institutions, particularly newly established ones, are doing away with formal departments or, at least, are developing formal and functional interdisciplinary areas. The decision to do so has usually not originated with the department, but has, instead, developed at the college dean's level, the provost's, or higher. What department of chemistry has voted to have a department of biochemistry that is coordinate and autonomous? Which department decides whether or not a new medical school is to be developed? Does a vote by the English Department to increase salaries produce the money by which increases can be realized? Is an expansion of a department of infectious diseases to precede or follow the expansion of Middle English studies? Many decisions for the whole institution are beyond the purview of a particular department; indeed, they involve not only the faculty and the president, but also the trustees and the student body.

Not only in the resolution of department decisions does the president have a role, but also in the matter of educational innovation. It is at this second point that I take issue with Dr. Fellman. It is my understanding that he perceives the president as being too busy with finances, public relations, and the physical plant to deal with the educational enterprise itself. Regarding the role of educational innovator, I can, perhaps, best cite my own experience.

When invited to the University of Kentucky as president, I was primarily concerned, as an educator, in developing the best possible means for providing the best possible opportunities for higher education within our constituency. I felt it my responsibility to set forth prospects, needs, and challenges from my vantage point as president. These academic proposals were, in reality, questions to which the faculty, as well as trustees and students, had the opportunity of reacting—by discussing, modifying, legislating. As president, I felt completely free to participate in the discussions as they progressed, with faculty or with trustees. The new academic plan which evolved for the total institution was indeed a result of "responsible participation" in decision making, as Dr. Fellman advocates, and I mention it as illustrative of an instance in which a president actively participated in the innovating process.

In this context of unifying and innovating, it is well to remember that the president is often a scholar, a seasoned member of the academic community who is familiar with decision making at various levels. Though he might be an "outsider" at a departmental meeting, as Dr. Fellman suggests, this is more a function of the delegation of interests than an exclusion. His administrative concern is not primarily with public relations, finance, and so forth, but is *also* with those areas, and this is my third comment. Because a president presides over a *whole* institution, he is concerned with academic promotional procedures, interdisciplinary alignments, the rights and privileges of faculty, as well as with other more unacademic administrative concerns. In regard to administrative minutiae, however, he spends no more time on a bus schedule (to use Dr. Fellman's example) than he spends on academic minutiae such as interviewing graduate assistants.

Though Dr. Fellman has given particular attention to decisions made at the department level and to the opportunities for the faculty to become more broadly involved, I myself, as a president, have a particular interest in the relation of the faculty to the trustees, and of the students to the trustees, in decision making. In my own institution, two of the faculty are nonvoting members of the Board of Trustees. They are there not as representatives of the faculty senate but as educational spokesmen who help immeasurably in the education of lay trustees.

In contrast, the argument that students be represented on the Board of Trustees has not seemed to me to be similarly valid. They are present at Board meetings and frequently speak on issues that are of concern to them; but I question that a student, who serves for one year, can be an adequate spokesman for his large constituency. Many student concerns with decisions relate, in fact, to the departmental or divisional level, though some of the student activists do interest themselves in trustee-made decisions.

A fifth point for discussion is Dr. Fellman's view that the president has "interstitial authority," by which I understand him to mean that authority which has been abdicated or relinquished by an indifferent, uninformed, disunified faculty. He writes that "Presidents are strong because faculties fail to exercise the authority that is within their group." In my perception, the authority of the president is not by default; it is inherent in his role. Dr. Fellman presents a plea for the faculty to "play a meaningful role in the process of making policy decisions." I believe that the administrative function is absolutely essential in any complex organization and calls for a variety of decision-making points.

Lastly, I agree with him that many faculty maintain their level of interest only at the departmental level. But there is a great variety of opinion among faculty themselves in regard to their own participation in decision making, ranging from those who have an interest in every phase of the university to those who get involved only in what goes on around them and otherwise wish to be left alone. Genuine interest and broad faculty participation is an asset to any institution. It encourages the devotion of faculty talents to the welfare of the institution rather than to the "parochial" interests of one discipline. Substantive and organizational decisions call for the involvement not only of individual professors and departments but also of committees, councils, institutes, schools, and colleges.

It should be acknowledged that university-wide committees and concerns do indeed require valuable faculty time and do not always seem to pay off. Faculty colleagues on my campus sometimes imply criticism of the "Senate pro" or deride a faculty member who is "doing committee work" instead of "his own." It is true that a faculty member who takes an active interest in broad issues and programs within the university will probably soon find himself an administrator—maybe even a college president! Wide involvement and encompassing viewpoint are helpful in a faculty member; they are essential in a president.

Decisions in a university are made at many levels. The immediate academic minutiae often involve the viewpoints of the largest numbers of persons with homogeneous interests. As decisions increase in effect and tenure, wider representation is involved in reconciliation, compromise, and modification. Here, representation of the interests of affected parties is paramount, and lines of communication must be made accessible even if, as Dr. Fellman points out, they are seldom used. As one of my colleagues has noted, "Flows of information within a university should be studied to see that adequate exposure is arranged, even though adequate assimilation may not follow."

In summary, I agree with Dr. Fellman's assessment of the importance of faculty participation in deciding academic affairs and with his emphasis on the importance of faculty interest in departmental decision making. I would advocate a broader concept of the president's role as resolver and innovator, rather than relegating him to other time-consuming but supplementary administrative aspects of the educational enterprise. We also need to encourage the faculty's communication with the trustees, acknowledging that many faculty prefer a lesser scope in decision making.

I am not fully persuaded we are in Dr. Fellman's Age of the Professor nor in his Age of the Department. It could as well be the Age of the Grant, the Age of Physical Expansion, the Age of International Service, the Age of Student Protest. One's view of decision making in the academic community is heavily coated by one's own vantage point. This is as true of me as of Dr. Fellman.

An End to the Age-Is-Wisdom Theory

EDWARD N. ROBINSON

WHAT HAS TO BE SAID about this problem must be said face to face—to provoke an argument, to arouse some emotion—because academicians are prone to consider this and other problems as intellectual exercises to which answers can be applied at leisure. The matter is far more serious than that, both in its implications within the university community and in its consequences for the society of which the university is a part.

The leadership of this country—the men responsible either directly or indirectly for the war in Vietnam, the oppression of the Negro, the dehumanization of the poor—is college trained. These men are incompetent, incapable of seeing past the existing structures and traditions, incapable of devising new ways for men to relate to each other and their society. Why is this so? For one thing, most of these men, like most of the people in this country, have never been asked to create, to think imaginatively, to take real responsibility.

In the average college classroom, success can be won through attention, collation, and repetition. That's the academic atmosphere. Then, there's the political atmosphere which requires even less participation. At most schools, students are expected simply to accept the rules laid down for them by their elders, on the basis of an age-is-wisdom theory, combined with a we-know-more-about-the-university-than-you-do professionalism. If students accept this kind of policy, what have they in fact done? They have accepted the fact that what most men say is their ideal is usually quite different from what they actually do, for most of these elders would express a belief in democracy and representative government. They have accepted the contention that they aren't capable of acting for themselves, of deciding what rules they should be governed by. They have accepted the role of the unthinking follower in a society already far too full of such people.

Of course, most students do accept this style of government. They become well-adjusted members of the American consensus, a consensus usually based on apathy—lack of interest in finding things out for oneself or the inability to do so—because they have never been encouraged to think independently. Their professors are the students of yesterday, and their knowledge is made up of the same kinds of things that they were and were not taught. It's quite upsetting to hear professors say that they are glad when students cause trouble over inequities so that they (the professors) are provided with an impetus to get moving. It's shaky when professors can live as members of a community and not see the injustices which exist in it until someone else points them out. It's frightening when professors say that they wish all the disturbances over various breaches of human dignity would die out, because these disturbances are forcing them to spend three or four hours a week on university committees trying to find solutions. And it should be pointed out that all these things *are* said in such situations; they aren't just creations of my imagination.

It must be admitted that often the faculty can't do much for the institution even if they want to, because a lot of universities are run behind closed doors, opened to only a very few people privy to the "necessary facts on which to base a decision." This is another variation of the Have-Faith argument which runs: I-know-things-that-I-can't-tell-you-and-they-have-affected-my-decision-in-ways-that-may-seem-strange-to-you. Not only does the question arise, Why is it necessary for the governors of a university to hide things from the rest of us? but we can also ask again, What kind of responsibility and involvement is developed by a system in which none of the leaders are responsible to anyone but themselves, and none of the constituents are supposed to know what is going on?

All this may sound like a rather heavy-handed exaggeration of a minor problem. A year ago, I would have agreed with you (though I at least have the so-called excuse of youth), but no more. A year ago, I wouldn't have thought that the Congress of the United States would believe that the answer to the problem of urban ghettoes lay in riot control bills and not anti-rat measures. I wouldn't have thought that the University of Michigan administration would comply with a subpoena of the House Un-American Activities Committee for membership lists, much less do it without consulting outside lawyers or the people on the lists. And most important, I wouldn't have thought that those people who consider themselves liberal would be incapable of seeing that what they call "moderation" in reacting to these injustices is, in effect, a way of perpetuating them.

The injustices within the university don't lead directly to people dying or to children going hungry or to minorities being made into second-class humans. But I think it's clear that the kind of attitudes the university fosters with regard to individual creativity, morality, and responsibility is the same kind of atmosphere which prevails in those circles where these greater wrongs are allowed to exist. And the university contributes directly both men and ideas to these circles. That is why it's important that we change things at the university, why it's necessary that we realize that there are a few things which take priority over new books or coveted peace and quiet, that is why we must start doing what we say we believe in.

All Have Major Roles To Play

J. BROWARD CULPEPPER

DR. DAVID FELLMAN HAS WRITTEN a perceptive analysis of decision making by the several constituents of higher education. I have the distinct impression, however, that he displays a certain bias toward the "party line" of the American Association of University Professors (AAUP). He correctly begins his paper by pointing out that the decision-making process is difficult to analyze because of wide variations in patterns of administration and operation among the some 2,000 institutions of higher learning in the nation. In order to draw meaningful conclusions when discussing who decides what, one almost is forced to deal with the individual institution. Dr. Fellman also recognizes that outside influences frequently have an impact upon decision making, but he rather carefully restricts his remarks to the four immediate constituents of higher education: the faculty, the administration, the trustees, and the students.

The Faculty Member: In recent years, the faculty member has played an increasingly important role in the administration of higher education: so much so, in fact, that Dr. Fellman suggests that this period could be called the Age of the Professor. He appropriately emphasizes that if the professor is to perform in this expanding role, he must recognize the necessity of accepting the responsibilities involved. This would require him to take part in broader issues and activities than those operating at the departmental level. Dr. Fellman states that any self-respecting faculty will demand the right to participate fully in institutional policy making. Undoubtedly, this is the AAUP position, but for most administrators and board members—and perhaps some faculty members—it is too strong a position. I would argue that the faculty member must be involved in decision making and in planning; ideally, he should have an opportunity to express his ideas and to make suggestions. But the governing board must have the final authority in determining policy. In the implementation of policy, it is again important to recognize that the professor should be given the opportunity to help formulate those procedures which will have an impact upon his teaching, research, and service activities, but the basic responsibility for implementation must rest with the administration of the institution. The Association of Governing Boards outlines these relationships and this distribution of responsibilities in its *Handbook for University and College Regents.*

The President: Unquestionably, the president should provide leadership for the academic family. If he is to be most influential and to have a reasonably happy institutional community, then he must involve the faculty and students in planning and committee activity relevant to all aspects of academic administration. Dr. Fellman goes too far, however, when he says that the broad powers of the president persist only because of the inability of the faculty to exert its own influence effectively and consistently. To realize the institution's objectives, the president should seek ways to tap the reservoirs of strength formed by the faculty and other constituents. This is easy to say but sometimes most difficult to bring to reality in the face of faculty indifference to institutionwide matters. The problem for the president, who operates "the communications system which links the components of the academic community," is to generate genuine interest on the part of *all* the constituents in helping to devise constructive plans which will enable the institution to attain its goals. Certainly, if he is to carry out his full responsibility, the president is more than a glorified "overseer" who spends long hours checking on food services, having timeworn buildings painted, obtaining donations, greeting visitors, and the like.

The Governing Board: Dr. Fellman notes that the governing board must relate the institution to its chief constituency and that the board exercises "final institutional authority." This statement makes it clear that the primary role of the board is to serve as a policy-making body under which the institution will be administered. The policies established by the board should reflect the desires of the chief constituency with regard to the role and function of the institution and should ensure the most advantageous use of the resources provided. I agree with Dr. Fellman that it is absolutely essential for the board to delegate much of its authority to those who are permanently on the job and especially to the president, who is responsible for the implementation of board policy.

The Student: It is unfortunate that Dr. Fellman has relegated the student's role in decision making to a footnote. The remarks he makes in the footnote are quite pertinent and indicate a possible expanding role for the student in policy making. The footnote should, perhaps, have been part of the text, so as to enhance its significance. Student participation in planning both his extracurricular and academic activities can be most helpful and rewarding for all concerned. As the main beneficiary of the academic process, however, it is inconceivable that basic decisions in policy making would be left finally to him. His inexperience in and of itself makes injudicious such a practice.

The Departmental Syndrome: Dr. Fellman is most accurate in that portion of his paper in which he indicates that the greatest number of faculty operate in management and administration only at the departmental level. Undoubtedly, the significance of the department has come about, in large measure, because of the development of very large academic institutions. This emphasis on the department also underscores the fact that the interests of most professors are directed where they should be: toward instruction, research, and scholarly pursuits. It is clear that, if the professor is to be the force which Dr. Fellman would like him to be in administration and decision making, he must be willing to move beyond the departmental level and to participate in various institutionwide activities. While it is the department head who is most frequently analyzed and criticized by the faculty member, it must be remembered that the board, through policy, and the president and deans, through administrative decisions, all have an important influence upon departmental activities. While the department can be envisioned by the professor as a cozy base of operation in the academic community, his interests and his energies must go beyond this haven of security if he is to exercise the authority necessary for a successful democratic administration.

The Decision-making Process: Administrative practices and decision making naturally vary among institutions and even among individuals at the same institution. In decision making, as Dr. Fellman says, some friction must inevitably occur, and the broader the participation, the more likelihood there is of conflict. It should be recognized that in the process of involving many constituents in decision making, time becomes an important factor. Insofar as it is possible, it is well to develop ahead of time a precise understanding of the procedures to be followed, so that when moments of decision arrive, action can be taken without the burden of disruptive, time-consuming conferences and exchanges. Further, it is important that each of the main constituents of higher education recognize that all have major roles to play and that each should respect the interests of the other. Team work, exchange of information, understanding relationships, recognition of rights, and knowledge of the duties and responsibilities of the other constituents will enable all to contribute most effectively to the successful operation of the institution.

LOGAN WILSON

Institutional Autonomy
And Heteronomy

IN THE LEXICON of academic discourse, *autonomy* is a word with a long and interesting history. It connotes a favored institutional condition, and impediments to it are, by definition, dirty words for those who view the ideal type of academic community as one characterized by self-governance, internal direction, and freedom from outside control. Its antonym, *heteronomy,* which often describes more nearly the realities of academic governance, is, oddly enough, a term that is seldom used. To understand how goals are determined and control mechanisms are established in American higher education, one must keep these polarities in mind.

Because it is doubtful that any campus in this country is now or ever was completely self-governing, the persistent academic concern with autonomy is somewhat curious. What does it mean, and to whom does it matter most? To what extent should students, faculty, and staff participate in institutional governance? With disorder on the campus becoming more commonplace, can all our institutions expect their outside constituencies to accord them as much autonomy in the future as they have in the past? If changing conditions require a reassessment of traditional goals and conventional evidences of autonomy, what readjustments must be made and what claims maintained? In view of the number and diversity of the parties involved, to whom should the answers to these and other critical questions be addressed? What common understandings need to be incorporated into public policy to ensure the best development and conduct of higher education in the United States?

For example, the United States National Student Association, which maintains that the present "system of higher educational institutions restricts the student's rights to democratic self-government," advocates a "student power" movement to effect complete student control over "all regulations of a non-academic nature which apply solely and exclusively to students . . ." At its Congress last summer, however, it expressed a willingness to share joint control with the faculty and administration in such matters as course requirements, admissions policies, financial aid policies, building and grounds planning, hiring and dismissal of faculty and administrative personnel, and grading systems and appeals on grades. By vote of those present at the convention, the organization's national office was given a mandate to "organize, educate, and aid individual campuses in the philosophy and implementation of student power."

Although some professors are under the illusion that there was once an academic Golden Age when *they* ran things without interference from anybody else, W. H. Cowley, in tracing the history of institutional governance, has refuted this notion. I agree with him that —as tax-exempt nonprofit institutions—colleges and universities exist to serve the general welfare and that full control of a profession or occupation by those who practice it directly, be they teachers, lawyers, merchants, clergymen, or civil servants, would constitute syndicalism rather than democracy.

There are those who would prefer syndicalism, of course, and there are others who see no need for any outside controls. Paul Goodman, for instance, has advocated doing away entirely with ". . . the external control, administration, bureaucratic machinery, and other excrescences that have swamped our community of scholars." J. Kenneth Galbraith recently expressed the view that "the faculty now governs and only the faculty can govern" in what he calls "the mature university." Although he hardly mentions the existence of administrative officers and relegates trustees to a purely ceremonial role, he concedes that it might be helpful for professors to bring students and alumni into an alliance with them.

"ESSENTIAL INGREDIENTS"

Academicians now hold positions of influence equalled by few other occupations in our society. They are granted considerable freedom to create, interpret, and disseminate knowledge. Because the colleges and universities in which they work must also be committed to the pursuit and transmission of truth, some institutional autonomy is a social necessity rather than an academic luxury. In short, even though contemporary centers of higher learning cannot be isolated from the supporting society, they must at least be insulated from improper constraints and undue interferences. As Sir Eric Ashby has very aptly put it:

> The arguments for university autonomy, like the arguments for academic freedom, are weakened by querulous appeals to tradition and privilege. The only effective argument is the pragmatic one. A system of higher education, like an airline, is a highly technical organization. If experts are not allowed to run it without interference from the state, it will collapse. The only effective policy, therefore, is for universities, like airlines, to be left to manage their own affairs.

In his recent book, *Universities: British, Indian, African,* Sir Eric sets forth what he considers to be the essential ingredients of institutional autonomy: (1) freedom to select students and staff and to determine the conditions under which they remain; (2) freedom to set standards and to decide to whom degrees should be awarded; (3) freedom to design the curriculum, recognizing, of course, the standards of professional bodies; (4) once having obtained external support, freedom to allocate it without being subject to further inspection; (5) and finally, the right to require nonacademics participating in governance to identify with the university and not to act as representatives of outside interests and also to delegate all academic decisions to the academics themselves.

Prior to the publication of this statement, I was in a small conference with the author when he referred to these "essential ingredients." As I listened to him, it crossed my mind that some of the best-known American institutions do not meet all these specifications. The University of California, for example, under the division of labor established by the California Coordinating Council, may admit no students except those in the top eighth of their high school graduating classes in that state. State colleges within that same system—which, incidentally, is considered to be the nation's most outstanding—do not have complete latitude to design their own curricula but must confine them within limits that are centrally determined. Throughout the country, moreover, most publicly supported colleges and universities do not have full freedom to decide internally how their funds will be allocated; and all institutions receiving Federal funds must open their accounts to governmental inspection. Finally, some lay trustees regard themselves as primarily obligated to interests outside the institutions, as is evidenced in the recent statement of one state university regent. Asserting a felt obligation to step in and override faculty and administration from time to time, the trustee said:

It is not only within the powers granted to the regents but it is their duty to grant or deny tenure or promotion to faculty members as they believe it is to the best interest of the university, even if such action is contrary to the recommendations of the deans and the administration. To do otherwise would admit to being a rubber-stamp board, to which I will not be a party.

❖   ❖   ❖   ❖   ❖

This can be done by giving instructions to the present administrative officers and seeing that these are carried out or, if this course of action does not succeed, then it is the job of the regents to override the administration or to change the administration if and when necessary. . . .

Other instances which indicate disregard for Sir Eric Ashby's "essential ingredients" of institutional autonomy could be cited. Our basic concern should be with general trends rather than particular instances, however, and in the absence of systematic data, I can only give you my own impressions of what has been happening.

GAINS AND LOSSES IN AUTONOMY

Looking at the vast diversity of American higher education, I would begin by noting that, in the matter of autonomy, no broad generalization about developments can apply to all institutions. I suspect that, in the main, junior colleges, former teachers colleges, and church-related institutions have more autonomy than they did a generation or so ago. Many junior or community colleges have broken away from the rather regimented controls imposed upon them by their close identification with public school systems; teachers colleges have not only changed their names but they have also shaken off much of the authoritarianism that once pervaded their governance and curricula; and church-related institutions are less under the dominance of religious bodies. In virtually all institutions, students and faculty are less submissive than they once were to external controls over their behavior. The growing diversity in sources of support has, in many respects, rendered colleges and universities less beholden to any single source of control. The force of tradition has been weakened, and the demand for conformity has correspondingly lessened. The performance of higher education's functions, moreover, has become more professionalized, with universal rather than particular criteria applied to the judgment of results. In short, I believe that these and other circumstances indicate significant gains here and there in institutional autonomy.

Along with these gains, however, there have been some losses. The weaknesses, as well as the strengths, of the traditionally loose arrangements in our system of higher education have increasingly been called into question in recent years. The unplanned and uncontrolled diversity resulting from local autonomy in policy making has already disappeared among public institutions in virtually all states. Issues relating to size, governance, programs, facilities, faculty and staff personnel, student clientele, and budget are less and less matters left to internal resolution. Drastic changes have taken place and are still occurring in patterns of decision making. Behind these changes, of course, is an intensified public, and hence political, concern with the greatly increased cost, complexity, and importance of higher education. In addition, it is more widely recognized that a rational approach to the interdependence of colleges and universities within a state or region is perhaps as essential as a proper regard for their independence.

There now exist only a small handful of states which have neither a formal nor a voluntary coordinating board or other agency for public higher education. The American Council on Education is conducting a comprehensive study of state-wide systems which will update existing information about such systems, analyze the key issues and problems they generate, evaluate their effectiveness, and attempt to assess future trends.

Pending this comprehensive assessment, let me give you some of my own opinions about these systems, coupled with some observations about the general situation in which we find ourselves. We would all agree, I trust, that higher education has become too crucial to the general welfare for its development to be left entirely in local hands. Many urgent problems cannot be adequately dealt with by individual institutions acting unilaterally, and piecemeal approaches do not yield satisfactory patterns. With the growing collectivism of modern life, more and more decisions and actions affecting the present and future of higher education are being transferred from the private to the public arena, and from the local to the state or national level. The spread of state-wide boards may thus be interpreted as a logical response to the functional need for more centralized policy direction.

In our kind of society, the emergence of such agencies has, in my judgment, been inevitable and in many respects desirable, but we should not overlook the fact that they, by their existence and nature, reduce the authority of the boards, administrators, and faculties of individual institutions. Considering the tendency of many academicians to resist the centralization of authority and to criticize relentlessly the actions of institutional trustees and administrators, it is indeed astonishing how silent they have been about this drastic reorganization that has taken place in the governance of public higher education since World War II.

These coordinating agencies have negative as well as positive reasons for being. Let me illustrate from the experience of one state which some years back had about twenty degree-granting public colleges and universities. The programmatic duplication among them and their competition for funds became so acute that the state legislature placed a ban on all new academic programs. True, there had been a Council of State College Presidents for some years, but their main purpose was to uphold a tacit understanding not to undercut one another in institutional hearings before the legislative appropriations committee. Seldom, if ever, was there much discussion of a voluntary approach to a more sensible division of academic labor among their institutions. To make a long story short, the legislature established a Commission on Higher Education to do for the institutions what they were either unable or unwilling to do for themselves.

This episode, I suspect, illustrates the negative side of the story in a number of other states. Prior to the development of systematic coordination, most states simply had congeries of institutions, some of which were indiscriminately established, inadequately maintained, and poorly directed insofar as serving the best public interest was concerned. With institutional rivalry, rather than careful attention to the real needs behind some of the seemingly endless expansion of local endeavors, it is no wonder that the rich diversity of the education enterprise was often displaced by a destructive divisiveness. Institutional autonomy run rampant not only unnecessarily increased the price of public higher education but also reduced its over-all effectiveness. When rapid population growth and other factors added to the spiral of rising costs, it became obvious to many states that a coordinating mechanism had to be developed.

But this is by no means the whole story: fortunately, there are many positive reasons for the growth of coordinating agencies. On all sides, there has been increased awareness of the need to distribute funds fairly among existing institutions and to have an orderly plan for their expansion and for the establishment of new institutions. An agency that reviews programs and budgets can well be looked at constructively as a means for implementing goals rather than as a device for keeping costs down. The less as well as the more affluent states are now convinced of the importance of education as an investment and of the advantages of central planning. Boards or councils specifically charged with policy responsibility for public higher education can usually do a better job of dealing with complex academic problems than can governors and legislatures, who must cope with the whole spectrum of public affairs.

Some states, as you may be aware, have successively tried different arrangements, but so far, they are not satisfied. The California scheme, widely regarded as a prototype and model, is now under fire within the state itself. A present difficulty in judging the effectiveness of a state-wide scheme is that input and output analyses for higher education are so underdeveloped that assessment is to a considerable extent a matter of individual opinion.

THE POWER OF DECISION

In the meantime, patterns of decision making continue to change. Federal actions, particularly since 1963, have contributed to the movement toward centralization and politicization. The Higher Education Facilities Act of 1963 required that state commissions be designated to develop and submit plans for the utilization of facilities funds under Title I. Comparable stipulations are found in the Federal enactments of 1965. In each instance, state governors were given important appointive powers. These moves reduce the possibility of Federal interference, of course, but only at the cost of imposing another layer of government agencies between academic institutions—private as well as public—and their sources of support.

For a number of years, moreover, decisions made by the legislative and executive branches of government in Washington have tended to reduce the autonomy of colleges and universities by increasing the *outer* rather than the *inner* direction of higher education. A well-known medical dean recently remarked that his office controlled only $200 thousand of his total $8 million medical school budget, all the rest of the allocations being determined largely by actions in the nation's capital. And although we often think of Harvard as being a model of independence, a noted political science professor there expressed amazement several weeks ago at how little control even Harvard now has over Harvard!

At this point, I want to emphasize that I am not attributing ulterior or sinister motives to anybody. If there is an organized effort anywhere to shatter the autonomy of institutions and destroy their integrity, I am unaware of it. Professors who serve on specialized panels in Washington are there primarily to help physics or cancer research or what not, and I am confident that creating an imbalance in colleges and universities is the last thing they have in mind. I would guess, too, that individual faculty and staff members who belong to organized regional or national groups that lobby for their own vested interests are not consciously trying to weaken the duly established procedures for determining priorities on their own campuses. I would say also that members of Congress and the executive branch generally bend over backward to minimize Federal control in programs intended to assist higher education. And finally, I would add that the increasing involvement of courts of law in the settlement of what were once regarded as intramural disputes is assuredly not a reflection of judiciary desires to undermine the authority of academic institutions. In spite of all such disclaimers, however, it must be acknowledged that these involvements inevitably reduce the number of policy decisions made on campuses as a corollary of increasing the number being made elsewhere.

These erosions of institutional autonomy may take place so gradually, subtly, or indirectly that awareness of what has happened often does not occur until well after the fact. Whereas faculty militants and others are still watching the main gates, where deliberate attacks on institutional autonomy were customarily launched in bygone years, it has often, in recent years, been difficult to differentiate between friend and foe among those who enter by the unguarded side and rear gates of the citadel of institutional independence.

I realize, of course, that the citadel, like the ivory tower, may no longer be an appropriate metaphor for the contemporary college or university. Even when a particular institution has no choice but to give up a part of its prior autonomy by entering into new arrangements, it may gain in support or influence. Moreover, for the purpose of cooperation toward common goals, both public and private institutions often enter voluntarily into agreements with one another or with other agencies whereby some of their individual autonomy is traded off for material benefits. The growing number of these institution-initiated consortia in the last decade or so attests to the increased interdependence of all institutions of higher education.

Dr. Eldon L. Johnson has said of such cooperative arrangements among institutions that they lie "between isolated independence and complete merger." Since the scheme depends upon voluntary association, it has no central power beyond that delegated by its members and thus escapes the element of compulsion found in externally imposed mechanisms. In his summary appraisal of the consortium or federation idea, Dr. Johnson has concluded:

> In retrospect, perhaps the crucial elements that assure distinction in cooperation among colleges are these: effective means of deciding what to undertake in common; willingness to undertake what will strike imagination, fix attention, and elicit participation by its high relevance; resources to command action and reward cooperation; and machinery for

keeping center and extremity in reasonable harmony and in mutual dependence.

The chief trouble with cooperation among colleges is that it matters little in the personal and academic lives of most of their constituents. . . . At one extreme, they can be motivated by what a cynical friend of mine quite correctly implied when he asked, "Are your colleges *hurting* badly enough to cooperate?" At the other extreme, they can be motivated by the realization that there is a whole range of imaginative possibilities in collective action which extend and supplement, rather than threaten, already excellent institutions.[1]

As colleges and universities have been drawn into a closer relationship with one another and with society at large, the concept of the institution of higher education as an individualistic, private enterprise has just about disappeared. In a society where conservative sentiments uphold independent enterprise as an organizational model, it is perhaps ironic that the model in higher education should be recognizably approximated only in proprietary and unaccredited institutions and in the secessionist "free universities" formed by dissident teachers and students. Everywhere else in the academic fold, the growing interdependence of institutions and their closer intermeshing with the surrounding society have predictably resulted in increased heteronomy.

One university president, Homer Babbidge, has contended that some institutions are surrendering control of their own destinies. He has maintained that their failure to take the initiative and plan for themselves has made them vulnerable to plans imposed from the outside. To offset the erosion of autonomy, he has urged every college or university to adopt a clear set of goals and a strategy to be followed, and to develop the resources to monitor itself as well as leadership strong enough and sensitive enough to ensure that goals are the touchstones of every action.

As I stated earlier, there is no such thing as a completely autonomous institution. At this juncture, I would add that there can be no such thing as a completely heteronymous institution. Even though it retains its name, a college or university that is transformed into a welfare agency, a public service station, or a supermarket catering solely to customer demand ceases to be an institution of higher learning. It may become quite useful to the community, but the metamorphosis sacrifices something essential to the integrity of teaching and research. That something is the minimum degree of autonomy neces-

---

[1] Johnson, "College Federation," *Journal of Higher Education*, January 1966.

sary for a college or university to be a critic as well as a servant of the larger society.

Although higher education per se no longer needs much protection against overt antagonists, it still must be shielded from well-intentioned but mistaken efforts that would transmogrify rather than transform the nation's campuses. What has been called the "inner logic" of intellectual endeavor cannot be debased without ultimately destroying the main reason for being of colleges and universities. The indirect effects of misguided student activists or militant teacher unionists, for example, can be just as corrosive as are open onslaughts from the outside. Measures that give financial aid to teaching, research, or public service may carry price tags of control that self-respecting institutions can ill afford to pay. Moreover, even the enlarged public interest in higher education, with the consequently increased politicization of decision making, contains a latent threat to the enduring purposes of institutions and to the autonomy they must have to achieve them.

In this changing climate, it seems to me that all who really care about higher education need to reassess the whole matter of institutional autonomy, put rhetoric aside, and take a hard look to discover what concessions should be made and what claims should be stoutly maintained. I have no bill of particulars to offer, and doubt that one equally suited to the purposes of all institutions could be drawn, but I am prepared to stick out my neck by giving a set of checkpoints regarding the minimum autonomy required by every college or university to remain viable as an institution of higher learning. These checkpoints would be as follows:

1. Every academic community must be able to exercise the functionally necessary control of its membership of faculty, staff, and students. Although public policy may legitimately influence this membership, outside agencies should not be permitted to dictate the entry, retention, or exit of particular individuals.

2. Consistent with the requirements of accrediting associations and recognized professional groups, each institution should be responsible for maintaining its own academic standards. With regard to other internal standards, to quote the decision of the California Supreme Court last April, "[The] University, as an academic community, can formulate its own standards, rewards, and punishments to achieve its educational objectives. . . . Thus, except for the applicable constitutional limitations, the relationship between appropriate University rules and laws of the outside community is entirely coincidental."

3. Conceding the right and the power of outside agencies to grant

or withhold funds and to influence their allocation, no institution should be deprived of the discretion required for their most effective internal utilization.

4. A sufficient degree of autonomy must be maintained for the institution's trustees, administrators, faculty, and students to exercise distinctive rights and shared responsibilities. Such rights and responsibilities should be respected both internally and externally.

5. In the realm of ideas, colleges and universities must be accorded the functional freedoms necessary for intellectual enterprise.

You will note that my itemization is less inclusive than the list of "essential ingredients" I cited earlier; indeed, it is admittedly minimal rather than optimal. In view of the erosions of institutional autonomy that are becoming widespread in this nation, however, I think it is high time for educational leaders everywhere to reach some basic understanding and to alert the general public about what can and what cannot be permitted if American colleges and universities are to maintain the integrity necessary for them to continue to serve the best interests of our society and of mankind.

KENNETH KENISTON

Responsibility for Criticism And Social Change

AMONGST THE MAJOR FUNCTIONS of the modern university, criticism is surely the most neglected. In the spate of recent treatises on the goals of higher education, much has been said about the transmission, extension, and application of knowledge, about teaching, research, and public service, and occasionally even about "innovation." But the critical function of the university is mentioned, if at all, in an apologetic aside, rather as if critical comments made by students and faculty members were merely the price the public must pay ("academic freedom") for the *other* valuable services performed by the university.

Were we to rely solely on these prevalent theories of higher education, we would find it impossible to understand most popular accounts of the American university. For newspapers, weeklies, and monthlies, radio and television, pay by far the greatest amount of attention to the critical voices that emanate from our universities. Student rebellion and protest are breakfast table topics; faculty teach-ins and petitions are headline news; the critical stance of "university intellectuals" toward government policies is constantly discussed; and the proper definition of the rights of university members to criticize our society preoccupies the public.

Nor could we infer from most recent discussions of our universities that in the past fifty years American higher education has become the prime source for critical analyses of our society. When criticism is discussed by the theorists of higher education, it is largely in parentheses—to minimize its importance and prevalence ("Most students are basically apathetic; most of our faculty are Republicans"), to explain it as a result of remediable defects within the university ("We must learn to pay more attention to our students as individuals"), or to defend it lamely and apologetically ("Academic freedom includes the right to be wrong").

Criticism, then, is the cuckoo's egg in the otherwise harmonious nest of traditional university functions. There can be no doubt that criticism is an actual function of the American university; indeed, our society has come to rely upon higher education to exercise this role. How much we take this critical role for granted can be seen by attempting to imagine what our society would be like if all students and faculty members were to be transformed overnight into uncritical apologists for the *status quo*. America would not only be quieter and less interesting, but unimaginably less vital and less promising. To the traditional functions of teaching, research, and public service, a fourth has been added—that of criticism—a function much discussed and maligned by the general public, but passed over in embarrassed silence by most articulate spokesmen for higher education.

In the remarks that follow, I will consider some of the reasons for the emergence of criticism as a major function of American higher education, some of the qualifications of the university for exercising this function, and some of the limitations upon its exercise. But before turning to these topics, I should underline that in speaking of the critical function, I am not discussing what is ordinarily referred to as "public service" or as "innovation." By *criticism*, I mean above all the analysis, examination, study, and evaluation of our society at large, of its directions, practices, institutions, strengths, weaknesses, ideals, values, and character; of its consistencies and contradictions; of what it has been, of what it is becoming, of what is becoming of it, and of what it might at best become. The critical function involves examining the purposes, practices, meanings, and goals of our society. It entails not merely the description of the past, the characterization of the present, and the prediction of the future, but the evaluation of the past, present, and probable future and the right to prescribe solutions, alternatives, and new directions, and to act in support of them.

Criticism, then, is distinguished from simple analysis and description by the presence of judgment. A critic not only characterizes, but condemns and praises according to his values. In this measure, he commits himself to a position vis-à-vis the object of criticism and to the values from which his position springs. Moreover, the responsible critic will usually do more than analyze and evaluate; he will propose, recommend, and advocate action that accords with his judgments and promotes his ideals, and he will condemn, oppose, and reject what he judges worthless or evil. Criticism implies commitment to a position, and its natural consequence is action. To separate critical thought from action is therefore to be blind to the fact that ideas have behavioral implications; to promote the first but suppress the second is to unman the critical intelligence. Similarly, any attempt to distinguish between "objective" and "partisan" criticism ignores the role of judgment and values in the critical process: for all judgments and values can be deemed "partisan" by those who reject them. What can be asked of criticism is not that it be objective, but that it be informed, regardful of facts, profound, generous, and intelligent. But to expect that it can be objective, confined to thought, or uncontroversial is to ask that it cease to be criticism.

One reason that theorists of American higher education have neglected to discuss the critical function is relatively obvious. The most articulate interpreters of the American university have been university administrators. By virtue of their difficult role, they are responsible to multiple constituencies: to their fellow college administrators; to their faculties and students; and, most relevant to this topic, to boards of trustees, alumni, state legislators, and public-spirited citizens with an interest in education. This last constituency finds the traditional university functions of teaching, research, and public service readily understandable and obviously important: they deserve support and grateful remuneration. Thus, in his search for the public and private support upon which his university depends, the administrator is, not surprisingly, inclined to stress those functions which are most unambivalently applauded by the public. Often embarrassed by dissenting students and protesting faculty members, he is likely to excuse rather than to justify their existence. Students, he explains, are young, searching, and uninformed; they will settle down; and in any case, dissenters are few in number. Faculty members are notably cantankerous and eccentric; in any case, they contribute to the public good in *other* ways. Academic freedom is, after all, a prerequisite for the adequate performance of teaching, research, and public service. The public must learn to accept a few weeds in the rich harvest of American higher education.

This neglect or dismissal of the university's critical function, however, not only fails to describe accurately the present role of higher education, but also defensively slights what should be viewed as one of the most valuable functions of the university in our rapidly changing and complex society. Indeed, the emergence of criticism as a major function of the university is intimately related to the changing nature and needs of American life. In modern society, the simple transmission of knowledge must increasingly give way to a critical re-examination of that knowledge; the extension of knowledge presupposes a critical analysis of what is worth extending; and the application of knowledge requires a critical study of which knowledge can be applied to what.

SOCIAL CHANGE, DIVERSITY, AND SOCIALIZATION

The traditional model of higher education is essentially a model of socialization. It is commonly said that the task of education is to "transmit" or "communicate" to the next generation the skills, techniques, knowledge, and wisdom of the past. In libraries, archives, and the minds of faculty members, universities have accumulated profound knowledge and insight about the past and present; teaching involves "passing on" this knowledge and insight to students. Similarly, the traditional model of research involves either the study of the past in order to disinter its enduring wisdom or the study of nature in order to uncover its eternal laws. And the traditional image of public service presupposes an established body of knowledge that can be applied to the solution of social problems—in short, a kind of technical assistance to the community. In all of these views, the older generation is seen as possessing knowledge, skills, and insights which can be conveyed in an uncomplicated way to the receptive young.

There are, to be sure, many variations on this traditional model. Some view the function of higher education narrowly as training: the simple transmission of skills to those who will eventually use them. We hear much today, for example, about the services of higher education in providing a reservoir of "skilled manpower" for the national economy. By others, proponents of the liberal arts, education is viewed less as the transmission of skills and more as a way of teaching students how to ask questions, how to analyze problems, and how to look at the world. Similarly, within the basic model of socialization, there is great disagreement as to how much "adjustment" to the existing society should be encouraged. Some few argue that universities should teach their students to work within the existing society; others define the goals of higher education as having to do with "the good life," a life that may not involve immediate acceptance of community standards. But according to each of these views, higher education serves its students and society best when it transmits to them skills, facts, competences, techniques of analysis, or values which originate in the past and which are assumed to be important, relevant for the present and future.

The durability of the model of socialization is easy to understand, for the assumptions upon which it rests have until recently been valid. For many centuries, the university was the prime repository of the learning and wisdom of the past; and scholars have traditionally been those who examined this past with an eye to distilling its implications for the present. As a description of the medieval university, the Renaissance university, or even the religiously oriented British university of the eighteenth and nineteenth centuries, the traditional model is largely accurate. Yet increasingly, "socialization" no longer describes what happens or what should happen in higher education. To assume that higher education can simply socialize youth presupposes social conditions that are fast disappearing from American society. For one, the increasing pace of social change invalidates the assumption that the skills, wisdom, and knowledge of one generation can be uncritically transmitted to the next; for another, the growing complexity of our society raises with urgency the question "Which society should the young be socialized to?" Increasingly, higher education, if it is to serve either its students or society, must assist the former to examine critically what they inherit.

To understand why traditional views of education are increasingly inapplicable to the modern American university, it may be helpful to consider those situations where these views still apply. The concept of socialization, for example, remains useful for analyzing those basic learnings that take place within the family and in primary schools: the acquisition of language, of elementary conceptual ability, of literacy, of fluency with numbers. There is no doubt that what is taught will continue to be applicable to any conceivable future; nor is it difficult to define with some precision what should be learned. Thus, what has been called "primary socialization" occurs and will continue to occur within the family and the primary schools even in a changing and complex society.

The model of socialization also remains relevant to the education of youth in static and simple societies. In most primitive societies, for example, social change occurs slowly and almost imperceptibly, when it occurs at all. In such societies, the wisdom of the past is clearly relevant to the present and future; the skills, life styles, and values that were good enough for a man's father are good enough for him and will be good enough for his children. Such traditional societies are highly resistant to change, and their "higher education" (initiations, age-graded learning, apprenticeships, and so forth) can appropriately consist in teaching youth the traditionally prescribed and socially established ways. Indeed, in most traditional societies, any form of education that leads youth to challenge the established ways only produces misfits.

A second characteristic of most traditional societies is homogeneity, uniformity, and the absence of individual choice. In many primitive societies, for example, there is only one adult role available to each sex: a man must be a hunter or a fisherman or a tiller of the land; a woman must be a wife and mother with prescribed economic duties. Equally important, traditional societies tend to be monolithic in religion, ideology, and life style. The questions "What shall I do with my life?" and "What shall I believe?" are answered before they arise by the wider society, not left up to the choices of the individual. And even in those traditional societies where a variety of adult roles exist, entry into these positions is rarely influenced by the desires of the individual, but is instead dictated by the accidents of birth to clan, caste, and guild. In any society where the options are few or nonexistent, educative agencies can appropriately limit themselves to training youth for the clearly defined slots they will fill as adults. There is no need to assist the young in choosing wisely in societies where they have no choices to make.

Until the relatively recent past—and certainly during the centuries that gave birth to our basic concepts of the functions of education —the model of socialization described relatively adequately the functions of such higher education as existed. But increasingly, in modern American society as in other advanced nations, the preconditions for the validity of this model—an unchanging and homogeneous social order—no longer obtain. In our society, perhaps more than in any other, change is the rule rather than the exception; unlike most traditional peoples, we have learned to welcome eagerly the revolutionary transformations that during the past century have repeatedly altered our physical, technological, social, and moral orders.

Thus, far from being able to predict that the wisdom and skills of the past will continue to be relevant in the future, our best prediction today is that the future will be different from both present and past. Who, a generation ago, could have anticipated the material conditions of life, the social problems, the moral revolutions, the changing values and standards, or the international dilemmas of today? And who can predict the technologies of tomorrow? Which skills, values, outlooks, and information, taught to college students today, will be useful and relevant to them in thirty years? Which job skills dare we uncritically "transmit" to youth? Which perspectives and values can we merely "communicate" in full confidence of their enduring validity?

Nor does modern American society meet the requirement of homogeneity. Indeed, the very term "society"—with its connotations of consistency and coherence—requires major redefinition as we move from the primitive to the modern world. Our social order is stratified, organized, differentiated, and compartmentalized in a hundred ways. Instead of one homogeneous society, we confront highly articulated sets, groupings, classes, regions, enclaves, and clusters of people, who happen to live within the same national boundaries, but who may otherwise possess few common values, patterns of life, and norms of behavior. Even those values once firmly associated with the "American way of life" have been vigorously challenged from within our own society. Indeed, virtually every generalization about America now requires qualification; every rule has its important exception; and every value ardently held by one group is as ardently rejected by another.

Thus, even if our society were unchanging, it would not be clear which subculture higher education is supposed to socialize students to. In *which* world will tomorrow's students live? The white upper middle class of the Eastern seaboard? The bohemian subcultures of New York or San Francisco? The academic environment of the small liberal arts college? The urban Negro ghetto? Clearly the answer will vary from student to student. Or if we consider the traditional function of transmitting values from the past, *which* values do we mean? Those of scientific optimism and progress? The romantic rejection of industrial-technological society? The values of free enterprise? The tradition of protest against social injustice? In our incredibly heterogeneous society, it is no longer possible to define precisely the institutions and values to which youth are to be socialized.

Few would deny that the content of higher education must change in a changing and heterogeneous society. But my argument here implies that in modern technological societies, the functions of education must change as well. Insofar as higher education today is content merely to transmit knowledge to students who are taught to assimilate this knowledge passively, it will prepare a new generation that has absorbed indiscriminately the obsolete along with the enduring. Insofar as research today consists merely of an unselective digging in the past for principles that will be extended automatically into the future, it will often be irrelevant to that future. And insofar as public service is defined to mean the uncritical application of existing techniques to uncritically accepted community goals, the university will fail to serve the community well in the long run. Most important, insofar as higher education encourages in today's students an outlook of acquiescent assimilation, it will fail to prepare them for a modern world in which the ability to examine, evaluate, criticize, and select is a vital necessity.

I am arguing, then, that to the traditional triumvirate of teaching, research, and public service, the function of criticism must be added. To assist the next generation in developing viable life plans, choices, commitments, and values, it is not enough that we present the past on a silver platter. By example and by direct precept, the university must teach its students to become informed, wise, sensitive, and humane critics of their legacy. Learning the facts must be but the preface to examining them critically; assimilating the past, if that past is to be useful, must be followed by analyzing, judging, and selecting the best from it. Indeed, recent years have suggested that many able American students are far ahead of our theories of higher education: they demand the right to criticize, to judge, to select, and to act in accordance with the results of their critical judgment. They insist, with increasing firmness, that their education be relevant to them and to the last third of the twentieth century. A vocal and perceptive minority has begun to point out with increasing indignation the gaps between what our society and our universities practice and what we preach. Although we may at times be distressed by the occasional shallowness of student criticism or embarrassed by its stridency, we cannot hope to silence it. Nor should we try: our task as teachers and administrators should be to ally ourselves with the critical intelligence of our students, demonstrating and teaching that criticism can be informed, wise, and deeply responsible.

Indeed, if any danger faces us, it is not that today's students will become the irresponsible revolutionaries of the next decades, but that through our failure to educate students in the proper and responsible uses of criticism, we will deprive the next generation of a critical intelligence that it will desperately need. The modern world brings with it not only enormous opportunities, but also aggravated problems and terrifying risks. What should concern us most is that we, as educators, may not sufficiently justify and strengthen the critical function of the university and the critical spirit of the young, that we will train a generation blind to the problems and risks of the twentieth and twenty-first centuries. Only if we actively encourage and teach today's students to be intelligent, informed, and selective critics of the modern world and the legacies of the past, will we adequately serve them and our society well.

TIME SPAN, THE NEXT GENERATION, AND THE WIDER SOCIETY

In considering the effects of rapid change and social heterogeneity upon the functions of higher education, I have so far emphasized the increasing importance of teaching a critical and selective stance to today's college students. But the critical function of higher education is by no means exhausted with a consideration of teaching students. On the contrary, over the last decades, American universities have also come to exercise this function in a far more direct way: by collectively acting as the watch-dogs, gadflys, defenders, Jeremiahs, and at times Cassandras of our society. Increasingly, the university has become the prime source of ideas about the nature of our society as a whole and about its future.

One of the distinctive problems confronting modern American society is that of assessing, understanding, evaluating, and guiding the directions of social change. This problem can of course scarcely arise in a static society, which has little need to reflect upon the meaning of change, since change rarely occurs. Nor does the question of who guides social change arise in the same form in planned and totalitarian states, whose political regimes are not subject to moods of the electorate, and where the state is responsible for the shape of change. And even in the emerging nations of the world, the major directions of social change are generally taken from the example of the industrial-technological nations. Our own society, in contrast, has resisted the model of total planning; and, being in the vanguard of technological innovation, we cannot look to other nations for models. Instead, we are committed to the proposition that debate, dialogue, confrontation, disagreement, and vigorous partisanship—coupled with a political system that acts to prevent any one group from remaining entrenched in power for a long period—represent the best way to govern our future destinies. Yet precisely because we have resisted so strongly any governmental efforts to plan and coordinate the directions of social change, the question of who is to assess, evaluate, and attempt to guide the long-range directions of our society has become more urgent. And increasingly, the university has stepped in to provide a much-needed critical commentary upon the transformations of our social order.

In earlier periods of American history, the question "Who is responsible for guiding social change?" was rarely if ever asked. For Americans have traditionally trusted that the logic of expanding industrialism would automatically produce the greatest good for the greatest number; and when undesirable social changes followed in the wake of industrial transformations, they were quickly dismissed as the unavoidable toll of Progress. But in the past three or four decades, it has become apparent that unplanned social revolutions have sometimes been destructive in a way that human intelligence might have prevented or corrected. We have become increasingly aware that the chronic transformations of our society have left a debris of avoidable or remediable social wreckage: the structural exclusion from our affluent society of a significant portion of the poor, the destruction of the core of our major cities, the defacement of the beauty of our countryside, and our frequent involvement in the support of foreign political regimes whose values are antithetical to our own.

In this critical examination of modern society, American universities have quietly but nonetheless decisively assumed the leading role. Higher education has become the chief source of analyses, evaluations, and judgments of our society: our proposals for reform, our critiques and defenses of the *status quo*, our prophecies of doom and our utopias almost invariably originate from the academy. With but few exceptions, our modern vocabulary of social analysis, our rhetoric of social criticism and reform, are the products of higher education. The university has given us our most powerful understandings of American social character, of the economy, of our psychology as a nation. Academics have analyzed emergent patterns of consumption and leisure, the human implications of the technological revolutions of the past decades, and the meaning and portent of our new role in the world. The most cogent voices of criticism, rejection, and protest have emanated from the universities. So, too, the most powerful defenses of American life, of our ideals as a society, and of the viability of our traditions have come from centers of higher education. And university students and teachers have intensified our reluctant awareness of the many discrepancies between the ideals we profess and the way we live.

The reasons for the pre-eminence of higher education as the "critical center" of American society are not difficult to find. The modern university at its best provides a more extended time span and a more inclusive scope of concern than does any other major American institution; and the experience and temperament of the academic community at its best encourages a concern with the next generation and a critical view of the existing society which permits the academic to detach himself from immediate pieties and verities in order to search for more enduring principles and ideals.

Like individuals, social institutions may be thought of as possessing time spans of greater or lesser length and as having scopes of concern that are more or less inclusive. In our society, most institutions are ill-equipped to exercise the critical function with regard to the long-range directions of society as a whole because they are bound by their objectives and their internal arrangements to a short time span and a scope of concern that is restricted to one defined sector of society. Industry and technology, perhaps the prime motors of social change in America, tend to focus on the immediate future of some single area of the economy. Typically, American industries plan no more than five or ten years ahead, basing their plans on short-range projections of supply and demand in one particular economic area. Similarly, political parties, despite their rhetoric of concern for the long-range welfare of our society, tend in practice to emphasize short-range electoral planning (four years and less), and therefore to be minimally effective in exerting long-range strategic influences over society as a whole. Even governmental agencies and regulatory bodies, despite their aim of providing continuity of administration, planning, and control, are generally incapacitated as social analysts, critics, or planners because of their fiscal dependence upon legislative moods and because of their sensitivity to changes in political administrations.

Compared with most other institutions in American society, then, universities more often permit at least some of their members to reflect in a relatively unhampered way upon the long-range meaning and implications of society as a whole. To be sure, universities have short-range and restricted objectives as well: grading students, publishing to avoid perishing, convincing the state legislature that the budget needs to be increased. And the academic may of course define his concerns in a narrow and departmentally limited way; many (perhaps most) academics do. But it is also possible for the university professor to take a broad view, to study the implications of one topic for another, to reflect, analyze, and evaluate in a leisurely and unpressured manner. Furthermore, the attainment of tenure protects the senior faculty member against having a parochial or sectoral definition of his role imposed upon him by external forces. Often sensitized by his professional training to the historical transcience of values and institutions once considered self-evident and eternal, sometimes willing to venture beyond his field to explore other areas, the academic is better placed and more strongly motivated than other comparable professionals in our society to take a long-range view of things and to attempt to understand not only the intricacies of some small microcosm, but the macrocosm of our society and the modern world.

Apart from its relatively long time span and its inclusive scope of concern, the modern American university possesses other characteristics that have made it the chief center of criticism of our society. The motivations and role of the academic profession allow it, when it desires, a more intimate involvement with the next generation than that afforded any other professional group. And to this encounter with youth, the academic brings a critical mind inclined to stand apart from the traditional pieties of any particular embodiment of the community. To be sure, these same qualities often make the academic community appear seditious, disloyal, and dangerous to those who identify themselves with the *status quo*. But these qualities also enable at least some academics, at some times, to put aside the immediate interests of their own position and take time to consider the welfare of the next generation.

Most adults are of course preoccupied with the next generation in one way or another. As parents, we are concerned with our children; and in most vocations, at least some adults undertake to pass on to their juniors the values and standards of their vocation. Yet in most situations, the concern of the older generation for the young is attenuated. Parents are linked to their children not only by concern and identification, but also by ambivalence, frustration, disappointment, and hurt, which may impede understanding and sympathy. Similarly, in most American occupations, a sense of responsibility to the next generation is often balanced or outweighed by an even greater sense of obligation to the previous generation, as embodied by the boss, the board of directors, or the traditions of the occupation. Indeed, in much of American society, the young and the old meet largely on the latter's terms: the new generation must accommodate itself to that which preceded it.

It sometimes happens in universities, however, that the relative weight of the younger generation is increased. At least some academics have chosen their vocation because they have a special concern with youth, and this concern sensitizes them to those they teach. It is not always mere lip service when academics comment on how much they learn from their students; nor is it an accident that the most accurate characterizations of today's youth often come from their teachers. Between teachers and their students, there can exist deep but generally unstated ties of understanding, sympathy, and identification. In recent years these ties have been reflected in the frequency with which faculty members have allied themselves with dissenting students and in the reluctance of students to attack openly their teachers. Whatever the actual merits of the case, it is the administration, not the faculty, that must generally bear the brunt of student dissatisfaction.

One reason for this bond between academics and their students is that the teacher must depend upon his students for a part of his self-justification. Insofar as he attempts to judge the fruitfulness of his efforts, a teacher must look to the future activities of the next generation, rather than his own. Thus, while his research and his services to the community may be important sources of professional esteem, the academic also looks toward the young to justify him. Whether he defines his goals narrowly, as reproducing his own academic kind, or broadly, as attempting to prepare youth to live wisely in an unknown future, his judgments of his own success as a teacher will depend upon the quality of his students' lives.

The academic vocation also allows—indeed demands of—the teacher an intensive exposure to those whom he seeks to educate. And it requires considerable imperviousness to remain unaware of the very real differences between this student generation and those which preceded it. Many faculty members *are* that impervious; but others are able to perceive the changing outlooks and needs of college students. Some of what the academic sees in his students is, of course, all too familiar from the years of his own late adolescence and early adulthood. But today, much of what he sees is also unfamiliar, and his vicarious participation in the outlooks of his students permits him to see the modern world not only through his own eyes, but through the eyes of his students as well. This "double vision" in turn creates at least in some members of the academic community a special preoccupation with the world in which their students will live, a heightened sensitivity to the factors that will help determine the options, resources, and dilemmas that will confront their students as adults, and a strengthened investment in guaranteeing that the society they will live in is adequate to their needs and potentialities. This intensified concern contributes to the American university's willingness to examine critically the direction and the future shape of our society.

Finally, the university's assumption of a critical role vis-à-vis American society is related to the intellectual style and outlook of those who choose an academic vocation. A generation of research has shown a distinctive correlation between antiauthoritarianism, the possession of a critical mind, and the choice of an academic career. The extent of this correlation is daily witnessed in the skeptical and iconoclastic outlook of many of the teachers and scholars who inhabit major university centers. More than other professionals, such men and women are disposed to challenge authoritative views, to trust the power of reason in ameliorating human difficulties, to identify with the underdog rather than the powerful, to favor a complex view of the world, and to question any solution that presents itself as beyond question.

The possession of such a temperament inclines a young man toward an academic vocation and, once he has chosen this vocation, constitutes an effective instrument in its pursuit. The critical atmosphere of many major universities serves to reinforce this temperament and the outlooks that it engenders; and the willingness of many American universities to defend the academic freedom of their students and faculty members has protected academics, more than any other group, from community pressures toward conformity and uncritical acquiescence. The scholarly pursuits of the academic tend also to reinforce and strengthen his critical perspective, pushing him beyond the immediate opinions of his time and place and often increasing his sense that the norms embodied in any historical community are relative.

In stressing the qualifications of the American university in exercising the critical function, I do not mean to deny its disabilities. For example, the university's long time span with regard to our society is rarely coupled with an equal time span vis-à-vis its own organizational needs: industry undoubtedly does a much better job than higher education in planning for its own future. And the university's potential for a broad scope of concern is often vitiated by departmental parochialism: thus, academics who might otherwise venture beyond their own disciplines are commonly restrained by the fear of provoking jurisdictional disputes or inspiring the derision of their colleagues. Furthermore, although the academic world is relatively protected against community pressures, the university can generate its own internal pressures toward conformity: for example, an implicit demand for uncritical rejection of the *status quo;* an unthinking attribution of all evil to University Hall, the Governor's Mansion, or the White House; an unexamined attitude of intellectual self-righteousness. But despite all its many disabilities, the American university has in the past decades shown itself capable, at least at some times and in some places, of a more sustained social analysis, criticism, and commentary than any other institution in American life.

Similarly, in underlining the critical temperament of academics, I do not mean to suggest that all faculty members are equally endowed with critical minds, much less that the academic is characterized by a sweet reasonableness. Nor do I mean to dismiss the valid criticisms frequently made of the "academic mind" and the "academic liberal." To those of us who pride ourselves on being members of the academic community, it is chastening to recall that the term "academic" is usually preceded by the word "merely": all too often, our views are in fact trivial, irrelevant, superficial, or uninformed. And surely, only a minority of academics are as sensitive to the needs and outlooks of their students as those I have described. But I do mean to suggest that during the past decades, American universities have gathered within their protective boundaries an unusual number of men and women whose temperaments and outlooks incline them to view the contemporary community and the modern world in a critical rather than an acquiescent spirit, and that this concentration of critical minds in the modern university helps explain its pre-eminent role as critic of our society.

In brief, then, the institution of higher education in America has become the major source of analysis, commentary, critique, defense, and reform in our society. It has come to occupy this position partly in response to our growing awareness that the unexamined and unguided logic of technological change has not automatically produced a humane, decent, beautiful, and just society or world. Compared with other institutions in America, higher education allows its members an unusual freedom to consider the long-range trends of society in a broad and inclusive perspective. Compared with other professionals, university teachers are likely to be particularly sensitive to and concerned with the next generation and with the social and human preconditions for their welfare. By temperament, academics are inclined toward skepticism, toward questioning, toward the examination of what has been given, and toward faith in the powers of human intelligence to resolve human problems. For all these reasons, then, the modern American university has become the prime critic of our society.

WHO IS TO CRITICIZE WHAT?

Even if we grant that the American university's exercise of the critical function is valid and essential both with regard to students and with regard to the wider society, the important practical questions still remain. Who is to criticize what? Should individual universities align themselves with particular critiques of the wider society or become lobbyists for social reform? In what circumstances is criticism legitimate, and by whom? Are there no limits on the exercise of the critical function? Should not the university be objective rather than partisan?

To clarify these questions, we must distinguish among three meanings of the term " the university," for according to our definitions, our answers will differ. First, we may think of "the university" as equivalent to "higher education": that is, as a social institution on a par with other major institutions like the family, the law, and industry. In my comments so far, I have largely been referring to the university in this institutional sense. But second, we may think of the "university" as the university community, the students, faculty members, administrators, and others who are associated with particular universities. In this sense, the university consists of the group of individuals who are united by the fact that they hold roles in a special kind of organization. And finally, we may think of "the university" as a particular organization—as Eastern Michigan University, the University of Mississippi, Johns Hopkins University. In this sense, a university contains an administrative structure, carries on relations with other organizations, has financial needs, sets admissions standards, hires faculty members, and so forth.

I have tried to make clear my reasons for arguing that the university as a social institution—higher education in America—not only does but should exercise a critical function in educating students and in commenting on the wider society. And in defining the critical function, I have noted that its exercise entails not only "objective" analyses of existing institutions, values, and practices, but the evaluation, judgment, rejection, and acceptance of what exists, coupled frequently with a commitment to alternatives to the *status quo*. In this sense, then, if the critical function is to be exercised by higher education, it entails the possibility that students and faculty members will make commitments, pass judgments, and carry on activities which will be taken as partisan. Thus, to justify the critical function, we must be prepared to justify its inevitable corollaries—evaluation, judgment, and commitment to action: to do otherwise would be to make criticism merely "academic" in the worst sense of the term. As one of the major social institutions in modern American society, then, the university must be critical, and that includes the right to be partisan.

I have also indicated my conviction that the members of the

University community not only have made but must continue to make critical contributions to our society. To be sure, the rights to analyze critically, to evaluate, to defend and oppose, to propose and reject, to campaign for and against are not limited to members of the academic community; they are rights that we possess simply by virtue of our citizenship in a democracy. But for reasons I have attempted to explain, members of the university community are disposed to exercise these rights with special vehemence and vigor and with results that are very much to the long-range advantage of our society.

The university as an organization, however, is in a very different position. As organizations, universities should act primarily to protect and promote the major functions of the institution of higher education: teaching, research, public service, and criticism. Thus, the tasks of the individual university as an organization must be distinguished sharply from the functions of higher education, that is, the university as an institution: the main task of the former is to maintain a climate in which, among other things, the critical spirit can flourish. If individual universities as organizations were to align themselves officially with specific critical positions, their ability to defend the critical function itself would be undermined. Acting as a lobby or pressure group for some particular judgment or proposal, a university in effect closes its doors to those whose critical sense leads them to disagree, and thus destroys itself as an environment in which the critical spirit can truly flourish. The task of a university as an organization, then, is to be neutral, objective, and dispassionate in order to preserve an atmosphere in which students and faculty members can discuss, evaluate, criticize, judge, commit themselves, and, when they choose, act.

This view implies that the university as an organization should not take upon itself the burden of enforcing community laws and standards. To be sure, members of the university are members of the wider community and are subject to its laws, just as they are free to strive to change these laws. But if the university as an organization implements or enforces community codes and regulations, acting as a substitute for law enforcement agencies, it assumes functions that are not properly those of higher education. One of the many disadvantages of the *in loco parentis* doctrine is that, under the guise of protecting students, it identifies the university as an organization with a particular set of community values, and thus, once again, closes its doors to those who would question or reject these values. Similarly, for the university as an organization to align itself with the deprecation or rejection of community values would undermine the free expression of those whose critical judgment leads them to stand staunchly behind these values.

In one respect, however, the university as an organization must be vigorously partisan and committed: to the defense of its right to exercise its own proper functions. A university must insist vigorously on its freedom to teach students what is known, to confront them with multiple viewpoints (that is, to a variety of distinct partisanships), to encourage them to reflect upon, analyze, and criticize what they learn. It must forthrightly justify the freedom of its faculty members to pursue their researches without community harassment, wherever these researches may lead. It must insist upon its own authority to decide when service to the community is consistent with its other goals. And, perhaps most important today, it must adamantly resist all efforts to limit the freedom of students and faculty members as individuals to comment upon, evaluate, criticize, and attempt to change the surrounding world. Specifically, this entails defending the rights of faculty members to hold deviant views and propose unpopular actions, of students to comment on off-campus issues and take part in off-campus causes, and of both students and faculty to mount action that overflows the ivied walls of the academy. In all these respects, the university qua organization should be a partisan proponent of the unencumbered exercise of its own functions and of the rights of its members.

Furthermore, each university has the obvious right to regulate its own internal affairs. Like any organization, a university must have standards regarding the quality of its efforts: of teaching, research, public service, and criticism. It has the right to demand honesty and decency from its members. It has the obligation to insist upon high standards of attainment and integrity from students and faculty members. It must attempt to develop patterns of self-government that embody within the university the ideals of free inquiry, discussion, and criticism. And inevitably, universities will differ, depending upon their traditions and circumstances, in their definitions of decency, in their standards of attainment, and in the ways they choose to govern themselves. But in this regard, it is easiest to err in the direction of excessive limitation, to be unduly fearful of the consequences of freedom. The steady movement toward allowing students more meaningful self-regulation and more consequential self-government, for example, has not brought with it chaos or license, but rather growing opportunities for responsible self-control.

In contrasting the generally neutral or objective position of the university qua organization with the critical and at times partisan stance that should be encouraged in students and faculty members, I do not mean to suggest that university administrators are condemned to a passive role. I began by noting the prevailing neglect or defensive slighting of the critical function of the modern American university. Partly because the critical function is unpopular with certain segments of the public, and partly because our theories of the university do not do justice to the realities of modern American higher education, the public has not learned to understand the contributions made by the university's exercise of its critical function. Particularly in a time like our own, with its strong pressures for unanimity, its frequent equation of criticism with treason, and its discomfort at the vociferous dissent of an able minority of today's students and faculty, the justification of the rights of higher education and of the university community to teach, inquire, serve, and criticize freely requires active commitment, missionary zeal, and higher persuasiveness from the spokesmen for the university.

Increasingly, then, the critical function must be added to the traditional triumvirate of teaching, research, and public service. Criticism must be seen not as the price to be paid for the services of higher education, but as one of the most crucial of these services. As our century progresses, as our society and the world become more complex, as the pace of social change accelerates, higher education that is not eminently critical will be increasingly useless. More and more, our society and the world will need young men and women who have not only assimilated the past and made themselves familiar with the present, but who have also become articulate, informed, and thoughtful critics of both, and in this measure have qualified themselves to create the world of the future. By teaching, embodying, and expressing the critical spirit, the American university will continue to contribute to our society's capacity for self-understanding and self-renewal.

Responsibility for Criticism And Social Change

FREDERIC W. NESS, PAUL DANISH,
NEIL O. DAVIS

Criticism Should Begin at Home

FREDERIC W. NESS

READING DR. KENISTON'S PAPER, I was reminded of the account of the wide-eyed lady who declared to Thomas Carlyle that she was willing to accept the universe. "Madam," he replied, "you had better." In similar spirit, I accept Dr. Keniston's major premise. He leaves me little choice! But in accepting it, particularly in my role as representative of the college administrator's viewpoint, I cannot ignore a minor uneasiness: If we in universities and colleges are, in fact, to serve as critics of our society—and it is implied that we may be its last ray of hope—I have difficulty in concluding that we are now equipped for the job.

Dr. Keniston presents a challenge which none of us can ignore. In nearly every phase of our lives, the facts of social change are overwhelming. But can we of academia function as effective critics of society unless or until we have become demonstrably self-critical, unless there is far more evidence of clear-eyed self-appraisal? I suggest that we should examine our own capabilities before we undertake the distractions of partisanship in external affairs.

We have at least three preliminary responsibilities before we accept the assignment of social critic. First, we must look objectively at our own prejudices as they relate to our obligations to a changing society. Second, we must appraise our capabilities for adjustment to rapidly evolving educational needs. And, third, we must establish standards for, if not limitations to, the exercise of our social involvement.

As for the first, we academics, as a profession, often instinctively

164

devote more attention to protecting our stewardship than to criticizing or enhancing its quality. Our negligence in developing really effective means for evaluating the quality of instruction is a case in point. Further, certain peripheral concerns of the academic marketplace, particularly in our universities, so transcend the traditional functions of college faculty that their effect is to produce deep-seated frustration on the part of those who turn to us for instruction. The gulf between faculty and administration—and I must point out that it yawns visibly even in Dr. Keniston's presentation—signals a prejudice antithetical to the most effective functioning of an academic community. And finally, under this first point, Dr. Keniston's claim for our status as a special group, somehow or other set apart from the general community, would seem to work against our acceptability as the primary critics of society.

To take the second point: Criticism should begin at home. Thus, it is vital that we—as a profession, as representatives of particular institutions, and as individual teachers and administrators—scrupulously examine our capabilities to adjust to the evolving educational needs of our society. There is little evidence that we are serious about improving our productive capacities in the face of tremendously enlarged and changing demands, that we are adequately planning for the future. Our faculty specialists provide highly rewarding consultative services to business and industry, and yet our own institutional management too often leaves much to be desired. Could we, if called upon—and we are being called upon—fully justify, through the quantity and quality of our efforts, the massive expenditures of public and private funds now being channelled into higher education? Since the probable fate of the critic is to be criticized, we should demonstrate our ability to adjust while, if not before, we demand changes of the society that we serve.

The third domestic responsibility we face is equally important and I mention it with some understanding of its delicacy. Dr. Keniston rightly points out that, to be effective social critics, we are obliged, as a social institution, to be partisan. But is there no point at which we, as a community of scholars, should feel obliged to say that some of our colleagues may be going too far in their practice of the critical function? Do we better serve the long-range interests of a free society by being tolerant of all displays of errant taste and faulty judgment or by occasionally insisting upon the exercise of restraint and responsibility? Recognizing that lines are excruciatingly difficult to draw here and that eliciting majority opinion can be a traumatic experience does not necessarily invalidate the question. (Ironically, the mores of the faculty seem to dictate a self-imposed deportment which requires greater restraint from those who might disagree with the advocates of change than from the advocates themselves.)

In this same connection, we must be constantly vigilant against the temptation to confuse our professorship with our citizenship, a distinction which *we* may understand but which involves a subtlety increasingly beyond the comprehension of the wider community. Further, the fact that we are more highly trained than the majority of our fellow citizens makes it all the more important that we support our opinions by fact and temper them with scholarly self-criticism.

If we project ourselves as critics of society, a re-examination of the concept of academic freedom and responsibility will be imminent. Already some of our colleagues use the campus as a medieval sanctuary from which they can safely mount attacks upon the *status quo*, thus assuming the provision of more liberty than may have been intended by the doctrine of academic freedom, and perhaps more than society, to which we must ultimately be accountable, will be willing to grant.

I would offer two final observations which are relevant to Dr. Keniston's argument and to my own tentative caveats. First, I believe that he was a little cavalier in evaluating the administrator's role. At the very least, we would seem to need him, in his new university function, as a consensus-taker. Moreover, as the person who stands in the demilitarized zone between college and community, and who, we hope, deserves his slightly elevated status, the administrator is the institutional representative who generally perceives the consequences and all too often pays the price of an outburst of unsophisticated criticism or intemperate action by his colleagues. Accordingly, it is the administrator who, perhaps covertly, must insist on the kind of internal self-criticism that is essential if the institution is to justify its place as critic of society.

Admittedly, my entire case is patently weak. The ineluctable fact is that the social ills which we must help correct through criticism have such urgency that the precautionary measures I have suggested represent a luxury that we can ill afford. It would be unwise if not immoral for the academic community—with its tremendous intellectual capacity—to withdraw into introspection and self-appraisal and not be counted among the vanguard of those who would effect constructive social change. I am, nevertheless, firmly committed to the view that our very special abilities and our unique place in society oblige us, like Caesar's wife, to hold ourselves as much above reproach as humanly possible. This necessity demands a degree of self-criticism which I could wish were currently more manifest.

Today's Students as Critics

PAUL DANISH

I FIND MYSELF in almost complete agreement with Dr. Keniston's analysis of the critical function of the university. Rather than offer a critique of a paper in which I find little to fault, therefore, I would like to present some thoughts on a related question: the role of the student as critic both within the academic community and as a representative of that community in society.

That today's student is a critic cannot be doubted. "Berkeley" has become a household word as a synonym for protest; deans who, three years ago, categorically stated "It can't happen here" are bracing themselves for the next onslaught; an article on the Generation Gap is guaranteed to sell a million copies of any magazine turned on enough to groove with it; and a growing cadre of retired student activists have embarked on highly promising careers as consultants on youth affairs to the Establishment. It should be abundantly clear by now that, in recent years, the prevailing climate of American student opinion has shifted in the direction of partisan criticism, social involvement, and political (as opposed to syndicalist) protest.

There are any number of concrete manifestations of this shift. The significance of student involvement in civil rights and the rise of the New Left are by now clichés, but their import remains. Less well known are such developments as increasing resistance to the corporate recruiter on the campus, the growing number of student-initiated experiments in educational reform, the decline of fraternities, and the end of the age of innocence in student government. Further, it would be facile to dismiss as escapist such phenomena as the rise of the psychedelic subculture and the advent of the gifted dropout. What all of these manifestations collectively indicate, I submit, is that students—both individually and as a class—are developing a much more critical style of life. The sooner educators face this fact directly (instead of trying to cope with it on a year-to-year basis), the happier everyone will be.

None of these points are particularly original, and an elaborate discussion of causes at this point would probably be even less so. Indeed, the subject long ago succumbed to overkill in both the scholarly and the popular press. Because a post-mortem is expected, however, it might be profitable to make a few random observations about the new conditions, their meaning, and their consequences.

THE INTERPRETATION OF STUDENT ACTIVISM

First, it is no accident that so many campus insurrections have centered around the joint questions of free speech and civil liberties. The attenuated state of basic human rights in the student community may have been tolerable when the college experience was a two- to four-year apprenticeship for the Establishment, but such conditions no longer prevail. America is rapidly approaching universal higher education, on the one hand, and increasing numbers of students are committing themselves to lengthy courses of graduate study, on the other. As a result, one's years in college can no longer be viewed as an initiation period for the power elite; indeed, the student comes to view his college days as an open-ended period of custodialization with no honorable conclusion in sight. In such circumstances, it is absurd to expect students to wait until graduation in order to assume full political rights. The student concludes that he who counsels patience has some ulterior motive, and since such counsel usually comes from those directly involved in institutional politics, this conclusion is eminently reasonable.

Second, entirely too much emphasis has been placed on student stress as a cause of campus unrest. It is often contended today that the political issues around which student upheavals swirl are really no more than flash points which ignite much more deep-seated grievances. In such an analysis, the freedom-of-the-forum issues at Berkeley three years ago are viewed as no more the cause of the subsequent disturbances than the assassination of the Archduke is considered the cause of The Great War. This is a seductive proposition, but it simply isn't true. Generally speaking, the causes of campus unrest are those which are explicitly stated by the restless. In other words, I am suggesting that depersonalization, alienation, and anxiety are not the stuff that demonstrations are made of; they are the symptoms of good, old-fashioned political suppression, which people are going to chafe under regardless of what name it goes by. When Thomas Jefferson drafted the Declaration, he was trying to get rid of a tyranny that—in the context of his times—had become intolerable; he was not trying to solve an identity crisis. I submit the same applies to the students at Berkeley in 1964 and at the dozens of campuses that subsequently experienced similar difficulties.

Third, as the foregoing analysis suggests, those who would interpret student political grievances as demands for more individual attention may be building for disaster. If "more individual attention" is ultimately interpreted as the imposition of the overprogramed sterility of secondary education on the universities, the reaction is going to be much more militant student demand for autonomy than anything we have yet experienced. What students are asking for today is the right to run their own lives, make their own decisions, and commit their own blunders. Those demands cannot be met by extending adolescence for another five years under the guise of humanitarianism.

Fourth, as Dr. Keniston has correctly observed, "it is the administration and not the faculty that must generally bear the brunt of student dissatisfaction." This is so for the obvious reason that the administration is the cause of most of it. The overwhelming majority of student grievances are the direct result of administrative, not academic, action. Let there be no mistake: the name of the game is still paternalism and all the arbitrary action and puerile authoritarianism that it implies. This is not to say that students don't have complaints with academic policy; far from it. A full share of the controversy has centered on publish-or-perish, required courses, pass-fail grading, teacher evaluation, and so on. But whatever the fallibilities of the faculty, it does not, as a rule, elevate the casual disregard of civil liberties and the abrogation of basic political rights to the level of a major premise. Further, its abuses are confined to the classroom; the administration's can occur anywhere, any time, and in connection with any aspect of human behavior. In one remarkable case, administrative disciplinary procedures were initiated against students for conduct which took place during a vacation, 1500 miles from the campus and 700 miles on the other side of an international border. For some reason, educators find it exceedingly difficult to grasp the fact that most student dissent is politically motivated and oriented. In other words, many of the hangups that are usually attributed to anonymity, anxiety, and Oedipus are really the work of LBJ and the dean of men. Although it might be unduly optimistic, I find the proposition that the administration erred in many of its decisions a much more acceptable explanation for the upsurge of student dissent than the contention that a generation of students is allegedly too fragile to stand the buffetings of an allegedly neurotic society.

Fifth, when the student assumes the mantle of the critic, he is going to be a partisan critic. I think it is fair to say that, even if such a thing as purely objective criticism exists, the American student has little interest in aspiring to it. The reason for this disenchantment with even the ideal of the objective critic is, I think, a generational antipathy to what might be called the "Kerr-McNamara Syndrome": the ability to predict the tragic consequences of a particular course of action and then to embark on it and follow it to its predicted conclusion. Dr. Kerr presented a brilliant analysis of developments in the modern university in his book, *The Uses of the University,* during the course of which he suggested that certain trends keep the undergraduates in a state of incipient revolt. He then pursued the policies he described and watched his campus crumble into chaos. Mr. McNamara meticulously predicted the results—or lack of them—of aerial warfare against North Vietnam in 1965, but, nonetheless, it was under his stewardship that this particularly military strategem was executed. If objectivity requires that the critic stand by while clearly incorrect policies are implemented (or even take part in their implementation), then I submit the American student wants no part of objectivity. Such objectivity, apart from raising serious ethical questions, would destroy his critical credibility and reduce the whole process of criticism to an utterly futile form of intellectual masturbation. If one's criticism is to be taken seriously, one's actions must be compatible with its conclusions. The student critic would seem to have little esteem indeed for the intellect that can ignore itself and blandly term the process "objectivity." A far more laudable goal for the critical scholar is partisanship and fairness. One can be fair and still have taste.

THE UNIVERSITY'S ROLE

What all of this suggests, of course, is that the university must devise a new relationship between itself and its student body, a relationship that is substantively different from anything that has served in the past. To observe that such a change is necessary hardly requires much vision; with projected enrollments passing nine million in 1975, with hundreds of thousands of students entering four- to six-year programs of graduate study, with a million returning veterans pushing up the average age of the freshman class, and with increasing numbers of middle-aged adults returning to the campus, it would be the height of fantasy to suppose that the higher learning could continue to operate on the proposition that its main mission is to provide a paternalistic apprenticeship for a socioeconomic elite. Students everywhere are subjecting their lives and their communities to more critical re-examinations than ever before. In America, almost by definition, the student's life revolves around the university. It is utter folly to assume his milieu will escape his critical attention.

Indeed, it would be most unfortunate if the university attempted to avoid such attention. Apart from the fact that any serious attempt to do so would unleash seriously disruptive forces in the academic community, such an evasion would waste a tremendously important educational opportunity. There can be little argument against the proposition that the college is a place of socialization. Socialization for life in a pluralistic society, however, is a matter of developing critical faculties, a process which can proceed in many ways, but which is inherently contradictory to the conceptualization of the student as a passive receptacle at the end of a conveyor belt of prepackaged wisdom and skills. Freedom cannot be taught with a whip, unless one considers goading a man into revolution a legitimate educational objective. It must be lived to be learned.

Specifically, students must be given a maximum amount of discretion in making the decisions which affect their educations. Major areas of policy and decision making must be marked out where students, either individually or collectively, have final authority. Such standbys as giving students advisory roles on university policy-making bodies are wholly inadequate. A much more constructive approach would be to give the administration such a role in extracurricular and cocurricular matters. The removal of police powers from the administration in these sectors could be of advantage to the administration, too, for it is functionally impossible to be a counselor and a cop at the same time. Students must be allowed to make their own mistakes.

In dealing with student criticism, the administration has only one prescriptive duty—to assure that the wellsprings of debate are not poisoned. Its job is to stop those who would prevent others from participating in the critical dialogue and to encourage all to participate. In order to perform this role, the administrator must hold equal protection to be the paramount administrative virtue. In concrete terms, this means that the University of California was wrong in barring off-campus peace groups while allowing the Marines to recruit and that students are equally wrong if they block access to a military recruiter. All too often, unfortunately, political considerations tempt the administrator to deal swiftly with inequities of the latter kind while winking at those of the former. He who values the development of the critical process as an educational objective cannot afford to do this.

It is my contention, then, that the university should encourage partisan criticism on the part of its students and that it should provide an environment in which it can flourish. It should encourage criticism because that is a condition of human freedom, and it should encourage partisanship in criticism because that is a condition of ethical development. It must also take steps to check those who would stifle the critical dialogue—whether they are demagogues in the polity, authoritarians in the bureaucracy, or ideologues in the student body. To assume such a position will by no means be easy; change never is, and, as a people, we seem to be developing a progressive distaste for conscious change. (On this point I disagree with Dr. Keniston. I think a convincing argument can be made for the contention that rather than welcoming change, American society is apt to stumble forward every time it's pushed.) Nonetheless, the rewards of assuming a new position are great, and the perils of not doing so are greater. As society becomes more organized, its members must become more critical, or freedom, individuality, and life itself will lose its meaning. Non-critical man is definitely a convenience in terms of efficiency; he doesn't make much trouble, and he doesn't cost very much to maintain. But, he isn't worth a hell of a lot either. The critical man can be invaluable, for only he possesses the necessary preconditions of creativity, both social and technological. Unfortunately, he is expensive, wasteful, inefficient, recalcitrant, irreverent, generally cussed, and incredibly noisy. Still in all, a higher decibel level among the undergraduates seems a small price to pay for the future.

The University Must Speak Up!

NEIL O. DAVIS

I AGREE WITH Professor Keniston's thesis that criticism is and must be a major function of American higher education and that the colleges and universities form the "critical center" of American society. Nor can I take exception, in theory at least, to any of his other arguments.

Harvard President Nathan M. Pusey has said:

> Simply stated, Harvard's purpose is to conduct research and to produce a continuing flow of highly trained people for a wide variety of careers; though at the college level, it is perhaps rather simply to provide rich opportunity to select individuals for intellectual and personal growth. ... But if we look more closely, surely we must agree it is more than this. Can it indeed be anything less than to contribute to the best of our ability to the furtherance of civilized life?

Reminding us that "civilization continues a precarious existence," Dr. Pusey lists a "formidable array of threatening problems" which include poverty, overpopulation, resurgent nationalism, cultural conflict, war, and ill health. The university, obviously, is obligated to train minds and skills to deal with these problems. But, and perhaps every bit as important, its job is to furnish light, leadership, and informed criticism as solutions to problems are devised.

In my part of the country, the university community too long remained timid about speaking out on the issue of racial injustice. Not even today does a very large or impressive segment of it say much about white supremacy and other myths prevalent in and afflicting our nation. Too often, the politician intones shibboleths concerning human relations, political problems, and great moral issues, while remaining untouched by the public examination and analysis that only the university can provide.

The university must speak up. It must be free to examine, experiment, teach, and inform the broader society outside the ivied walls. It must speak critically whenever and wherever appropriate. Objective criticism is the ideal, but the university ought to admit that, in projecting and defending values, it must make judgments, and when this happens, partisanship rears its head.

Emphasis needs to be given to Professor Keniston's perceptive distinctions: the university as social institution (higher education), the university as a community of scholars, students, and administrators, and the university as a particular organization. The disgruntled alumnus and the outraged politician is seldom interested in making such distinctions, and even those who try to do so have difficulty in drawing the lines clearly. Indeed, a major obstacle to the university's assumption of the critical function is the problem of identifying these three universities to the public. How do you make the unhappy legislator or prominent donor understand the difference between the university speaking as a particular organization, and as a group of teachers and students? It is crucial that the public understand this distinction, for it is one thing to take high ground and lay down the principle of freedom and quite another to deal with the Wallaces and the Women for Constitutional Government.

It seems to me that the university community has not yet devised a strategy to have its cake and eat at least a piece of it too. May I suggest one?

The university has the responsibility, first, to provide a strong base of academic excellence on which every activity operates and is judged. A professor speaks with considerably more authority and freedom if he comes from an institution of recognized high merit. A trustee representing a prestigious institution finds it much easier to defend the principles of free inquiry and free criticism than does his counterpart from a college or university that the public considers mediocre.

The average trustee knows far too little about the institution he represents. And how can he defend what he does not know? Generally, administrators have made little effort to inform the trustee about academic principles, programs, and aims. His support, more often than not, is courted on the basis of nostalgic loyalty, rather than on educated understanding and conviction.

Nor do very many educational institutions seem to think it is important to inform the opinion-maker, be he politician, banker, or labor leader. Some of the larger staffs with the most generous budgets are to be found in university public relations offices which generally limit their activities to sending out news releases having to do with campus queen contests, the exploits of the athletic teams, and student elections. Infrequently do these offices bring to the campus representatives of the various public and private interests to hear and participate in seminars having to do with social issues or the eternal truths. Public awareness of what the university is for and what it is doing leaves much to be desired.

Perhaps more important than any of these considerations is the university's obligation to be a university in truth as well as name. This stand calls for conviction and courage. A long time ago, at the outset of the Scopes case debate, the editor of *The Montgomery Advertiser*, later to be a Pulitzer Prize winner for his attacks on the Ku Klux Klan, approached a public university president and expressed enthusiasm over the opportunity that the institution had to make a real contribution by bringing scientific light to the shrill and heated discussion in Alabama. The embarrassed president replied that his university had enough problems without becoming embroiled in the evolution controversy. From that day, the editor, not a college man himself, had no use for that president or even for higher education.

It is often difficult, of course, for a university to take a stand. But the administrator will find it much easier to do so when his institution has built on the rock of academic excellence and has kept its governing board and the public informed about institutional goals, accomplishments, and future possibilities.

Finally, while failure to speak—even when explained as strategy— can hardly be encouraged, sometimes a proper posture can be silence. In several instances, leaders in higher education in the South spoke eloquently without uttering a word when, despite being under strong pressures from political officers to denounce school desegregation guidelines, they chose instead to say nothing. Their silence, by contrast with frenetic statements from governors and others, made the point.

W. ALLEN WALLIS

Institutional Coherence
And Priorities

To say that a college or university has coherence is to say that there is an intellectual pattern to its activities. Its curricula may all be projections from a central core, carrying the essence of the core concepts further in special directions. They may all be foundation stones that support a central, overarching school or department. They may reflect a common method of study, or a common point of view, or concern with a common problem. They may represent an elaborate interweaving of subjects. An institution may be said to be coherent when each part has a close intellectual relationship with several other parts, and through them with all other parts.

The distinction between a coherent and a noncoherent or conglomerate university is not unlike that between a corporation whose products are related in their manufacture, distribution, or consumption, and a corporation that is simply a collection of businesses whose only relation is that they are owned by a single holding company.

My own institution, the University of Rochester, illustrates the difference: at some stages of its history, it has been coherent, at other stages, conglomerate, and today it has elements of both at once. It was founded in 1850 as a small, private, nonsectarian, liberal arts college for men. Under the influence of a local lady, Susan B. Anthony, it became coeducational in 1900, but otherwise it remained unchanged until about the time of the first world war. Then within a decade the Eastman School of Music, the College of Medicine and Dentistry, and the Memorial Art Gallery in Rochester were all founded and placed under the university's charter. But because they made little impact on one another or on the original College of Arts and Science, these acquisitions constituted, in effect, a conglomerate university, not unified

even by a common heating system (in Hutchins' figure), for only the
Art Gallery and the college were located together. During the next
forty years, this conglomeration evolved into a coherent institution as
first the biological and physical sciences and then the humanities and
social sciences developed faculties and graduate programs comparable
to those in medicine and music, and as these separate parts were con-
solidated geographically. Even today, however, the institution retains
some degree of conglomerateness, in that the School of Music, the
Art Gallery, and the humanities departments are at different locations.

Coherence in a college or university is created, maintained, and
strengthened by giving a consistently high priority to those goals that
promote coherence. On the one hand, energetic efforts are made to
fill in gaps and to round out programs that will increase coherence; on
the other hand, opportunities are grasped or spurned according to
whether they create coherence or conglomerateness.

Although coherence has obvious merits, one should not presume
that it is always preferable to conglomerateness. There are at least two
situations where conglomerateness contributes much to a university.

The first, which again may be illustrated by the history of the
University of Rochester, is related to long-range growth. Had
Rochester, at the time of World War I, rejected the colleges of music
and medicine and the Art Gallery (as, indeed, in the nineteenth century it had rejected engineering) on the grounds that they were not
compatible with the small-scale, undergraduate, liberal arts education
to which the so-called university was then confined, the subsequent
development from what was actually a college to a university in fact
as well as in name would have been most difficult, and this development, as I have argued elsewhere,[1] was essential if the institution was
to achieve a significant role at a high level of quality.

Conglomerateness is also desirable in situations where an institution has exclusive responsibility for the higher education of a certain
constituency (usually political, as a state or city, but possibly religious, ethnic, or occupational). In such cases, one of the institution's
most useful functions is to serve any of its constituency's legitimate
interests in higher education that are not being met elsewhere, regardless of whether the resulting institution maintains its close intellectual coherence. Indeed, it is perhaps fair to criticize certain
public institutions on the grounds that they are so concerned with
academic coherence—with institutional image—that they fail in their
responsibility to render services not otherwise available to their con-

    [1] Wallis, "The Plight of the Small College," *Atlantic Monthly*, November
1965, pp. 124–26; Letter to the Editor, *Atlantic Monthly*, March 1966, p. 50.

stituents; they seem bent more on emulating the most prestigious private institutions than on serving the unmet needs of their citizens.

The notion that each university can have its own institutional coherence, and its own set of priorities which derive from and contribute to that coherence, presupposes a variety of academic freedoms. These seem all to be diminishing. As they dwindle, universities are likely to have less control over their own priorities; consequently, conglomerateness is likely to prevail over coherence, both within institutions and among them. The fact that lip service to academic freedom is increasing should not be allowed to obscure the fact that academic freedom itself may be waning.

THE ABSENCE OF FREE SPEECH ON CAMPUSES TODAY

Consider, for example, one of the most basic of academic freedoms, freedom to present controversial views on the campus. On few campuses in America today does such freedom truly exist. Stokely Carmichael can speak without hindrance, but George Wallace creates so grave a threat of disorder as to preclude the possibility that he would be listened to calmly and fairly. Senator Fulbright would be given a respectful hearing on any campus; few would dare invite Secretary McNamara, since his appearance would almost certainly precipitate tensions, probably protests, and possibly disorders that would prevent free and open discussion. Timothy Leary enjoys freedom of speech on most campuses, J. Edgar Hoover on few; Nelson Rockefeller and Robert Kennedy on many, Richard Nixon and Hubert Humphrey on few. Even when a speaker manages to deliver his speech, and an audience manages to hear it, if he has entered the campus in the face of pickets, or with security forces in evidence to protect him, it cannot be claimed that he has enjoyed more than a mockery of a free, full, academic presentation of his views.

University administrators cannot take steps to preserve genuine freedom of speech for unpopular speakers without incurring the charge of suppressing free speech. The man who must present his views after running a gantlet of hostile demonstrators or while confronted by insulting placards is certainly not being given a rational hearing; yet to bar the placards and their bearers or otherwise to uphold decorum would be regarded—especially by faculty members— as a limitation on academic freedom and would lead to tension and disorder so great as to cause more damage to the university than is caused by simply avoiding unpopular speakers. Furthermore, the fact that many faculty members exhibit conditioned responses to any charge that academic freedom has been violated or even threatened should not obscure that freedom of speech cannot be preserved for some without limiting it for others, once either party to a disagreement rejects generally accepted standards of decorum, fair play, discussion, and mutual respect. Once these standards are disdained, genuine freedom of discussion cannot possibly take place, and no matter what steps are taken—even if none are taken—there will be real truth to the charge that academic freedom has been compromised.

Note that these infringements of freedom of speech commonly occur when nonacademic figures come to the campus to talk about nonacademic subjects. Their appearances are usually heralded by assertions about the importance of being involved in the big issues on which the welfare of the human race is said to depend, and by condemnation or ridicule of the academic, sequestered in his cloister, concentrating on trivialities like the structure of the nucleus, the nature of good and evil, the genetic code, the conditions of economic growth, English poetry of the seventeenth century, or the cause and cure of arthritis—"trivialities" being defined implicitly as those matters about which no politician, popular pundit, or propagandist is at the moment creating a clamor.

None of the other traditional academic freedoms is as conspicuously corroded as is freedom of speech on the campus today. Others, however, are tarnished. The element that is common to all the corrosive and tarnishing influences is the contaminating effect that follows when universities assume a role of influence and power in practical affairs beyond the academic realm. Involvement in the affairs of others invites involvement by others in the affairs of the university, and this involvement by outsiders results in restraints on the freedom of the university to establish its own priorities and thereby to maintain its own coherence.

LIMITATIONS ON THE FREEDOM OF FACULTY MEMBERS

The academic freedom of the individual faculty member is granted not as a privilege but as a means of obtaining a service to the university, and thereby to society, that cannot easily be obtained unless the faculty member has complete freedom to choose his own subjects for study and to publish and teach the truth as he sees it, motivated by no other consideration than truth. Academic tenure is granted for the same reason that life tenure is granted to Supreme Court justices: to minimize considerations of the economic self-interest of the professor. No one need suspect that he teaches the views he teaches just to keep his job.

Today, however, other powerful interests have come to bear on professors besides just keeping their jobs. One widely used college textbook, for example, advocates views which its author had refuted earlier in a more sophisticated technical treatise; one is led to wonder whether the author now believes what his textbook teaches, or whether he simply recognizes the commercial reality that the views presented in the textbook are more acceptable to most teachers, who will thus be more inclined to adopt it. To take another common situation, it is more and more often the practice of foundations and government agencies to support not the work of a university but the work of a specific faculty member; since grants to faculty members affect their prestige directly and their remunerations indirectly, may not the desire to receive such grants influence the views they express, in particular their praise or criticism of the work of those who give grants? Many faculty members involve themselves deeply in public affairs and even in partisan politics (indeed, it has been alleged of one historian that each of his brilliant books on American history is at heart a political tract for a contemporary presidential campaign) and such involvements also create conflicts of interest.

Less and less does tenure serve to resolve these potential conflicts of interest. Tenure, therefore, comes to be viewed as merely a sort of special economic privilege of professors. This view—widely held even by faculty members—weakens what has been an important support for academic freedom.

As faculty members seek not only truth but also power, prestige, and pay from outside the university, the single-mindedness and disinterestedness of their pursuit of truth is increasingly called into question. Consequently, their claim that they should be free of restraint and responsibility—and the support given to this claim by administrators and trustees—is received with increasing skepticism. As faculty members become more and more subject to outside influences, an institution's capacity to set its own priorities and to establish or strengthen its coherence is further limited. Indeed, these outside influences—which have become capable of directing the activities of faculty members at a time when universities themselves, in the interest of academic freedom, are conscientiously restraining themselves from direction of their faculties—constitute a powerful force for conglomerateness.

RESTRICTIONS ON INSTITUTIONAL AUTONOMY

The freedom of universities to establish their own priorities and patterns of coherence has been eroded as the importance of funds from the government has grown. The constraints operate not because these funds are of public rather than private origin but because the source of funds is centralized. He who pays the piper calls the tune; but he who pays part of the salary of one player in a symphony orchestra does not program any concerts. In order to be eligible for Federal funds, several states which until recently maintained two or more independent institutions, often rather different in character, have imposed central coordination and planning on their institutions. Under pressure from the Federal government, this central planning is being extended—though so far only nominally—to private institutions. He who calls the tune wants only one tune, or if more than one, then tunes that are harmonious to his ear.

That it is the centralization, not the governmental source, that brings about this loss of institutional autonomy can be seen by comparing the effects of the GI bill after the second world war with the effects of recent Federal funds. Under the GI bill, the money reached universities as the result of millions of independent decisions by veterans about where to present their vouchers. An institution could establish the pattern of coherence that it felt would best serve some prospective students. New York State's Regents Scholarships and Scholar Incentive Awards are another example of the way funds from a central source can support higher education without reducing institutional autonomy. The point is that funds, even though they come from a single source, can be disbursed in decentralized ways that preserve the integrity of the institution.

Such is not the case, however, with recent government support, which tends to take the form of grants rather than purchases of services. Purchases, because they can be based on the quality of the final service, leave the institution free to decide which services it should offer and to follow its own judgment on how to attain quality. Grants, on the other hand, have to be rationed in some way; and the way is necessarily formal, mechanistic, and above all uniform—in short, "bureaucratic" in a literal, not a pejorative, sense. Thus, a college with a large physical education department may be denied a Federal grant for a new library, whereas a second college academically inferior in every way may have an identical application granted, the reason being that the first institution will show a smaller percentage increase in total academic space, because the formulae applied by the Federal government count space for physical education as academic space. Actually, of course, quite apart from the problem of what space should be counted as academic, we may question whether percentage increase of academic space is a meaningful indication of where a grant will be most useful. At any rate, whatever the formula used, those institutions that best fit it will be aided, and those which best carve out their own special pattern of academic coherence may be passed over.

Funds from an excessively large private source can have as unbalancing an influence as government funds; that is to say, in accomplishing their particular objectives through universities, large private agencies may diminish the autonomy and diversity of our system of higher education.

Another nongovernmental force that often hampers an institution's ability to establish its own pattern, to experiment, and to innovate, is the accrediting agency. Those accrediting agencies which are organized by groups of colleges and universities may operate in ways bearing more than a little resemblance to the ways of industrial cartels. Others, supported by departments or professional schools, may exert outside pressure on a university in behalf of one of its constituent parts—or against one of its parts if that part is out of step with corresponding departments or schools at other universities. Still other accrediting agencies are controlled by special-interest groups; this is the case with several professions.

A strong institution can sometimes refuse to yield control of its curriculum to these outside agencies, but such resistance is unusual. Students are reluctant to attend, and donors to support, unaccredited institutions. In some cases, a student is not allowed to take the examinations required for professional licensure unless he has a degree from an accredited institution; so even if his preparation is superior to that specified by accrediting formulae, he is prevented from demonstrating this competence. Moreover, in at least one instance, Congress has specified that funds should be restricted to institutions accredited by a certain professional association whose interests only partly coincide with those of students and employers of graduates, and only partly favor quality in education. More commonly, Congress requires merely the approval of some "nationally recognized accrediting agency," an undefined phrase which presumably means an accrediting agency that is accredited by the National Commission on Accrediting.

Each type of accrediting agency is attempting to do good, at least by its own lights. But even if we grant that they protect some students from shoddy or perhaps even fraudulent schools, it would still remain true that in the aggregate their value is negative: their beneficial effects do not offset the harm they do by hindering improvements in curricula and by limiting the power of each institution to set its own priorities and to establish its own pattern of activities, coherent or conglomerate as suits its circumstances.[2]

---

[2] Among the disadvantages of accrediting, cost should not be overlooked. During the academic year 1966-67, for example, Bradley University, an institution

THE MANAGEMENT OF COHERENCE

The foregoing account of current hazards to institutional integrity, emphasizing as it has the tensions created by outside influences on student life, faculty activities, and administrative policy making, may seem to have prepared the way for conclusions rather different from those that follow.

It may seem that since the threats arise from the baneful effects of the university's involvements with the outside world, the remedy is to withdraw, to convert our institutions into ivory towers, sequestered monasteries. But that way madness lies: Most problems of individuals and institutions arise from relations with other individuals, institutions, and society; and the autistic university would be no more viable—or admirable—than the autistic individual. As Ortega y Gasset puts it,

> Not only does [the university] need perpetual contact with science, on pain of atrophy, it needs contact, likewise, with the public life, with historical reality, with the present. . . . The university must be open to the whole reality of its time. It must be in the midst of real life, and saturated with it.[3]

My conclusion, then, may sound moralistic. The university must have the strength of character to resist these encroachments, and even to bend them to its own ends. To have *strength* of character, it must first have character, and it must be aware of its character. The university, though it is very much a part of society, has a distinctive role to play. Government, business, journalism, art, war, religion—these are not its roles, yet it has intimate and extensive relations with each and with much else.

We must define the university's central and unique role in order to differentiate it from the many institutions and activities with which it is in close association. From the definition, we can then devise tests of whether particular activities are congruent with that role and of how intimate and extensive the university's relations with other institutions should be.

Once the university sees its own role clearly and adheres to that role, it will be in a position to resist encroachments. If the university— through its principal spokesmen and policy-makers—assumes the

---

of 275 faculty members and 4,850 full-time students, went through four reaccreditations. According to T. W. Van Arsdale, Jr., its president, the cost was 1,350 hours of faculty and administration work, plus 835 hours of secretarial work, plus $5,700.

   [3] Ortega y Gasset, *Mission of the University* (Princeton, N.J.: Princeton University Press, 1944), pp. 96–97.

posture of an innkeeper, making itself available to serve any paying customer who may enter, refusing only those so blatantly unrespectable that they will repel other paying customers, then it can expect to be treated as such. If it assumes the posture of a patent-medicine huckster, claiming that it will create prosperity (or, in the more fashionable phrase, "stimulate economic growth"), eliminate inequality, ennoble justice, improve government, elevate art, cure disease, resolve labor disputes, prevent war, and purify the air, it can expect to be treated as a huckster.[4] But if it has a clear view of what it can do and what it should do—of what its special mission is—it can command respect for that view.

It is not appropriate here to enunciate the central character and purposes of a university, against which proposed activities should be tested.[5] What I would emphasize here is the diversity of American colleges and universities. With college education on the way to becoming nearly universal, and graduate degrees more common than undergraduate degrees used to be, the importance of diversity is increasing. One of the most serious dangers to our system of higher education is that uniformity and homogeneity may very well result if the external pressures exerted upon our institutions are not countered by the firmness of their own individual characters.

The way to maintain an institution's coherence and its control over its own priorities, then, is not to try to turn back the tides undermining our freedom and independence (though perhaps we can at least stem these tides), nor to flee into isolated ivory towers (though perhaps we can clarify the division of labor between universities and the rest of society), but to define, to keep clearly in mind, to explain within the university, and to assert forcefully to the outside world the special purposes and modes of action that maximize a university's value to society. Hammer blows on one side of a sheet of metal will leave it misshapen and formless if there is nothing on the other side; but if on the other side there is a firm, well-shaped anvil, the pressure of the hammer will delineate clearly and firmly the character of the solid form beneath.

[4] Mark Twain, in *The Gilded Age*, a novel published nearly a century ago, used as a part of a plot to defraud the United States government the claims that a university would (1) create economic growth in its environs (the "Route 128 effect") and (2) help Negroes. "Plus ça change. . . ."

[5] I do, of course, have views on this subject and have published them: "The Importance of Error," *University of Chicago Magazine*, November 1962, pp. 14-16; Inaugural Address, University of Rochester, *Rochester Review*, June-July 1963, pp. 10-19; "Centripetal and Centrifugal Forces in University Organization," *Daedalus*, Fall 1964, pp. 1071-81; *The Contemporary University*, ed. Robert S. Morison (Boston: Houghton Mifflin Co., 1966).

Institutional Coherence and Priorities

ROBERT S. POWELL, JR., MRS. HENRY B. OWEN,

JAMES E. ALLEN, JR., JOHN WILLIAM PADBERG, S.J.

The Necessity for Ongoing Dialogue

ROBERT S. POWELL, JR.

IT WOULD BE COMFORTING to those who now exercise power in our universities if they could feel that the real threats to institutional coherence and rationality stem largely from competing and conflicting pressures from outside their institutions. But a closer examination of our universities will, I think, suggest a more basic reason why our institutions of higher learning lack clear priorities and direction. The central difficulty has very little to do with competing pressures and influences. Even if the government and the foundations were not pillaging the time of our faculties with juicy research contracts, even if there were no encumbering strings attached to the big Federal grants, even if students did not riot every time a conservative spoke on the campus, and even if state legislatures let universities run their own affairs—even if all of these traditional bogeymen were suddenly to disappear, the problem of establishing within our institutions some sanity and rationality, or some focus, would be just as formidable as it surely is today.

The present crisis springs from the lack of strong and purposeful leadership within our institutions. The cause lies *within* our institutions: in the inability or unwillingness of those now making decisions to confront and answer the question: "What is this place for?" I submit that our institutions have lost any real sense of educational purpose and that the increasingly strong encroachments and pressures on our universities from the outside are *symptoms* of that loss of purpose, not causes of it.

If those now running our universities had the will and the purpose to establish a scale of priorities, to extract from their experiences a rational philosophy of education, and to make that philosophy operative within their institutions, I have no doubt that it could be done. But that will, that purpose, is sadly lacking. Faculty senate meetings are spent in bureaucratic wranglings about how to settle the competing interests of the various disciplines, rather than in intelligent discussions of what the institution is all about and how its task of educating people can best be accomplished. Administrators, having disclaimed any serious responsibility for the academic matters (matters generally viewed as the responsibility of the faculty senates), are mostly concerned with making a good name for their school nationally, securing big government contracts, building more buildings, and furthering public relations. In short, both groups—faculty and administrative personnel— have the power and ability to start a serious discussion about the purposes and priorities of their institution, but neither group seems really to want to (or knows how to), and it is no wonder that outside pressures come in for so large a share of the blame.

Our institutions lack not only strong and purposeful leadership, but also any well-defined and thought-out *raison d'être* which makes sense for the twentieth century. In a way, the absence of such a philosophy is understandable. Thinking is hard work. The development of a coherent and integrated philosophy of education is a very difficult task, since it carries with it the formulation of a more general philosophy of life and concept of society. Yet, one can have very little sympathy for the leaders of our universities and colleges who cannot find time to do this thinking, if one realizes the consequences of their preoccupation with less important matters. An incoherent, fragmented process of educating people can only lead to incoherent, fragmented people, who, in turn, have their predictable and visible effects on our society. There is certainly very little sympathy for the administrators' plight in that part of the academic community which feels most strongly the corrosive effects of incoherence in the student body.

Writ large, the message of contemporary student unrest is simple and straightforward: The American student has lost faith in the leadership of our colleges and universities and thus in the education they offer. Amid all the very sincere pleas for patience and understanding— such as the one made in Dr. Wallis's background paper—students see five, maybe ten, truly imaginative experiments initiated each year by the leaders of our 2,600 colleges and universities, experiments aimed at testing new and different processes of learning, new goals, and new priorities. I dare say that there is more hard thinking going on in the U.S. Office of Education about what our universities ought to be doing than there is in all of our faculty councils put together. Consequently, in the absence of any agreed-upon aim for education, in the absence of a general philosophy for the educative process, and without any present national guidance or policy, it is no wonder that our educators feel themselves left at the mercy of pressure groups and external influences. And neither is it any wonder that the American student feels that, if any coherent philosophy is to be forthcoming, it will have to be developed within his own ranks.

A first step in the process of defining priorities and goals is to re-order traditional authority relationships which have for so long militated against serious discussion about purposes. As Theobald puts it:

> Education has not yet caught up with the fact that the educational pattern of the past, in which it was assumed that the old know and the young must learn, is no longer valid. We are teaching young people to respect authority at a time when authority is no longer possible, and when we ought to be struggling together to understand the world in which we live. We still say to them "listen and learn" rather than "strive with us." [1]

In the last twelve months alone, over sixty experimental colleges have sprung up on our campuses, all of them student-initiated. Some were exciting, others were less so; nevertheless, each of them, in one way or another, was trying to hammer out a new model and a new process of education which freed people to learn in their own best way. That, in itself, is refreshing when compared with the awful stagnation that has characterized far too many of our institutions.

In other words, if our institutions are really serious about wanting to make a new effort to define themselves and their purposes, the first —and I think the most important—step that they can take is to reorder the process of decision making within the institution, so that that process reflects the very best educational philosophy available to us. This further suggests that the decision-making process should serve as a model of the educational process we would most like to see emulated throughout other parts of that institution, from the classroom, to the student government, to the faculty council. Students must certainly participate in this process, and not simply because a great deal of helpful thinking about education has recently come from within their ranks. Students must be a full partner in the discussion about institutional priorities and coherence because they and their needs represent the *sine qua non* of the institution's existence.

Our institutions will find no tight equation available for establishing their priorities and goals and for assuring the coherence they need.

---

[1] Robert Theobald, "On Education," *Kaiser Aluminum News*, I (1967), 8.

If an institution truly wants to set priorities and goals for itself, it must, above all, find a way of creating and encouraging an ongoing dialogue among its constituents. Within the institutional community, everyone who has a stake in the outcome of that dialogue must have a full role in it at the outset. This includes the students, it includes the alumni if they're seriously interested, it includes the trustees, and it includes the faculty and administrative personnel. The problem today is that no one seems to want to begin such a conversation on those terms. It is true that those terms might very well fundamentally alter the traditional authority relationships within the institution; but as I suggested earlier, those traditional relationships have been one of the biggest barriers to a fruitful discussion of academic goals and priorities. By freeing people to participate fully, honestly, and openly in the determination of these goals and priorities, we may not only be encouraging them to do the maximum amount of hard thinking that is necessary, but also we may bring about a new and better way of learning and decision making.

The "Whole Picture" of the University

MRS. HENRY B. OWEN

AT A TENDER age, I was coached in the rudiments of baseball by my college-president father. My most vivid recollection of that coaching is of his repeated admonition, "Keep your eye on the ball. You can never be a shortstop if you do not learn to keep your eye on the ball . . . How can you ever hope to play left field if you don't keep your eye on the ball? *Keep your eye on that ball!*"

To me, President Wallis is saying the same thing when he states that, once the university clearly sees its own role and adheres to that role, it is in a better position to decide what its priorities must be, what action to take or not to take. So complex is society, however, so many are the demands upon the college and university, so enticing the grant or gift—even though it may throw the university off-balance—that it is difficult to keep one's eye on the ball, especially when the university "ball," it seems, has streamers floating from it in all directions. Just the same, the core is there. As President Wallis says, "We must define the university's central and unique role . . . From the definition, we can then devise tests of whether particular activities are congruent with that role."

Many trustees of many institutions are quite unprepared for the part they must play in helping to shape the goals of their institutions.

Nor is it their fault. Consider, for example, that popular alumnus who has recently been appointed to the board of his *alma mater,* and who visualizes it as the same institution that it was when he graduated forty years ago. He has had little opportunity to understand the real changes that have taken place during those forty years. Or take the example of the new trustee. He may be a well-known and highly able business man, already on many boards and committees, but none of his experience has given him insight into the complexities of a modern university. How do you acquaint these members of governing boards with the unique role of their university in today's society? Or take the hundreds of other sincere, intelligent, conscientious men and women who wish to serve their institutions wisely but who lack perspective on the university as a whole? They have no contact with the students, most of whom they regard as potential demonstrators, though they may sympathize with the student rebellion against inadequate teaching and an IBM-card existence. They are mostly unaware of the graduate student group. They hear about the faculty, are proud of its scholarly reputation, are pleased because of the grants that come their way, but have no knowledge of the complications those grants may create in matters of campus unity, loyalty, or cohesiveness. Unaware of the pressures and tensions within and without the university campus, they have slight comprehension of the need of their college or university for relevance to today's world.

Trustees may widen their horizons by intelligent reading or by guidance from other trustees and associations, but who bothers to define for them the complex role of their own institutions? The president could, but is sometimes hesitant to do so. His trustees are always pressed for time, and so is he. A board chairman might, if he has had long and wide-ranging experience on his board and has a truly broad perspective of his institution and its component parts. Although many months are required if a new trustee is to assimilate all that goes into the role of his university, he is usually introduced to his new responsibilities by an array of Pertinent Facts: the fall football schedule and an explanation of how to make out his expense voucher. Oh, he attends board meetings, approves building plans, authorizes expenditures. But what does he really know about a university? How can he add to the cohesiveness when he lacks vision of the whole of which he himself is an important part?

It would be ideal if the administration and the trustees could see eye to eye on the role of their institution, could frankly and thoughtfully discuss the possible enlargement of that role or its adaptation to new conditions. But in all too many cases, they have never even exchanged ideas on the true nature and purposes of their college. Yet these men and women are the same ones who, with the administration, are charged with setting priorities and guiding the over-all destiny of the institution.

I agree with President Wallis that cohesiveness can be maintained by continuous, courageous, and honest appraisal of the central role of the university and its relationships beyond the campus boundaries. It can be maintained by an intellectual unity that encompasses activities far from the campus and that may even include a certain degree of conglomerateness as a part of the total pattern. I do not understand, for instance, why President Wallis feels that his institution retains "some degree of conglomerateness in that the School of Music, the Art Gallery, and the humanities are at different locations." This type of conglomerateness is also true of a junior year abroad, a land-grant college's far-flung extension services, or a university project in Pakistan. Our idea of "cohesiveness" may develop a new meaning, but the over-all intellectual framework and direction can still exist.

If you are a picture puzzle fan, concerned with fitting into place the hundreds of little pieces that make up the whole, you know that an initial glance at the complete picture enables you to fit the parts more easily into place. I pose, therefore, a final question to both President Wallis and the panel: Is there a way by which, given a greater degree of communication between the component parts of the academic community, the "whole picture" of the university can be perceived? To what extent can we develop a common awareness of the role of the university and of the need for cohesiveness in effectively fulfilling that role?

The Attitude and Performance
Of Government

JAMES E. ALLEN, JR.

I SHALL ADDRESS my comments on President Wallis's paper to the question of how the growing importance of government funds and activities affects institutional coherence and priorities, with particular reference to New York State.

As Commissioner of Education for New York State, I also hold the title of President of the University of the State of New York. This unique university comprises all the educational institutions in the state: elementary, secondary, and higher, public and private. It is incorporated by the state and subject to the general supervision and visitation of the State Board of Regents, who are responsible by law for coordinating the planning and development of the component parts of the University into a unified whole. They do not participate in the internal affairs of these institutions, except to approve the machinery of institutional government when they approve charters and to set standards when they register and approve curricula.

Higher education in New York is considered, both in law and tradition, to be a joint enterprise of all the private colleges, now numbering about 140, and the network of about 70 public institutions that make up the State University of New York and the City University of New York. Thus, the University is a conglomeration, to use Mr. Wallis's word, of institutions, each with its own identity and independence of control and operation, loosely bound together under the superintendence of the Regents to form a coherent educational system for serving the citizens of the state. The basic philosophy of the Regents is "unity with diversity."

Until recently, few states have made any significant attempts to institute such a system. Since 1960, however, the *laissez faire* attitude has undergone rapid change, and today, nearly every state has established a new planning agency for higher education or augmented the authority of existing agencies to include this function. While most of these agencies are concerned primarily with publicly supported institutions, the needs and concerns of private institutions are increasingly being considered through the creation of "superboards."

There is no need to dwell here upon the reasons for the increased role of the states in higher education. Society's needs and the demands of a growing population for increased opportunities for higher education are forcing every state to examine the adequacy of its educational resources. Furthermore, many of the recent Federal education acts have placed added responsibilities at the state level and have stimulated the formulation of guidelines for administering a variety of grants that benefit colleges and universities. In New York State, for example, Federal funds for higher education, administered by the State Education Departments, have jumped from virtually nothing to $44 million in the last three years.

The extent of the state's responsibility for the financial plight of private colleges is a matter of increasing concern. In a number of states, such as New York and others on the Eastern seaboard, the private colleges and universities have been the dominant source of higher education opportunity, and they continue to enroll half or more of all students attending college in those states. But rising costs and competition from public institutions are causing many private institutions to look to state as well as Federal sources for direct and indirect financial assistance.

President Wallis has said that, whether the effect of growing government participation in higher education is good or bad, the maintenance of an institution's powers of self-determination will depend, in large measure, upon the ability of each college and university "to keep clearly in mind" and "to assert forcefully to the outside world the special purposes and modes of action that maximize its value to society." This is certainly a strong determining factor, but of equal importance is the attitude and performance of government in its relationship to higher education. For the educator in government, the task of shaping this attitude and directing this performance is dual in nature. He must recognize that the government's responsibility to meet needs is broader and more general than that of institutions, and he must also recognize the specific requirements of the institutions. This is no easy task, for there is much in both these areas of responsibility that tends to make them incompatible. To achieve a balance that will meet the objectives of both requires awareness and flexibility. The very nature of government is adverse to individuality, whether personal or institutional, and constant vigilance must prevail if we are to achieve the objectives for which government exists, with as little sacrifice of individuality as possible.

The fact that the pressures generated by government—political considerations, public opinion, special interests, and so forth—generally lead to an emphasis on the more general goals at the expense of the particular is recognized by higher education. This knowledge operates to add another dimension to the task of the institution that seeks to preserve its powers of self-determination. Not only must it forcefully assert its special purposes and modes of action to the outside world, but it must move into that outside world in an effort to have a part in directing those forces that will affect its scope of self-determination. To elaborate President Wallis's figure of speech, not only must the university seek to be a well-shaped anvil, but it must also seek to have some control over the pressure of the hammer.

The greatest pressure bearing upon institutions of higher education today is government involvement. If the institutions are to influence this involvement, a threefold effort is necessary: First, to "educate" the educators in government as to the requirements for autonomy and academic freedom; second, to actively assist those educators in government who educate other government policy-makers or administrators; and, third, to aggressively support those policies and programs that help to ensure that the effect of growing governmental participation in higher education will promote institutional freedom and integrity.

Teaching as the Condition of Coherence

JOHN WILLIAM PADBERG, S.J.

FROM HINTS by Dr. Wallis in this paper and from statements in his other writings, it seems obvious to me that, for him, the education of the young is the central focus, the key to the pattern, the heart of the activity of a college or university. With this view, I wholly agree. Around this central focus, the other parts of the total picture of the university arrange themselves; only in relation to this most basic activity does the rest of the organism function. Of course, as Dr. Wallis elsewhere remarks, this does "not imply that teaching is the only activity" of the college or university. But he seems to weaken his case when he continues, "nor [does it] even [imply] that other activities are not equally important." I wonder what other activities *are* equally important. Is it not the university's receptivity to this impossible multicentricity that has blurred the focus, obscured the pattern, entangled the priorities, and often made the university not just conglomerate— a possible blessing—but quite incoherent, an unmixed evil?

It is foolish and, what is worse, useless to deny or wish away the multiple research and public service functions of higher education. They will not and cannot be conjured out of existence, for not only can they force the institution out of a self-serving solipsism, but in doing so, they can also contribute richly to the depth and diversity of teachers, students, and the institution alike. When they assume, however, equal importance with teaching—the "only university activity that depends wholly on the university"—then coherence becomes disorder and priorities get out of control.

It is indeed true that institutional coherence and a clear set of priorities presuppose a variety of academic freedoms, and as such freedoms dwindle, so too will the coherence and priorities. Among the obstacles to academic freedom that Dr. Wallis lists are: the absence of free speech on campuses, limitations on the freedom of faculty members, and restrictions on institutional autonomy.

It may be that the reverse is also true, that academic freedom, in its turn, assumes and depends upon the existence of proper priorities and institutional coherence—a coherence that rests upon the university's awareness of its unique role, the central focus of which is education of the young. The university must see itself, or at least must want to be considered, as an institution committed to the critical examination of the tenets, principles, laws, dogmas, and ideas that make up the varying body of truth and to the active training of its students in both the manner of such investigation and the use of its product. That such is the present central focus of higher education is debatable. I would simply maintain that if the university does set such priorities, it will have far less trouble in resisting the encroachments on free speech, on faculty freedom, or on institutional autonomy.

It is too much to hope that student yahoos—radical or reactionary —will ever completely vanish from the groves of academe, but if day in and day out, the university stresses the creation of an atmosphere wherein there is critical and open examination of ideas, then there is at least some hope that both Carmichael and Wallace, or Kennedy and Nixon, can be heard on the same campus and can have their messages received with the attention they deserve by students and faculty. When the university ceases to be a haven for the faculty member who treats teaching as simply the burdensome price to be paid for the solitary pleasures of his own private world of research (an attitude tolerated and sometimes encouraged by the university in the interest of bigger grants and better prestige), then, perhaps, students will have less reason to vent their frustrations in intolerance, and faculty and administration will have less cause to react in panic-stricken breast-beating.

The freedom of the faculty to teach is, however, jeopardized. Power, prestige, and pay from outside the university do indeed work against a faculty member's single-mindedness in the pursuit of instructional goals. This is, indeed, a major problem in the universities. And what administrator, what trustee, what dean or departmental chairman, what student does not welcome the "great man," the "international expert," the "renowned author"? What university can resist the temptation of the power, prestige, and financial gains that come with the addition to its faculty of such a personage? We all fail, in part, to resist these temptations, but if the university keeps its internal teaching function in central focus, it will take a harder look at the possible disadvantages of hiring the "great man," and, as far as possible, it will reward with its own versions of power, prestige, and pay those who most successfully perform in the teaching function.

Finally, institutional autonomy is restricted by Federal financial involvement and by accrediting demands. Here, Dr. Wallis has done us a great service by clearly pointing out that the danger does not come from the source of funds itself, but from the centralized character of the formulae governing their disbursement. I wonder whether institutions of higher education have the intestinal fortitude and can intelligently cooperate to acknowledge and to proclaim directly and repeatedly two facts: First, that they—both public and private universities and colleges —need unconditional governmental support, either by direct grants to the student or by across-the-board help to the institution; Second, that because our government wants and needs these institutions, it cannot, even if simply as a matter of national public policy, afford to let them degenerate. There are formidable risks in making such statements. But I think that not to make them bears even more formidable implications and bodes dangerous results. The need for help—and help with a minimum of direct governmental interference—is obvious. He who pays the piper does, indeed, now call the tune, but unless we devise some system whereby institutions retain their autonomy and individual characters, we shall all be marching to the same tune: a disastrous outcome in a society that has prized and prospered from institutional diversity.

Do universities and colleges in this country have enough confidence in themselves and in their central focus on teaching to insist on that explicit support for the diversity necessary to examine the various approaches to knowledge? Do they also have enough confidence in themselves and enough respect for other views to accept gratefully the benefits of accrediting agencies, and to resist, singly or in concert, when such outside agencies encroach on their autonomy or intrude on an institution's freedom to experiment and innovate?

We must be convinced that the academy, according to its own best lights, should serve first the student—not the nation, not the state, not the predominant ideology, be it governmental, ecclesiastical or even educational. Unless this is so, higher education will throw away its autonomy, sacrifice its coherence, subvert its priorities, and finally and most tragically, deny its inmost purpose.

PART III

Fresh Perspectives
On Goals

RICHARD H. SULLIVAN

Coordination for the Definition of Goals

AT THE OPENING of the Fiftieth Annual Meeting of the American Council on Education, special recognition was given to the organizations that founded the Council in the first months of 1918. Few of the 1918 papas would have predicted such numerous progeny. The family's growth has been remarkable. Its structure has changed. The constituencies we represent and the constituencies we serve bear only modest resemblance to those of a half-century ago. Yet within the Council, and because of the Council, we are still a family. We share common purposes, parallel opportunities, persistent perplexities.

I speak as a member of the family both personally and symbolically, not as an external, arm's-length critic or observer. I have served on Council committees and boards and have worked with its staff. Like the other member associations, the one I represent, the Association of American Colleges, has benefited from the Council's leadership and its coordinating efforts. The other member organizations and institutions that have employed me have relied on the Council for studies, information, publications, identification of problems, and formulation of policies. I am inclined to view this anniversary more as a beginning than as an ending. Where we have been together, important as that has been, is of less consequence than where we are going.

One historical curiosity deserves mention here. According to its *Bulletin* of March 1918, the Association of American Colleges, at its annual meeting in January of that year, had passed, without a dissenting vote, a resolution "approving the establishment of a Federal Department of Education with a Secretary in the President's Cabinet." For its time, that was indeed forward-looking—by more than three decades, as events were to prove.

Immediately following that Chicago meeting, the officers held a conference with other association representatives. From that came the "Emergency Council on Education," which by the following July was given its present name and charged with responsibilties in times of peace as well as of war. The record of that conference reports that the AAC's resolution, to have a Secretary of Education in the Cabinet, was "the chief subject of consideration." [1] It is fortunate for all of us that other and broader subjects were discussed. Had the Council been charged solely with carrying out that one fine resolution, the first three decades of its life would have been most frustrating and could scarcely be described as a glowing success.

The wartime problems in 1918, however, made visible the need for an "adequate coordinating agency" [2] to deal with a range of issues and a variety of relationships between education and the Federal government. In the intervening half-century, the growth of both has been remarkable. Higher education is now funded from an increased variety of sources. It is led and staffed by vast numbers of teachers, researchers, administrators, and support personnel. It includes huge and complex universities. It includes many small colleges of simple structure. It reaches not only students from all kinds of backgrounds, but also a more than quadrupled proportion of the age group. It grants more graduate degrees than it granted bachelor's degrees not so long ago. It encompasses an almost unlimited set of courses and curricula. Its research enterprises reach around the earth, touch the moon, seek out the most distant stars, and soon will lead to harvesting and mining the oceans. It probes the mysteries of the tiniest matter and the enigmas of the largest social organizations. It defies exact analysis and even description.

Changes in the American Council on Education mirror that growth and that increased diversity. Nevertheless, threads of continuity can be discerned. Two functions of the Council, the need for which led to its creation, remain its most distinctive characteristics.

THE COUNCIL'S RELATIONS WITH THE FEDERAL GOVERNMENT

The first function or responsibility is to represent the corpus of education, and particularly of higher education, to the Federal government.

[1] Association of American Colleges *Bulletin*, March 1918, p. 3.
[2] *Ibid.*

Monitoring the traffic in the other direction, from the government to our institutions, is almost equally important. As the Council looks to the future during its fiftieth anniversary year, I should expect to find very wide agreement on one proposition: Whatever other functions it serves, the Council should keep at the top of its priority list the necessity to enhance the relationships between higher education and the Federal government.

I single this point out for special comment not from any belief that the Council has failed either to perform this complex task or to accord it the requisite priority. Indeed, I agree with Senator Wayne Morse that one primary reason for the recent passage of an extraordinary range of measures, relating "quantitatively and qualitatively" to education, had been that by the 1960's "at long last the educational segment of our country moved forward as a united body in support of all the various pieces of education legislation." [3] In his Annual Report for 1966, President Logan Wilson reviewed the "notable gains in unity of effort" [4] in this sphere. He generously noted that other agencies, associations, and institutions had made their own significant contributions to that effort. It is also the case that the Council's role and activities have been vital, crucial, and indispensable.

My positive reasons for discussing this subject, together with any concrete suggestions I can offer are closely interrelated. I have somewhat arbitrarily divided them into three parts.

First, the Federal government's involvement in education is complex, diverse, and constant. It touches all our lives. It touches them every day. It is extraordinarily influential over the practices, processes, and outcomes of decision making within our institutions. This involvement will continue. In all probability, it will increase. Shifts in Federal programs, policies, and priorities for funds and in Federal attention to different kinds and levels of education and to different types of institutions, as well as changes in the geographical distribution of Federal funds, affect a great many of us from moment to moment. A few timely examples should suffice. Graduate school enrollments for 1968 cannot be predicted or planned for without full regard to the impact of Selective Service policies. Support of and planning for basic research in the universities are very heavily dependent on Federal budgetary decisions this year and next. The ability of students in a number of states to borrow funds for college expenses this fall was affected by week-to-week Federal decisions during the summer. These are cliff-

---

[3] Quoted in American Council on Education, *Annual Report, 1966*, p. 1.
[4] *Ibid.*

hanging situations. For the period immediately ahead, constant vigilance and continuous activity are required on behalf of higher education, and required particularly of the Council. This is the year-to-year, month-to-month, and even day-to-day necessity.

Second, one can separate out from that sometimes frenetic activity, a number of policy questions implicit in the present array of Federal programs and their continuations and logical extensions. Such analysis is crucial both in the definition of the Federal role and influence and in the resolution of institutional health, freedom, and responsibility. Rather than trying to catalog the issues, I will illustrate them by one example.

We have long said that a major purpose of the university is to extend through research the range and depth of man's knowledge and understanding of himself, of society, and of nature. It has now been determined that it is in the national interest for the Federal government to support such research and to do so on a large scale. On the exact relationship between those two statements and on the implications of such a determination rest the detailed methods of Federal funding and administration. These methods, in turn, have a major impact on college and university finance, faculty personnel policies, facilities and equipment, commitments, and priorities.

Two quite contradictory views are now expressed. Some spokesmen believe that the Federal government should pay the full direct and indirect costs of any basic research it supports. Some others are as equally convinced that the universities should share in the costs of basic research. The first view may give insufficient attention to the possibility that, in the absence of a given piece of such support, the universities may still have the obligation and the desire to pursue such basic research. The second view may slight the possibility that, in the absence of the universities' commitment to a particular field, the national interest may require that it be created and fully funded. Analyses of university dependency on the government and of the nature of faculty loyalties could be added, to round out the example. I shall not pause for that, since a long list of equally complicated examples is available. It does seem urgent to me that we initiate a critical and creative examination of present Federal programs, particularly of their underlying assumptions and basic policies, together with their effects on both government and institutions.

This examination would be difficult even under ideal conditions. A voluntary organization like the Council may find it especially arduous as long as its committees and staff must also stay on top of the day-today operating decisions, discussions, and crises resulting from Federal action or immediate and short-range planning for action. Yet it is vital to us all that neither task be neglected.

Third, we must confront truly long-range questions of Federal support of and influence on higher education. Whatever answers are proposed will be subject to political review and political decision. Politics is "the art of the possible." Present Federal programs have evolved within the limits of what has been possible at any one point and over a series of points in time. This will always be the case at any given moment. But we should stretch those limits cumulatively over a long period. We should be able to achieve what now seems impossible. To do that, we must have more clearly in view and agree more explicitly on the truly desirable patterns for the Federal share, the Federal responsibility, the Federal methods, and the Federal influence.

In fiscal year 1966, total Federal support of colleges and universities was more than $3 billion and represented nearly one-fifth of higher education expenditures. Twenty-five institutions each received more than $25 million from the Federal government. Seventy-nine institutions each received more than $10 million. At the same time, from 1963 to 1966, there were shifts toward a more even distribution of funds geographically and toward inclusion of support for more small institutions. In 1966, more than 2,000 institutions received Federal dollars.

Many of us believe that even more Federal support and an even wider distribution will be required. The partnership in any case is now very real, influential, and (I think) indissoluble. We should chart out our long-range preferences, and we should be frank and open in working out the necessary compromises among different kinds and levels and needs of institutions, for these are affected unevenly and unequally by each Federal program. Balance is possible only through the totality of such programs. We need to set the short-range steps, changes, enactments continually against a backdrop of the long-range desiderata. Unfortunately, however, we are not agreed within the family on answers to some hard questions.

Again, let me give not a catalog but two examples. Should the Federal government provide unrestricted grants for the general expenses of operating our instructional program? If so, how can this be best done, done most equitably and efficiently, done without surrender of institutional autonomy, done with sufficient institutional accountability? What is the best mix of Federal support for quantitative expansion and Federal encouragement for qualitative improvement?

As a nation, we have virtually accepted the moral and practical responsibility of guaranteeing advanced educational opportunities to the able but needy student. What part of this commitment must be subject to Federal solution? If this goal is a responsibility of the nation, as I believe, and if it is in the national interest to have an educated people, Federal scholarships and grants-in-aid are both needed and justified. We have accepted that principle at the graduate level. It must be reexamined with respect to undergraduates. The various and ingenious plans for financing higher education heavily through student loans and repayments may be, in part at least, evasions of a fundamental responsibility to directly recognize and positively nurture talent, for the national welfare as well as for the individual's advancement.

Many of our associations are to some degree grappling with one or more of these thorny questions. The Council has not neglected them. Nevertheless, we need to give them even more attention. In today's setting, the Council, as the principal coordinating agent and honest broker of such ideas, has not only special obligations but a special opportunity.

The commitments we now have in Vietnam are enormously complicating and inhibiting every decision about every other section of the Federal budget. Some day, somehow, suddenly or gradually, those commitments and costs will be greatly reduced, and the pressures to apply Federal funds toward several large but now thwarted investments in our internal economy and society will, in a sense, burst loose. The pressure for more Federal support of higher education will be among them. We can be ready with a thorough and defensible set of plans, based on several carefully formulated alternative assumptions about the level of possible funding. If $7 billion instead of the 1966 level of $3 billion is available, what balance, what priorities, and what methods are wisest? Or if $10 billion is available, what would one add? Without such plans, we can only back blindly into the new situation, improvising as we go. I would suggest that the Council take the lead in establishing a representative commission of review and planning for the Federal part in the post-Vietnam world of higher education. I believe that other associations that are Council members, as well as the institutions we all represent, would lend their full cooperation.

THE COUNCIL'S COORDINATING FUNCTION

I referred earlier to the two functions or responsibilities that have long been the Council's distinguishing characteristics. The second of these is the task of coordination. Originally, this referred only to the coordination of Federal government and higher education, but the challenge has broadened. Higher education is now big and growing. It is diffuse and diversifying further. It is employing more widely new methods of planning, cooperative effort, and sharing of controls and responsibility. Generally applicable distinctions between purely public and purely private institutions are harder to make with certainty.

The Council is well along with a study of state-wide systems of higher education, giving special emphasis to coordinating bodies. I think the time may be ripe for a thorough review of the complex array of national associations. The Council, because of its broadly representative nature, is better situated than any other organization to stimulate and sponsor such a review.

In the past fifty years, and particularly since the Second World War, there has been a very significant growth in local, state, interstate, regional, and national bodies. The isolation and splendid sovereignty that characterized institutions in another era are out of date. Interinstitutional cooperation in many forms is now taking place and will (wisely, in my opinion) develop much further. These operations are going to take a lot of the time and attention of key administrators. Associations of faculty members and researchers and specialist administrators, in many combinations and for many purposes, have multiplied. They too take time and attention—or they're not worth having.

At the Council's annual meeting three years ago, Russell Thackrey, in pointing out a number of the problems arising from the growth of such organizations, said: "The multiplication of organizational activity in higher education has had, as a by-product, a strong tendency to fragment the representation of the college or university *as such* in relationship to the legislative and administrative branches of the national government and to the foundations, corporations, and individuals who provide private funds for educational purposes. It has also placed increasingly heavy demands on the time and energy of many individuals who are called on, in various capacities, to participate in these activities." [5]

A review such as the one I propose should look for any significant gaps in representation, to see whether certain kinds of institutions or of academic personnel are not well served. It is, for example, no secret that many of the smaller private undergraduate colleges of arts and sciences believe they have an insufficiently clear or influential voice in Washington. We are re-examining that complaint in our association, and it is appropriate that the Council as well do so. Despite expressions

[5] Logan Wilson (ed.), *Emerging Patterns in Higher Education* (Washington: American Council on Education, 1965), p. 238.

of gloom and doom, such institutions continue to be an integral, vital, and influential part of our family enterprise. If my figures are correct, more than 40 percent of all institutional members of this Council are private four-year colleges with enrollments of less than 2,500 students each.

As another example, relating to associations with individual rather than institutional members, I believe that there is not now an appropriate member of the American Council of Learned Societies to represent broadly the scholarly field of religion. This deficiency too is being studied by others. It should be nevertheless a part of the over-all review I suggest. An examination of duplication of effort—of overlap in the activities of two or more associations—might be even more timely and of greater consequence than a study of such omissions. Conceivably, some associations could achieve greater strength by merging; the merged organization could then represent special continuing interests by divisional arrangements, standing committees, and the like. If some duplication were eliminated, communication would probably be improved. We all have too much to read. Much of it repeats what we've read somewhere else. A surprising part of it is now generated by the national and other associations themselves. And yet the natural instinct is for each new organization to start its own newsletter, bulletin, journal, quarterly. Through planned and cooperative restraint, we might become more effective. Any one of these gains might be small in itself. But many of them would affect the same rather small group of educational leaders, and for them the accumulation of several small improvements could be a significant help.

I give very high marks to the separate efforts of the existing associations to improve themselves and to provide better service and ideas to their members. As each of us carries on the tasks of self-examination and self-improvement of our respective associations, however, we are bound to our own precedents, commitments, and clientele. Each of us is under pressure to keep proving ourselves. We are all subject—the Council itself and all the others—to the harsh question of that Kentucky voter in Alben Barkley's district years ago, "What have you done for me *lately?*" Only through a collective and frank review will we be able to answer that question cooperatively, rather than one by one and competitively. I think, on the whole, we can be much more certain that we will remain properly competitive than that we will succeed in being properly cooperative and not duplicative. Competition, at least within limits, is in the nature of things. Cooperation and coordination must be continually induced.

It is clear that in higher education we are dealing with new and changed conditions which control us, and which we, in turn, attempt to control and ameliorate. The society, the value systems, the normative limits of behavior, the institutions of fifty years ago are all intensely modified. In some senses, that earlier period was the Age of the Presidents in higher education and I trust that this age has not yet come to an end. We have, more recently, been living through the Age of the Faculty, and we now confront the combination of much greater faculty participation as managers in the educational enterprise and faculty union drives for collective bargaining as employees. Either role may be desirable at some places and at some times, according to the judgment of those involved. Their simultaneous manifestation in any one place is puzzling. We have entered already what historians may properly call the Age of the Student. His drives, his needs, his contributions present and potential, his plea for relevance, his need for freedom, and his rights to participation preoccupy many of the best minds among us. His impatience can be annoying, his awkwardness and inconsistencies can be baffling, if not self-defeating. He is, in any case, nearer the center of our stage, and that is most desirable. In whatever new guises, the essential tasks remain for our open and evolving society, for the Council, and for all of us: to make our colleges and universities strong centers of teaching and of learning, strong centers of scholarship and discovery, responsive and responsible, free, truthful, and unafraid.

SIR JOHN WOLFENDEN

British University Grants
And Government Relations

A FUNDAMENTAL PROBLEM in a great many countries is that of the relation between the universities, on the one hand, and government, on the other. And by government, I mean any government, of any political complexion, in any country. For fundamentally the problem in itself is the same anywhere. What differs, from one country to another, is the attitude towards the problem of the parties who are involved in it.

The basic relationship between government and the universities is one of tension. I see nothing in this situation which calls for alarm, disquiet, or distress. Tension, I am told by my physicist friends, is a necessary condition of movement and action—and just for once I believe what the physicists tell me. Fruitful tension occurs in other fields besides this one: in a happy marriage, in an international alliance, or in the struggle of an artist with his materials. I see nothing wrong in tension.

Where there sometimes is something wrong is in the attitudes of the parties toward it. It is wrong, in my view at least, if a government, *because* it pays the piper, insists on the right to call all the tunes he plays. It is wrong, in my view at least, if universities, *because* they are autonomous institutions, claim the right to ignore the society which supports them. These, of course, are extreme positions which nobody holds, or at least admits to holding. But if either party approaches the problem in this frame of mind, there will inevitably be not just tension but friction; and friction, my same physicist friends tell me, is apt to generate heat, and in certain conditions, explosion.

THE DIVISION OF RESPONSIBILITY IN BRITAIN

All the universities in Britain, including Oxford and Cambridge, receive grants from public funds toward their capital programs and toward what we call their recurrent expenditure and you call their operational budgets. Last year, the public contribution in Britain, under these two headings taken together, was £214 million. It amounted over-all to 90 percent of the capital spending of the universities and to 75 percent of their recurrent expenditure. You may wonder why it was £214 million and not, say, £250 million or £185 million. The answer is that, after the universities had individually made known to the University Grants Committee what they believed their needs to be and after the University Grants Committee had made their assessment of those representations and advised the Government on the basis of their assessment, £214 million was the amount of money which the Government decided to make available for the universities collectively.

That rather complicated sentence reveals, conceals, or contains one of the basic principles of this whole matter. At no point do the universities in Britain directly confront the Government. It is the duty of the University Grants Committee to assemble the necessary facts, proposals, aspirations, and hopes, and then to offer its own global advice to the Government. That advice is always, by strict convention, confidential. Similarly, once the Government's decision is made, it is the University Grants Committee which allocates to each university the sum which, in its collective wisdom, it thinks right. Again by strict convention, these allocations are never questioned—or, for that matter, individually defended—by the Government. The duty of making these allocations is the responsibility of the University Grants Committee and nobody else, and it is accepted as being so both by the Government and by the universities. This does not mean that universities are always satisfied—I live in London, England, not in Utopia—but it does mean that if any university wishes to protest, it does so to *me*, and that trying to lobby Members of Parliament or putting up university chancellors to make speeches in the House of Lords will get them precisely nowhere.

What I have said so far has omitted a great deal of detail. But I am anxious to establish the fundamental principles, and the function of the University Grants Committee as honest broker, go-between, interpreter, buffer, or what you will, is the most fundamental of all. Within recent months, there has been a decision to empower an official with the resounding title of Comptroller and Auditor General, to have access to the books and papers of the University Grants Committee and of the universities. The advice which the University Grants Committee gave to the Government on this question is as confidential as all its advice and I do not propose to reveal it here. What I can say, and I think it is important, is that these powers recently conferred on the Comptroller and Auditor General are, by the nature of his office, to be exercised on behalf of Parliament, not on behalf of the Government. Of course it is possible that financial scrutiny on behalf of Parliament might lead to pressure that the Government should intervene more directly in policy decisions made by the University Grants Committee and by the universities. But on this point, and on the position of the University Grants Committee in general, let me quote from the statement of the Secretary of State for Education and Science in the House of Commons on July 26, 1967, when he announced the decision:

> The Government do not propose to alter the present well-tried and flexible arrangements for financing universities by the capital grants and block recurrent grants made available and distributed on the advice of an independent University Grants Committee. We shall therefore preserve the present system by which block grants are allocated to universities by the University Grants Committee with the consequent freedom of discretion on the part of universities as to how they should be spent. It is no part of the Comptroller and Auditor General's duty to question policy decisions or decisions reached on academic grounds. His function is to comment and advise on the propriety, regularity and efficiency with which monies voted by Parliament are administered by those to whom they are entrusted. . . .
>
> The existence of an independent check on how the universities spend public money should serve to reassure Parliament and the public. It need not infringe the academic freedom of the universities. It does not denote any lack of confidence in the existing system whereby the University Grants Committee stands as a "buffer" between the Government and the universities. It was in this spirit that the Public Accounts Committee made its recommendations. It is in this spirit that the Government accept them.

That seems to me to be pretty explicit.

UNIVERSITY AUTONOMY AND COOPERATION

One other fundamental principle I must make clear. I am not, as Chairman of the University Grants Committee, director-general of the universities of Britain. I am often tempted to think that my job would be a great deal easier if I were. But that would be fundamentally wrong, because each university is an autonomous, chartered, responsible corporation; and the whole essence of a university's life requires that it should make its own decisions, within its known and predictable income, and determine its own priorities. This is the doctrinal basis for the practical procedures by which we make our financial allocations for several years ahead and make them, so far as recurrent grant is concerned, as block grants not itemized or earmarked for specific purposes. It is expected, and accepted, that each university will, in broad terms, operate within the proposals which it has submitted to us and on which its grants have been based. But within those broad boundaries, each university works out for itself its own detailed priorities.

Now if we all simply left it at that, there might ensue nothing but wasteful anarchy. We now have 44 universities in Great Britain—just twice as many as we had ten years ago—as well as a considerable number of nonuniversity institutions in which a substantial amount of degree-level work is done. If each of these did exactly what it liked, the chances of the emergence of a coherent and efficient over-all pattern would be infinitesimal. So the problem which is posed to us is how to introduce coherence into a situation that involves 44 institutions, each of which could theoretically—and, indeed, practically—do just what it damn pleased.

Fortunately, it can truthfully be recorded that the universities, individually and collectively, are just as well aware of this problem as the Government, or Parliament, or the University Grants Committee. They now recognize that it no longer makes sense, if it ever did, for every university to try to do everything; and policies based on a false etymology of the word "university" are much less prevalent than they were in the days when each one of a small number of universities was trying to "establish itself" by the multiplicity and variety of its offerings. Last month, I attended a large and enthusiastic two-day "Conference on Coordination between the Universities." The important thing about this was that it was convened and organized on the initiative of a group of universities, not by me, still less by the Government. I well know that to most American educators there is nothing new or surprising about enterprises of this kind, and indeed, it may be surprising that, in the British context, this kind of thing calls for remark at all. The point, and my purpose in making it, is to show that, inside our system of relationships between Government, the University Grants Committee and universities, this kind of activity can and does take place; and it can and does arise spontaneously from within the universities themselves. It would be misleading to give the impression that interuniversity collaboration is complete or that the University Grants Committee is content simply to sit on the sidelines hopefully but passively waiting for it to develop. From time to time, we actively intervene to suggest that University A might discontinue this or that line of teaching; at the moment when recurrent grants for a forthcoming quinquennium are fixed, we indicate, with discreet (I hope) but pretty intelligible emphasis, what our hopes and intentions are in the allocations of the grants we make; and we are continually (almost continuously) urging on the universities the need for more efficient use of men, materials, and money. And they are not slow to respond. But it must all be done within the two fundamental principles of ensuring economical outlay of public funds, on the one hand, and of maintaining the responsible autonomy of each university, on the other.

THE UNIVERSITIES' OBLIGATIONS

And the ultimate purpose of the whole operation?

I am, by temperament and experience, disposed to mistrust antitheses, disjunctions, or even distinctions which seem to be logically tidy and complete but which on examination are found not to correspond to the real world in which we actually operate. It is not, in real life, that we have to decide whether the function of a university is teaching *or* research, whether the ultimate purpose of a university education is to fulfill the highest potentialities of the intellect of the individual *or* to make sure that the needs of the community are met. This is not an either/or situation: It is that much more complicated and untidy affair, a both/and relationship. Indeed, there are not simply two factors in the relationship, there are several. A university, if I may stick out a multiform neck, has many functions. I cannot enumerate all of them, but I venture to suggest some of the duties and responsibilities which a university, any university, has in our present age and circumstances. (And for me, at any rate, there is little comfort to be derived from antiquarian dogmatism. I am interested in universities in present-day fact, not in some idealized and romantic picture of them in Italy in the fourteenth century or in Germany in the nineteenth.) Among the elements which are present as a matter of observable fact in any university today are, at least, these: the education of the country's best brains up to the limit of the capacity of those brains; the pursuit of knowledge and intellectual discovery for its own sake; the transmission and the reasoned criticism of the culture of which the university is a part; and the twentieth-century equivalent of the fulfillment of those moving words in the ancient Bidding Prayer, "that there may never be wanting a succession of persons duly qualified for the service of God in Church and State."

I have deliberately spoken of the balance between teaching and research rather than of a conflict between them. And I dogmatically assert that the keeping of this balance is the responsibility of the faculty—or what we call the academic staff. Under our British system, as I have said already, the recurrent grant which is made to a university is a block grant for each of the five years ahead. A university's application to the University Grants Committee is itemized in great detail, and the details are very carefully scrutinized. But at the end of the day, the allocation of public funds to the university is, with very rare exceptions in very special circumstances, a block sum, without strings. Decisions on how these funds are to be deployed inside the university rest solely with the university itself, including the decision on how much money is to be spent on teaching and how much on research. There are, of course, other research funds besides what flow to a university through the University Grants Committee; there are funds from the research councils, Government departments, contracts with industry. But in these cases, too, as well as with what I will arrogantly call "UGC money," the decision whether or not to undertake this or that piece of research rests with the university. When I say "the university," I may well seem, to American ears, to fall short of proper precision. But, with all due respect, that is exactly what I mean. Recommendations about such decisions as these are made by the university senate, usually on the initiative of the heads of the various departments. Before a proposal gets to the senate, it has been exhaustively, and exhaustingly, discussed at departmental meetings, faculty boards, and senate committees. When it comes to the senate itself, there will be any amount of what is euphemistically called "professorial in-fighting"; and this is so whether we are talking about the carving up of the University Grants Committee grant, or about the decision to embark on a particular line of sponsored research which may seem to some faculty members to be (you know the words) distorting the pattern of the university's growth. Eventually, there is a senate decision based on genuinely (I was going to say "purely") academic grounds.

Now comes an important point. This academic decision goes forward to the university council, the continuing body which is ultimately responsible for the university's financial affairs. This body has a majority of nonacademics: business men, industrialists, lawyers, whatever— and a substantial minority of members of that same senate who sit on precisely equal terms with those whom we affectionately call the "lay" members. In my experience of trying to run a university, I never encountered a division on my council between the academics on the one hand and the nonacademics on the other. And I have never known a senate recommendation on an academic matter to be rejected by the council except for the simple reason that there was no money for it. This is what I mean by "the university," and that is why I boldly say that such academic decisions as the balance between teaching and research are in effect taken by the faculty itself. Of course, there are stresses and strains; of course there are occasions when bargains have to be struck between Professor A and Professor B; and of course sometimes a vice-chancellor is accused of being two-faced. But these are elements in any normal real-life organization. The essential doctrine is that a university is an autonomous and responsible body, and that it makes its own decisions inside its known income.

Rather similar considerations apply to the other big question—and I will paraphrase the words of the Bidding Prayer into the secular words, "the deployment of scarce and highly skilled manpower." Here, there is an added complication, at any rate for us in Britain. The considerable expansion of university education which resulted from the Robbins Report was based on two principles. The first is simply demographic; that is, we have to meet the consequences of the behavior of mothers and fathers in the postwar years. The second is that we have to provide university places to fit the qualifications with which young men and women are equipped when they emerge from school and wish to take their education further. With the first of these criteria nobody can argue: The existing children are undeniable facts. The second does produce difficulties, and I freely admit that, so far, we have not mastered them.

There are two factors here which are very hard to reconcile. It is a fact, regrettable or not according to your point of view, that the majority of our boys and girls, when they leave school, are qualified for university places in the humanities or the social sciences. It is also a fact, regrettable or not according to your point of view, that the national need is for more scientists and technologists. We have increased the number of scientific and technological students in our universities from 35,000 to 85,000 in the past ten years. This October, there will be some 1,500 available but unfilled places in these areas; and well though I know the semantic difficulties about defining an unfilled place, the fact remains that too many young men and women are coming forward from the schools qualified in subjects other than these and not enough qualified in science and technology. I do not know the answer to this problem. We have not yet reached the point in Britain where children of thirteen or fourteen can be directed into particular studies; we have not yet succeeded in per-

suading them that there is a future in science and technology as exciting as in history or economics; we have not yet recruited teachers who
can inspire their pupils toward these studies; and we have not yet
persuaded industry how best to use highly qualified graduates in science and technology. We have, in short, not yet educated public opinion to a real respect for the technologist.

But, to come back to the point of doctrine, it is theoretically within
each university's responsibility to do what it chooses about this situation. Each university could, if it so chose, entirely ignore the question
of the nation's need and do merely that which was right in its own
eyes. Mercifully, university senates and councils are not composed of
introverted, self-regarding half-wits. They recognize that, whereas universities in Britain were once small private corporations existing on
fees and the endowments of pious benefactors, they are now intimately
enmeshed in a society which financially supports them, and, at the
same time, tolerates a remarkable degree of autonomy for each institution.

In that situation, I have no experience of irresponsibility on the
part of any university in the face of demonstrated national need. They
have collectively increased by 25 percent their intake of medical students over the past ten years; they have planned for more technologists than in the event the schools have produced; and they have diversified their offerings, if I may borrow a phrase from U.S. educators, in a
way which in my undergraduate days would have been unthinkable.
And this they have done, I repeat, by their own decisions. We, from
the center, make them aware of the national situation; we encourage
this or that form of development—electronics research, it might be, in
preference to Assyriology—and we try to prevent, as I have said before,
everybody from trying to do everything. But, again, I am not director-
general of the universities of Britain, even when it comes to ensuring
that they meet the needs of the nation.

I spend my life walking a tightrope. We in the University Grants
Committee operate on what we call the Principle of Equal and Opposite Unpopularity. If we were too popular with the universities, the
Government would suspect that we were in their pocket; and con-
versely. I can only say that I am humbly proud to be involved in an
operation which, as I see it, combines, as well as can be expected in
this imperfect world, the proper autonomy of the universities and the
proper degree of responsibility for the expenditure of a considerable
amount of public money.

McGEORGE BUNDY

In Praise of Candor

THE FORD FOUNDATION continues to make more grants and appropriations to American colleges and universities than to anyone else. We yield to none in our concern for the health and strength of these institutions. Government aside, we have been and we are the largest single source of their new funds. Colleges and universities may approve or disapprove of our particular actions, but I hope they would agree that they have no cause to complain of the direction of our effort. Drawing upon this record of the organization I represent, and also upon my own continuing sense of membership in the academic profession, I would like to discuss one of the problems we face as members of the American community of higher learning—the problem of explaining ourselves economically.

I shall refer sometimes to universities, sometimes to colleges, and sometimes to both, and I beg the reader to hold me to no rigorous accounting of the argument as it applies to one or another class of institutions. What I learned at Harvard eighteen years ago has been confirmed at the Ford Foundation in the last eighteen months—the college and the university, in the whole of our national environment, are essentially inseparable; we cannot make much sense of either one in isolation from the other.

The first point to be made about the economic problem of the higher learning is that it exists. I deeply believe that what has been true for a century is still true today: that there is a dramatic need for new and larger resources in the colleges and universities of our country.

My second point is not so simple or pleasant. It is that this first proposition—so clear and so persuasive to those concerned with higher education—is not at all clear to the people of our country, and not easily demonstrated to any skeptical or careful questioner. *We* may know in our bones that the needs of our colleges are more urgent than ever; we may even know from our balance sheets that the deficits predicted so long are now becoming a brutal reality; we may be able to demonstrate, case by case, that this contract or that loan or the other gift is more needed than ever. In this or that contest with regents or with governments, with trustees or with professors, we may be able to argue persuasively our desperate need and our consequent claim to indulgence. But as a whole, and to the country as a whole, we have not made our case.

NEED TO PROVE OUR CASE

One surface reason for this failure is simply that our colleges and universities, over the last twenty years, have experienced an expansion that is without precedent—in buildings and in budgets, in students and in professors, in reputation and in rewards, in power and pride, and in deserved prestige. As we try to tell our countrymen that we are faced with imminent bankruptcy, we confront the painful fact that in the eyes of the American people—and I think also in the eyes of disinterested observers abroad—we are a triumphant success. The observers seem to believe (and I myself believe) that the American campus ranks with the American corporation among the handful of first-class contributions which our civilization has made to the annals of human institutions. We come before the country to plead financial emergency at a time when our public standing has never been higher. It is at the least an unhappy accident of timing.

But what is much more serious is that with the tools now available, we cannot really prove our case. We simply do not have the facts and figures that we need. Let me emphasize that I do not say that the facts and figures do not exist; I say only that we do not have them. We do not have them for the simple and fundamental reason that as a class, neither colleges nor universities—public or private, large or small, old or young—have ever made it their business to learn and to tell the whole story of their resources and their obligations, their income and their expenses, their assets and their debts, in such a way that the public can fully and fairly judge their economic position.[1]

Even on relatively straightforward questions of financial reporting, most of us are still remarkably reticent. The annual financial report of

---

[1] In this sweeping assertion, I am not talking about our ordinary budgets, but about the whole range of considerations which affect our present and future economic strength. Nor do I mean to say that there is no college or university which has not *tried* to do this job. I mean rather that, as a class, we have not done the job and that therefore there is no *general* understanding of the situation, and no background against which specific disclosures can be judged.

the average institution of higher learning is comprehensible only to its writer, if to him. Let me emphasize here with all the force I can that I charge no one with fraud or even with negligence. The reasons for the deficiencies in our accounting are many, but, in my judgment, they do not include weakness of mind or of conscience among our administrators. They are more subtle and more difficult than that.

THE EXCUSE OF ARBITRARINESS

Even the smallest of our colleges and universities is a complex organism. Every modern accountant knows that it is no easy matter to give a clear account of even the simplest business firm, but there are a number of well-understood concepts, with a special and simple and central role for net earnings. A college is not so fortunate. It is a not-for-profit institution, which is a simple and straightforward way of saying that its balance sheet is not the measure of its achievement. Different institutions can and do take very different views of the value of their buildings, the uses of their endowment, their obligations for maintenance, their reserves for depreciation, and the true costs of such different activities as admitting, housing, feeding, teaching, expelling, flunking, and ignoring their students. The best single illustration of this problem, I have always thought, is the question of allocating the costs of a major university library. This is the place that draws the professors that write the books and lecture the boys and attract the graduate students who fill the corridors. This is the place that devours the funds that pay for the pages that no one reads for a hundred years. This is the place that attracts the gifts that lower the taxes, and pamper the pride of the bibliophiles. This is the penance of presidents. To whom should it be charged?

The example demonstrates that the allocation of costs is always somewhat arbitrary. There is much force in the argument that a university is a single institution and that all its income and all its expenses are best considered together. Yet, on a proper modern view, the fact that financial analysis is difficult is no excuse for avoiding it. Above all—and I think this is my central point—complexity is no excuse for obscurity. The educational meaning of our financial facts and figures may sometimes be arbitrary or indeterminate, but the facts and figures do exist and they need to be more openly and fully reported than they are now.

From this point onward, I think, my observations may well be more relevant to private than to public institutions. Certainly my own direct experience, both in Cambridge and in New York, has been mainly with the private sector. I do not know, by chapter and verse, if what I have to say applies to public institutions as well; and I have often heard colleagues in the great state universities explaining how open and complete their financial accounting has to be. I do not here question this claim, but I do make bold to suggest that they may wish to question it themselves. I have not found it self-evident that the accounting of the public institutions is really more enlightening than that of their private counterparts; and a skeptic may ask if their openness is not more apparent than real. I would suppose that the president of a public university knows many things about his budget that he does not publish to his legislature. And if I may build speculation on speculation, I will say that such calculated reticence has been as necessary in the past as it will be inappropriate in the future.

But what I assert as speculation for public institutions, I can urge with more assurance and conviction for the private institution. As first evidence for this position, I cite the fact that we are much more candid than we used to be, and that it is good for us. We have learned to make public our policies and practices for scholarships, loans, and financial assistance. And we have even soothed each other by exchanges of information on our grants to athletes. A more recent and a much more significant change is in the field of faculty salaries where the AAUP has forced us all to reasonably full disclosure—not of the salaries of individuals, but of maxima, minima, and averages at every rank. There are some among us who suppose that these relentlessly public statistics are themselves a cause of the continuing and painful (to us) increases in faculty salaries. They blame the messenger for the bad news. The truth is we are all afloat in a world in which, for the first time, the laws of supply and demand are setting the level of faculty salaries, and until there is an end to the current pattern in which next year's value exceeds this year's price, faculty salaries will continue to go right on up. Moreover, whatever the pain to administrators, this upward movement of faculty salaries is probably the best result of market economics since the paperback book.

A PROPENSITY FOR CONCEALMENT

But while we have learned to make public information about tuition, scholarships, and salaries, we still do not report—and sometimes do not know—other critically important costs. One simple and striking example is the cost of buildings. We often put price tags on such enterprises before we have the money, but we seldom tell anyone afterwards just what the final bill was. The desire to minimize costs of construction—to say that we got a good bargain—is deep in all of us, both as individuals and as institutions. But in the case of college buildings, such reticence does much harm, for it gives an incomplete public picture of the real capital costs of a modern institution. In particular, it tends to hide the costs of quality.

A still more serious omission among most of us is the cost of maintenance. Here, we tend to hide the truth not only from others but from ourselves. I will venture the guess that there are few administrators who can plead innocent to the charge that they have failed to predict the real annual costs of a new building. Driven by both necessity and ambition, and knowing better than most of our friends the true importance of adequate construction, we have developed a built-in propensity to conceal our light bills from ourselves.

And one more area in which too many of us do not know what we are doing—and still more of us do not tell all we know—is, of course, the field of charitable investment. I forbear to comment further on this subject because the Ford Foundation has just begun a large-scale study of the whole question, but will emphasize that there is here no question whatever of a suspicion of wrongdoing, but rather an acknowledgement of the habit of reticence based upon natural traditions of discreet trusteeship, and upon the fact that no one can spend imprudently sums that have been prudently hidden.

Along with all these traditions, complexities, and innocent errors, there goes a larger reason for our incomplete reporting: It is that so many of us have not fully trusted those to whom we were reporting. The economic case for a great modern university is much more complex than the ordinary emotion of alumni loyalty. The reasons for heavy real deficits in a time of special effort and imaginative growth are sometimes too subtle for ready explanation even to one's board of trustees. The academic entrepreneur (and the term is a compliment, not a complaint) has had many of the same problems of timing his revelations as his counterpart in the business world. Many of the greatest of our academic leaders in the past have been among those who told us least about where their dollars came from and what they did with them.

CANDOR AS A REQUIREMENT

But we are moving now toward another age. In this new age—whether the institution is public or private—it will be held to a new level of accountability by Federal and state agencies of government working at a new level of sophistication. The bureaucrats and the committees will be eager to know more than academic administrators have yet been able to tell them, and in this eagerness, they will be proper agents for the public. I suspect there is consensus among us that we have no choice but to seek a drastic increase in the levels of public support for both private and public institutions. But the consequence for us all is a new requirement of candor. In their economic affairs, our colleges and universities must now become open—to themselves, to each other, to public authority, and indeed to all.

As we move in this direction, of course, we shall face many obstacles. Not the least is the fact that once we learn to tell just where we are, we shall come under relentless pressure to tell where we have been, and where we are going and why. We shall have to move from static reporting to marginal analysis. The penalty of successful reporting will be an unending demand for more. Such research is, of course, its own justification; moreover, the more we learn these techniques, the more we shall be able to persuade our friends to pay our bills, and make real our dreams.

I recognize that I have made an argument that is much more stated than proved, but I have no apologies to make. The testing of a proposition like this belongs not to refugees from academic administration, or to philanthropic friends of the colleges and universities, but to the practicing administrators themselves. Just as the brave beginnings I have cited are the product of decisions made inside our colleges, so must be the necessary decisions of the future. Much of this new openness will have to be achieved by common effort, just as much of the cause of our present reticence is an outdated competitive secrecy.

Let me close with a still wider and less argued proposition—that the prescription which I have offered in economic affairs may also apply to other parts of the community of higher learning. If it be true that the first need for effective future financing is that the university should be open, may we not speculate that a similar answer will be appropriate to such hotly argued questions as the governance of universities, the role and responsibility of students, the proper powers of the professors, and the relation between the campus and the citizen. To me, at least, it is a tempting hypothesis that the tension and turmoil of the present may yield in the end to increased openness, at every level and in all directions. Denying the apparent contradiction between privacy and communication, and relying upon the community of interest which is the essence of the university, I choose to believe that this hypothesis is right; and that the resolution of our troubles will be found by the means of reason in the process of candor.

SAMUEL B. GOULD

A New Objective

I HAVE OFTEN WONDERED how many times, in how many places, and before how many audiences the goals of higher education have been discussed and analyzed. It would appear that we are never done with the subject. I am not implying that so much attention to goals and objectives is a waste of time. On the contrary, even when it tends to be repetitive, such consideration has merit. For one thing, it keeps reminding us that there *are* goals, or there *ought* to be—a point that people, even educators, have a way of forgetting occasionally. For another, it is necessary because goals have been known to change or to need changing, even in such a traditionally immutable field as higher education.

The American Council is to be congratulated, therefore, for asking the question "*Whose* goals for American higher education?" I do not know whether it did so diffidently or boldly, innocently or knowingly, artfully or ingenuously. The use of that interrogative pronoun, however, creates a vastly different arena in which to debate, an arena where many others besides educators have a right to stand and be heard. Nor could that usage come at a better time in the life of higher education, for if any college or university today has so much as an ounce of complacency left, it must indeed be blind and deaf to everything going on around it. All of us stand in need of frank self-assessment, and we must face up to the results we discover.

If our self-assessment as an educational establishment were preceded by our self-assessment as a nation, we might see our present inadequacies and our future roles as educators more clearly. We hear every day that we live in a world of swift change, and just a glance around us tells us this is true. All change, however, does not necessarily exemplify worthwhile progress. I would suggest, for example, that we have in recent years developed a tolerance or even a taste for violence that is apparent not only in those theatrical, television, and literary representations which seem pathologically fascinated with all that is worst in man, but also in real life, where headlines about or even actual experience of mass lawlessness and cruelty as well as individual acts of violence leave us unmoved and undistressed. We have become conditioned to snipers and blood and mayhem and riots, much as some of us in past wars were deliberately conditioned to these and other brutalities as part of our military training. We have developed a similar tolerance or taste for opposition to law and order that can ultimately take us back to the jungle. Under the guise of concern for the protection of freedom, we are fostering a new and vicious kind of permissiveness. Finally, it is apparent that what we have already witnessed is only a beginning. There is far worse to come, since we as a nation are making promises that cannot possibly be kept; we are offering quick panaceas for an illness of the body politic that may soon turn out to be malignant.

Does the formal system of education have any responsibility in all this? Are we justified in our aloof or tentative attitudes toward our role in society, especially when society is crying out for help? Is it possible that a new objective of the broadest and most pragmatic sort is emerging for higher education: an objective made necessary by contemporary circumstances; an objective that grows out of the mistakes of the past century? I think it is not only possible, but essential.

THE GOALS OF THE CONSTITUENCIES

But first, we should perhaps ask how today's college or university is being judged, and by whom.

New conceptions about college and university life are evolving, disquieting conceptions to those who think of these institutions of higher learning in traditional terms. There is, for example, *society's* present attitudes toward the university. On the positive side, the university has never been more in the public or private consciousness. It has never received more attention or support. Its scholars and scientists have never been more sought after, more handsomely rewarded, more highly honored. Its students have never been more numerous or, generally speaking, more able. Its buildings and other facilities have never been more splendid. All this is common knowledge.

But there are dissident voices also, and these voices are strong and accusatory. Some critics maintain that the university follows rather than leads public opinion, and that, out of timidity, it has forsaken its role of intellectual forthrightness and honesty. It is said to be subject to external pressures as never before: pressures from Federal and state governments, from business, from social organizations. The lure of money from foundations and public agencies tempts it to stray far afield from its earlier and more time-honored missions. Its purposes and values have become so vague as to be unidentifiable or misunderstood; it is all too much concerned with self-preservation and financial stability. As one outspoken educator has commented, "The multiversity, which will do for the society anything the society will pay for, exists to flatter the spirit of the age." [1] Or, as another has said, "Education, far from being a vehicle of social change and advance as is so often assumed, can prove to be a prison of outworn ideas, a mechanism of obsolescence." [2]

It is unnecessary for me to catalog the internal and external relationships of the university—relationships with faculty, with students, with administration, with government agencies, with foundations, with potential or actual donors, with alumni, with the community. What *is* necessary is that we stand up to the realization that every one of these constituencies has *its own* goals for higher education, goals which may not necessarily be those of the university itself. And then it is equally necessary for us to ask ourselves *whose* goals are the ones we are working toward, ours or theirs? Who is making the basic determinations, and for what reason? And are these determinations the appropriate ones?

Suppose we take a sampling of these goals, starting with those of the general public. We are at a time in the life of our society when the desire for higher education has reached an unprecedented level. The college degree has become as essential as the high school diploma. It represents an open door to employment and a higher place on the social ladder. Whether the degree also represents intellectual achievement and growth is another matter, irrelevant to a good many who seek it. In their view, the important thing is to have it. One goal of the general public, therefore, is the availability of higher education to all.

Even those of the public not so concerned about acquiring a degree may have in mind specific goals for higher education. The increase of leisure time, the rapidly accelerating obsolescence of much training in professional and technical careers, the growing appetite for intellectual development, the effects of automation, the reconsideration of the

[1] Robert M. Hutchins, "The University and the Multiversity," *New Republic,* April 1, 1967, p. 16.
[2] Alexander King, "Revolution in Education," *The Listener,* Sept. 1, 1966.

place of women in our society—these combine to give a new importance to continuing education of many sorts. Our citizens expect and even demand that colleges and universities provide such programs. Nor do they feel that these are low in priority as higher education maps its future.

Paralleling this goal is the equally tempting one of making education completely free at all levels. Our citizens are steadily moving toward greater understanding of the viewpoint that higher education is not only in the interest of the individual; it is, rather, in the national interest and therefore should be provided to all who can benefit from it, regardless of their financial situation. Many people propose, as a direct opposite to the "free education" philosophy, that complete support be provided to higher educational institutions through a system of deferred student payments, to begin after graduation and continue throughout a person's lifetime; payment would be based on a percentage-of-income formula and collected as part of the income tax. The attractiveness of this proposal is not difficult to understand: it holds promise of relief for our financially hard-pressed institutions. What it means to education philosophically and socially, however, is a question that deserves the most careful scrutiny before such a proposal is accepted.

Legislators and other government officials have their own goals for higher education. While these differ according to circumstances, they all seem to converge in the single idea that government should be much more actively involved in determining what is to happen in our institutions. The huge expenditures for Federal and state aid to both public and private education create a marvelous opportunity for those in political life to be heroes, either as champions of the ultimate in support or as guardians of the public purse. And the increasing attention given by the news media to campus activism and any other independent tendencies of institutions makes politicians all the more sensitive and eager about their role as determiners of educational directions. While these attitudes are entirely natural, the latent dangers in some of these goals should not be overlooked.

The disadvantaged of our country have their own goals for higher education. They have historically been denied entrance to colleges and universities, either flatly because of race and color or because of inability to qualify. They look upon most of our patient and well-meaning efforts to rectify the situation as altogether too slow and too unrealistic. They seek instantaneous change, change that will immediately right the wrongs of a hundred and more years. And many of them are not in a mood to discuss present college or university standards or curricula, if these are to be any sort of bar to their entrance.

The business, industrial, and professional world has its goals for higher education, too. Certain kinds of education and research are very necessary, even fundamental, to the representatives of this world, and they are voicing their expectations more and more clearly and emphatically. In some instances, they have discovered that they, too, can be educators; thus, they are advancing plans for creating their own institutions and perhaps for granting their own degrees. Such objectives have far-reaching implications that demand our serious consideration.

Groups or segments within colleges and universities themselves have *their* separate goals. The most prominent groups can be found among students and faculty. The student relationship to the college or university has become a matter of national concern, not just for us but for laymen as well. Manifestations of unrest are strong and frequent. More and more institutions are discovering a new militancy on their campuses as students express dissatisfaction with the *status quo*. The university faces a wide and contradictory range of accusations: it is charged with naïveté on the one hand, and intellectual craftiness and dishonesty on the other; some say it is too specialized in its functions and thus too close to the practical world, while others maintain that it is completely irrelevant in its purposes and programs; objections are raised about its callousness and impersonality, while other accusations are voiced about its overprotectiveness of students. Undergraduate education is considered by many to be archaic, and the inadequacies of graduate education come regularly under fire. Every control the university exerts is attacked, and every attempt at maintaining an orderly process is challenged.

The power of student activism cannot be minimized, nor can its potential for creating and maintaining unrest be taken lightly. Unrest and tension on a campus can and should be dynamic factors for university good, but certain elements of the current student movement openly advocate such unrest as a means toward total disruption and destruction. Statements of the Students for a Democratic Society and some aspects of the most recent convention of the National Student Association make this clear. They reflect goals of extreme negativism and even anarchy which, if assiduously pursued, could make the Berkeley episodes seem like mere warm-up exercises.

Another internal force, with its own set of goals for education, is the faculty. Their goals are centered upon two elements: their advancement within their own discipline and the improvement of their working conditions. Faculties are not nearly so much concerned about the objectives of education in general as they are with their academic disciplines in particular. The university is now merely a convenient base of operations from which a faculty member works in the interests of his discipline and from which he moves quickly when a more attractive base is provided. There are, to be sure, occasional faculty members who like to dabble in administration or campus politics, but most prefer to be left alone. And those who do not so prefer are very often preoccupied with the goal of strengthening their profession rather than with goals of the total university.

These, then, are only some of the constituencies and their goals. They touch higher education directly, yet they are tangential in their respective effects. Together and severally, however, they represent what has occupied most if not all the attention of colleges and universities in recent years.

REGAINING THE INITIATIVE

The real question, however, goes beyond a query about the goals of others. It is, rather, what *our own* goals, as institutions, are. And the very fact that, to reach this point of discussion, we have first had to identify so much that impinges upon us from internal and external sources should make us pause and remember why this is so.

The blunt truth is that, as institutions of learning, we have allowed our initiative to become dulled and our courage eroded. We have allowed ourselves to be led along pathways not of our own choosing and have not often enough made plain what our own pathways are. We have frequently taken refuge in broad platitudinous statements of objectives; then we have compounded our error by doing very little to fortify these statements with specific programs that show we mean what we say. And rarely have we re-examined our goals in light of the needs of contemporary society, except in scientific or technological aspects; thus, in the eyes of many people, we are not reaching to the heart of our reason for being.

What I am saying is that *we* should be the originators of whatever process is necessary to determine our own goals, and that, thereafter, our actions should reflect in every possible way our efforts to reach them. If these objectives correspond in some ways to those of others, it may be advantageous both to them and to us; there should be no question, however, as to who makes the choice and establishes the priorities: It is the educational institution itself, through its duly constituted authorities. There should also be no question about how diversionary temptations are to be treated.

But how is the institution to choose? Who will select the goals? The educational administrators, or the faculty, or the students? I should think all of these and other constituencies as well, but working in close association rather than independent of each other. And, through the interplay of the several constituencies, I should hope that broad objectives of higher education would emerge, shaped to interpret a college or university's own estimate of its place in the totality of higher education. There will never be full agreement on these objectives, nor is consensus even desirable; there *can* be clarity, however, as to what the institution means and intends to do once it has charted its course. With this kind of clarity, the validity of the university's goals, both the timely and the timeless, can and should be the subject of a never-ending discussion.

Surrounding the relatively broad objectives which individual institutions may select and make more specific are even broader ones representing the great urges of the American people. These urges and aspirations differ greatly in some respects from those of other nations and even from those in our own country in earlier centuries. You will recall Sir Eric Ashby's description of the university conceived by Wilhelm von Humboldt less than two hundred years ago when he founded the University of Berlin: ". . . a society of teachers and students existing not one for the other but both for the sake of scholarship; a society sufficiently insulated from the world to be able to live according to its own inner logic; whose members seek intellectual solitude and are given the freedom to pursue it; able to reflect without having to decide, to observe without having to participate, to criticize without having to reform." [3] One could argue, of course, as did von Humboldt, that the objectives of higher education should be determined without regard for the needs of the people, that universities are beyond national or even international considerations and need take no notice of society except to comment upon it. This would be a difficult attitude to defend, however, even for the most aristocratic among us. The tempo and temper of modern America are such that the university choosing this as its major objective would find itself seriously questioned. Higher education is moving farther and farther away from the objective of creating an elitist cult. Such elitism has not been ruled out completely, but it is not as great a preoccupation as some would prefer it to be.

[3] Sir Eric Ashby, "Higher Education in Tomorrow's World," *University of Michigan Sesquicentennial,* April 26-29, 1967.

Instead, America approaches higher educational objectives as pragmatically as it does just about everything else. And it refuses to be intimidated or made ashamed of the hearty cheerfulness and generosity with which it plumps solidly for the ideal of educating everybody to his greatest capability for the sake of the ultimate good of the whole society. It will frankly agree to shortcomings in reaching this ideal, but this does not deter its continued dedication to what it thinks is appropriate for a democracy.

The objective of educating for the good of the total society is one that reaches beyond the compass of any single institution of learning. It has several elements within it, each of which may serve as a point of emphasis or concentration as a college or university determines its goals. An institution may not find it necessary or possible to incorporate all the elements; indeed, only the largest and most diversified of institutions could be expected to do so. Furthermore, all colleges or universities cannot be expected to educate at all levels. This is common knowledge and represents our general agreement that the diverse nature of American higher education is a great strength, one that we should try to protect.

THE GREAT AMERICAN OBJECTIVE

The elements of the "great American objective" can be readily identified and summarized. They all relate to—indeed, center upon— the growth of the individual. Some of them can be dealt with quickly since they are what all of us have been striving toward for many years. Only one element is different or new.

To educate for individual growth means to work toward the development of a person who can, as a result of his education, find for himself a stable economic life technically or professionally; who can discover richer and deeper patterns of living through his cultural awareness and appreciation; who can take an active or even leading part in the expansion of knowledge and the pursuit of truth; who is constantly aware of and receptive to the swiftness of change in modern civilization; who can be moved to an understanding of and a desire for world peace; who understands the responsibilities of freedom together with its rights, and insists upon these responsibilities and rights for others as well as for himself; and, finally, who is motivated to help solve the major social problems of our age. This is an all-inclusive statement, I know, and it repeats a great deal of what most of us have been setting forth as objectives for many years.

If there is one point of departure, one element that is new, it is that relating to the university's involvement in domestic social problems. Some of us, in our rather cautious and tentative espousals of the philosophy that led to the establishment of the Peace Corps, have accepted the validity of the tremendous student desire for involvement in the amelioration of illiteracy, poverty, and disease in underdeveloped countries; in the main, we have done this tangentially, nevertheless, so that the Peace Corps is not only government-sponsored but also government-operated. Ours has been the limited role of accepting responsibility for certain kinds of training on a contractual basis. We have added little creatively or academically to what the Peace Corps administrators themselves have organized as a program. And the major thrust, of course, has been international.

The time has come for us to recognize that, within our own country, we now are facing problems of illiteracy, poverty, and disease, and the resultant disorders these are spawning in all our cities; of a sizable proportion of our citizenry who are untrained and incapable of maintaining economic independence in our technological world; of the steady deterioriation of that most priceless asset of democracy—the dignity of the individual. What we have seen and experienced up to now is the merest prelude to what lies ahead. The time has come for us to recognize that there are no short-term solutions to these problems, that the millions upon millions of dollars being poured into present programs for the disadvantaged have little or no foundation in a master strategy that encompasses the immensity of the task and that sets forth what we ultimately hope to achieve, as well as marking clearly the steps that will lead to achievement. A new and grander strategy is necessary, and we as leaders of educational institutions must take the initiative in its formulation.

Furthermore, we must begin to concentrate as never before upon the resources available to us in moving toward the objective of a new educational pattern, designed for the betterment of the millions of undeveloped talents among our disadvantaged young people. These resources include the knowledge and experience of the faculty, the idealism and social zeal of students, and the traditional power of colleges and universities to make their presence felt within the communities surrounding them. This power, which transcends the political or the partisan, can elevate the problem to a new plateau of national interest and place it in a perspective of the next two decades. Colleges and universities must use this power, and in doing so must make clear that what is to be attempted will take the education of several generations of students to complete.

If we cannot win national support for our efforts, then we must try to persuade state governments to help; if state governments are unwilling, then we must do what we can independently by establishing smaller models of action. But, above all, we must put squarely on the line our potential worth in this all-encompassing struggle that can either engulf us or open a new vista for America.

In actuality, there is nothing very new in the concept that colleges and universities should take leadership in solving a major national problem. For over a hundred years, the land-grant colleges have done so, and in the process have compiled a fantastic record of change and achievement in agricultural development, through direct educational assistance, training, and research. In this enterprise, political involvement has been negligible; Federal funds have been turned over to the planning and directing agency, namely, the institution itself. There is no reason to believe the same process is not possible as we consider an attack upon urban problems. Surely, they are of at least equal consequence; surely, the educational establishment can cope with them on a state-wide basis; surely, higher education must take the initiative in encouraging and even insisting on such a program.

If it is true, as some maintain, that colleges and universities represent a reservoir not only of intellect but also of imagination, and thus are the most natural and productive sources of creative leadership, then it is time we proved this to be so. The most crucial problem in our country's history awaits solution. It will not be solved except through the most massive and untraditional broadening of the nation's educational base. What do we propose to do about it? Are we going to climb back into the tower and pull the ladder up after us? Are we going to continue to beat the dead or dying horses of teaching vs. research, or private vs. public education, or students vs. administration? Are we going to continue to preach and profess and pontificate about human dignity, and never lift a finger to save it at the moment of its possible extinction?

We are the great laboratories of the world, laboratories capable of dealing with more than man's material ambitions, his defensive capabilities, or even his philosophical dreams. In a world of change, we are the single greatest instrument of change, "the vehicle of social change and advance." In this tortured period of national life, we are faced with an unprecedented opportunity and with the choice of rejecting or embracing it. We should remember that the thinking elements of our nation are waiting to learn what our choice will be.

EPILOGUE

WALTER LIPPMANN

The University
And the Human Condition

I AM FREE of the obligation to offer solutions of the problems which occupy so much of the time of the governing authorities in the academic world: how to raise money, how to appease the alumni, how to get around the trustees, the state legislatures, the foundations and the Pentagon, how to ingratiate themselves with the chamber of commerce, the board of trade, and the clergy, how to tranquilize the egos of the faculty, how to deal with the students in their academic lives, their ideological lives, and their sexual lives, how to be cheerful and good fellows with the excessively inquiring reporters. About all of these preoccupations I shall have nothing to say. This leaves open to me the broad, unrestricted field of the human condition and what the universities ought to be doing for it and about it.

I

The proposition with which I am starting is that as men become modern men, they are emancipated and thus deprived of the guidance and support of traditional and customary authority. Because of this, there has fallen to the universities a unique, indispensable and capital function in the intellectual and spiritual life of modern society. I do not say that the universities today are prepared to perform this spiritual and intellectual function. What I do say is that a way will have to be found to perform these functions if the pursuit of the good life, to which this country is committed, is to continue and to be successful.

For modern men are living today amidst the consequences of emancipation from established authority. The dream of Franklin and

Jefferson, as Mr. James A. Perkins describes it, was of "an open society, free of both ecclesiastical and civil control, with little to fear from the uninhibited search for truth and for experiments in the application of truth." [1] The preponderant majority of our people in America today have arrived at such an open society. They have found, I submit to you, that as they are emancipated from established authority they are not successfully equipped to deal with the problems of American society and of their private lives. They are left with the feeling that there is a vacuum within them, a vacuum where there were the signs and guide posts of an ancestral order, where there used to be ecclesiastical and civil authority, where there was certainty, custom, usage and social status, and a fixed way of life. One of the great phenomena of the human condition in the modern age is the dissolution of the ancestral order, the erosion of established authority, and having lost the light and the leading, the guidance and the support, the discipline that the ancestral order provided, modern men are haunted by a feeling of being lost and adrift, without purpose and meaning in the conduct of their lives.

The thesis which I am putting to you is that the modern void, which results from the vast and intricate process of emancipation and rationalization, must be filled, and that the universities must fill the void because they alone can fill it.

It is a high destiny. But it must be accepted and it must be realized.

II

Before we can proceed, we must ask ourselves why, in the quest of a good life in a good society, we now turn to the universities rather than, let us say, to the churches or the government. We do that because the behavior of man depends ultimately on what he believes to be true, to be true about the nature of man and the universe in which he lives, to be true about man's destiny in historical time, to be true about the nature of good and evil and how to know the difference, to be true about the way to ascertain and to recognize the truth and to distinguish it from error.

In other times and in other places, the possessors and guardians of true knowledge have been held to be the appointed spokesmen of a universal and indisputable tradition and of divine revelation. In the western society to which we belong the traditional guardians and

[1] Perkins, *The University in Transition* (Princeton, N.J.: Princeton University Press, 1966), p. 15.

spokesmen of true knowledge have in varying degrees lost or renounced their titles to speak with complete authority. The hierarchy of priests, the dynasties of rulers, the courtiers, the civil servants and the commissars have to give way . . . and there is left as the court of last resort when the truth is at issue, "the ancient and universal company of scholars."

Having said this, I have not forgotten how often the professors have been proved to be wrong, how often the academic judgment has been confounded by some solitary thinker or artist, how often original and innovating men have been rejected by the universities, only to be accepted and celebrated after they are dead. The universal company of scholars is not an infallible court of last resort. Not in the least. On the contrary, it is an axiom of modern thought that the very process of thinking evolves. In human affairs nothing is infallible, absolute and everlasting. There are no courts which can anticipate fully the course of events. There are none which can take account of the unpredictability of genius. Nevertheless, in the modern world there exists no court which is less fallible than the company of scholars, when we are in the field of truth and error.

This court, this universal company of scholars, comprises all who study and teach in all the universities and institutes of the world. The colleagues of each scholar are his peers, those who have qualified themselves in mastering and obeying the criteria by which, in a field of knowledge, truth and error are judged.

The company of scholars is all over the globe, and its members are duty-bound to hear one another.

Insofar as the communication among them is adequate, so that a physicist in California is aware of the experiments and criticisms of a physicist in Peking, there exists the best possible insurance available to mortal men against the parochialism, the stuffiness, and dogmatism which are the chronic diseases of academies.

III

I have said enough, I hope, to reassure anyone who might think that I am glorifying the professors and attributing to them more power and authority than they are entitled to have. I do not mean to do that. I have had my share of controversies with a good many professors. What I do say is that the community of professors is in the modern world the best available source of guidance and authority in the field of knowledge. There is no other court to which men can turn and find what they once found in tradition and in custom, in ecclesiastical and civil authority. Because modern man in his search for truth has turned away from kings, priests, commissars and bureaucrats, he is left, for better or worse, with the professors.

And while we must treat the verdicts of the professors with a vigilant skepticism, they do have a certain authority. It comes from the fact that they have vowed to accept the discipline of scholarship and to seek the truth by using the best intellectual methods at the time known to contemporary men.

To make sure that I am not overstating my thesis, let me repeat. The community of scholars is the court of last resort in those fields of inquiry and knowledge about which scholars, as scholars, are concerned. Thus, if a professor is charged with the murder of his colleague, the court of last resort is not the faculty of his university or the faculties of all the universities. It is the judiciary of the state in which he lives. For the scholar is a scholar only part of the time and in part of his activity. In the role of murderer he is outside the field of scholarship.

But if a professor is alleged to have murdered his colleague a hundred years ago, as in the case of Professor Webster at Harvard, the court of last resort *today* about his guilt or innocence a century ago is not the judiciary of Massachusetts. It is the historians who have studied the evidence now available and have been confronted with the findings of all the historians who have read the history of the case. After a hundred years, no one is more qualified than are the historians to judge the case.

Reflecting on this we come close, I think, to the essential principle of academic freedom. In his relations with the laws of the land, a professor is as subject as any other man to the laws against murder, robbery, cheating on the income tax, driving his automobile recklessly. The laws for him, as for all other men, are what the law-enforcing authorities say they are. The professor has no special privileges and no special immunity.

But in the field of truth and error about the nature of things, and of the history and future of the universe and of man, the state and its officials have no jurisdiction. When the scholar finds that two and two make four, no policeman, no judge, no governor, no legislator, no trustee, no rich alumnus, has any right to ordain that two and two make five. Only other scholars who have gone through a mathematical training equivalent to his, and are in one way or another qualified as his peers, can challenge his findings that two and two make four. Here, it is the community of scholars who are the court of last resort.

It follows that they are the court of last resort in determining the

qualifications of admission to the community of scholars—that is to
say, the criteria of appointment and the license to teach. No criterion
can be recognized which starts somewhere else than in the canons of
scholarship and scientific research. No criterion is valid here because
it emanates from the chamber of commerce, or the trade union council,
or the American Legion, or the clergy, or the newspapers, or the ADA,
or the John Birch Society or any political party. The selection and the
tenure of the members of the community of scholars is subject to the
criterion that scholars shall be free of any control except a stern duty
to bear faithful allegiance to the truth they are appointed to seek.

A judgment as to whether a scholar has been faithful is one that
only his peers can render. The supreme sin of a scholar, qua scholar,
is to lie, not about where he spent the previous weekend, but about
whether two and two make four.

IV

If we say that the vocation of the scholar is to seek the truth, it
follows, I submit, that he must seek the truth for the simple purpose of
knowing the truth. The search for truth proceeds best if it is inspired
by wonder and curiosity, if, that is to say, it is disinterested—if the
scholar disregards all secondary considerations of how his knowledge
may be applied, how it can be sold, whether it is useful, whether it is
good or bad, respectable, fashionable, moral, popular and patriotic,
whether it will work or whether it will make men happier or unhappier,
whether it is agreeable or disagreeable, whether it is likely to win
him a promotion or a prize or a decoration, whether it will get a good
vote in the Gallup Poll. Genius is most likely to expand the limits of
our knowledge, on which all the applied sciences depend, when it
works in a condition of total unconcern with the consequences of its
own findings.

Believing this, I hold that the university must have at its core a
sanctuary for excellence, where the climate is favorable to the pursuit
of truth for its own sake. In our conglomerate and swarming society, the
last best hopes of mankind lie in what is done, and in what example
is set, in these sanctuaries.

I do not think of them as monastic establishments shut off from
the stresses and strains of the human condition. I think of them as
societies of fellows within the great corporate institutions that our universities have become, as societies where the relatively few who can
pursue truth disinterestedly will find the support and sustaining
fellowship of their peers.

V

Since man's whole knowledge of things is not inherited and must be acquired anew by every generation, there is in every human society a culture, a tradition of the true and the false, the right and the wrong, of the good which is desirable and the bad which is to be avoided. This culture is rooted in the accepted version of the nature of things and of man's destiny. The accepted version evolves and the encyclopedias become outdated and have to be revised.

Since the prevailing tradition rests on the prevailing science, it follows that modern men must look to the company of scholars in the universities to guard and to preserve, to refine and enrich the tradition of civility. They have to revise the curricula of studies and the encyclopedias of knowledge.

This does not mean, of course, that the scientists and the scholars are to be regarded, much less are to regard themselves, as a mysterious elite of the initiated who can lay down the law of right and wrong, of good and evil, in human affairs. It does mean that insofar as religion, government, art, and personal living assume or imply that this or that is true or false, they are subject to the criticism and judgment of the company of scholars. The prevailing and accepted science of the time is the root from which grow the creations of poets and artists, of saints and prophets and heroes. The science of an age is the material with which inspiration and genius create.

VI

I am more than a little concerned as I proceed, that you will think that I am erecting a very high tower on a very small base, that I am nominating the professors, whom you all know so well, to carry too great a responsibility. All I can say is that the human condition in the modern age brings us to what I have been talking about. The dissolution of the ancestral order and the dethronement of usage and authority in modern society have left us dependent upon man's ability to understand and govern his own fate. Necessarily therefore, we are in a high degree dependent upon the men whose lives are committed to the pursuit of truth.

The responsibility may be too great for the professors to carry. But somehow—since the responsibility must be met—we shall have to learn to find men who will tell us how to find the professors who can carry the responsibility. And if we are ever to find them, we must begin by realizing the need to find them. If they cannot be found, modern man is indeed adrift on a trackless sea.

VII

So, I venture to proceed. There is still something more, still another great function which the universities and their scholars cannot neglect, indeed cannot escape.

For there is more to the task of learning than to discover more and more truths than have ever been known before. That something more, which may mark the difference between mediocrity and excellence, is the practice of a kind if alchemy, the creative function of transmuting knowledge into wisdom.

Wisdom, says the *Oxford English Dictionary*, is "the capacity of judging rightly in matters relating to life and conduct." It is "soundness of judgment in choice of means and ends." The development of the capacity of judging rightly is something different from, and in some ways much more than, the capacity to know the truth in any particular field of knowledge, or to have mastered the art of applying this knowledge to some desired end. The capacity to judge rightly in a choice of both means and ends cuts across the specialties and the technologies, and it is, I dare to say, the hallmark of a liberal as distinguished from a utilitarian or vocational education.

We may say, I think, that knowledge is made into wisdom when what is true about the nature of things is reshaped to the human scale and oriented to the human understanding, to human need and to human hope. As this is done, the findings of scientists and scholars are transformed into the humanities, and the materials for a liberal education begin to appear.

The universities, therefore, are not only the depositories of wisdom. They are also laboratories where alchemists work, whose function it is to transmute knowledge into human wisdom. If the scholars do this, insofar as they do this, they transcend the sterile controversies about the two cultures, the scientific and the humanistic, and they learn to transcend the intellectual puzzle about specialism and generalism. For knowledge transmuted into wisdom places the sciences and the humanities within one universe of discourse.

Can it be done? There is no need to doubt that it can be done. The most revolutionary of all the intellectual achievements of the modern age has been man's increasing mastery of the art of discovery and invention. The reshaping and reorientation of knowledge, so that it is humanly accessible and viable, is the task of philosophers, of the masterminds in the special fields of learning, of the advanced students in the field of education, and of the great teachers themselves. It would be a feeble kind of defeatism to deny that man, who is penetrating the secrets of matter and of life itself, is unable to make usable the knowledge he is able to acquire.

VIII

A liberal education is concerned with what Plato calls the "royal science," the science that needs to be possessed by the rulers of the state. The education of a prince who is destined to be the king has from time immemorial been the primary function of education. Now that we live in a time when, as Huey Long truly said, every man is a king, it is still the prime function of education to instruct and to train the future rulers of the state.

It cannot be said that there exists as yet an adequate royal science. It is the task of the scholars to invent and compile the royal science of the modern age, a science which can in some measure be absorbed by all who vote, and can educate the comparatively few who will actually govern.

The heart of this science will be a presentation of the history and the practice of judging rightly in a choice of means and ends. Such a body of wisdom must be composed and compiled and made communicable, if the supreme teaching function of the institutions of learning is to be successful. This is their necessary business if they are to be more than laboratories of research, institutes of technology and vocational centers for careers.

For they cannot neglect the highest function of education which is the education of the rulers of the state. Quite evidently, it is not easy to discover what should be taught to the future rulers of a modern state, how they are to be made to acquire that capacity of judging rightly, which is the essence of wisdom. We are only at the frontier of modern, democratic education, within sight of the promised land. Those who come after us will have to make out of the accumulating knowledge of the specialists, a body of available and usable wisdom. The political scientists and the educators of the coming times will have to explore what is as yet a largely unknown continent—this royal science for our age. They will have to extract from the infinite complexity of knowledge what it is that the rulers of the state need to know.

Quite evidently, the ruler of a state, the President of the United States for example, cannot master all the branches of knowledge which bear on the decisions he must make. Yet he must have enough knowledge of a kind which will enable him to judge rightly whose judgment among the specialists he should decide to accept. He must learn the art, which is not described in the textbooks as yet, of listening to experts and seeing through them and around them. The educators of the future will have to extract from the whole body of nuclear science for example, what it is that the President and the Congress and the leaders of public opinion need to know about nuclear science and the behavior of great powers when they are confronted, let us say, with a treaty prohibiting the testing of nuclear weapons. Out of these extracts from the body of knowledge, the educators must design the curriculum of our own royal science.

IX

I have been meditating out loud about one central theme: that in the modern age, as the ancestral order of usage and authority dissolves, there exists a spiritual and intellectual vacuum of discipline and guidance which, in the last analysis, can be filled only by the universal company of scholars, supported and protected and encouraged by their universities.

AMERICAN COUNCIL ON EDUCATION
Logan Wilson, *President*

The American Council on Education, founded in 1918, is a
council of educational organizations and institutions. Its purpose is to advance education and educational methods through
comprehensive voluntary and cooperative action on the part of
American educational associations, organizations, and institutions.